# CHINA IN
# WORLD
# POLITICS

# CHINA IN WORLD POLITICS

John R. Faust
and
Judith F. Kornberg

LYNNE
RIENNER
PUBLISHERS

BOULDER
LONDON

Published in the United States of America in 1995 by
Lynne Rienner Publishers, Inc.
1800 30th Street, Boulder, Colorado 80301

and in the United Kingdom by
Lynne Rienner Publishers, Inc.
3 Henrietta Street, Covent Garden, London WC2E 8LU

**Library of Congress Cataloging-in-Publication Data**
Faust, John R., 1930–
   China in world politics / John R. Faust, Judith F. Kornberg.
     p. cm.
   Includes bibliographical references and index.
   ISBN 1-55587-413-4 (alk. paper)
   ISBN 1-55587-427-4 (alk. paper : pbk.)
   1. China—Foreign relations—1976– 2. China—Politics and
government—1976– I. Kornberg, Judith F., 1954– . II. Title.
DS779.27.F38 1995
327.51'009'049—dc20                            94-38876
                                          CIP

**British Cataloguing in Publication Data**
A Cataloguing in Publication record for this book
is available from the British Library.


Printed and bound in the United States of America

5 4 3 2 1

# Contents

# Tables

# CHINA IN
# WORLD
# POLITICS

# Introduction

The end of the Cold War and the collapse of the Soviet Empire have undermined much of the global power structure familiar to political leaders, researchers, and students of international politics. In this book we will look over the shoulders of the decisionmakers in Beijing to see how the emerging global system of the 1990s has brought about both new opportunities and risks to China's aging leaders. Ever since Western imperialism reached China's shores over three hundred years ago, outsiders have greatly influenced China's policy choices. In the chapters that follow, we will try to see whether in the 1990s China will finally emerge as a major world actor, influencing events at both the regional and global levels, or whether it will remain largely a reactor to events beyond its shores.

With the tide of communism receding outside China, we will ask whether Marxism and Leninism were not ends in themselves inside China, but instead means to achieve the more basic goals of China's leaders both before and after the triumph of Mao Zedong in 1949: freedom from foreign imperialism; unification of the Chinese nation; creation of effective political power (rule for the people but not by the people); order and stability; and promotion of prestige and well-being through the Four Modernizations—agriculture, industry, science and technology, and military capability.

We will also ask whether Adam Smith has finally triumphed over Karl Marx inside China, as seems to be the case not only in the West but also in Eastern Europe, the former areas of the Soviet Union, and most of the Third World. Though many China-watchers are predicting that it is merely a matter of time until an economic marketplace in China is followed by a marketplace of ideas as well as individual and political freedoms, we will look at current developments and trends inside China and suggest a number of possible alternatives, leaving it up to the reader to assess China's future. For example, these options might include a combination of marketplace investment, production, and distribution of goods with the continuation of many socialist values and practices as well as the preservation of Chinese traditions. Even if in the long run individual freedom and mass political participation triumph in China, are these viable policy choices for China in the foreseeable future? This line of reasoning takes into account the emergence of such practices in the West only after several centuries of marketplace development, the triumph of science and technology, the achievement of mass consumerism, and the near universality of basic education and literacy. In the West, universal adult suffrage and individual rights were not achieved with the Declaration of Independence or the French Revolution. Beijing's leaders might argue even today that most Western societies have basic deficiencies not only in political freedom and individual rights but also in safety and security of the people, human decency, and essential economic and social needs such as meaningful work and adequate health care. Beijing's leaders might further argue that although many Marxist prescriptions for achieving human well-being have largely been discredited in the 1990s, most Marxist criticisms of the First and Third Worlds remain valid in the post–Cold War era. From the Beijing perspective, is it not reasonable to argue that there must be better ways to achieve China's well-being than by adopting Western policies that have produced so many undesirable social, economic, and political results in much of the First World, most of the Third World, and much of Eastern Europe and the former Soviet Union in the 1990s? In each chapter we will challenge the reader to place him- or herself in the role of the Chinese decisionmakers and examine the risks and opportunities of different policy choices. After looking at the policy problems and the supporting data for different policy choices, we will ask a number of questions at the end of each chapter about future possibilities and offer suggested readings for further study.

## CHINA IN THE COLD WAR

In order to understand China's current choices, in Chapter 1 we will look at the remarkable evolution of Beijing's policies during the Cold War years. With all the twists and turns from 1949 to 1989, culminating with the tearing down of the Berlin Wall and the student demonstrations at Tiananmen Square, we will point out continuities in Chinese policy, such as the continuing efforts of the Chinese Communist Party (CCP) to legitimize itself in the eyes of the people through the mobilization of mass support for a combination of traditional Chinese values (the Mandate of Heaven and the Middle Kingdom). We will see how the CCP has appealed to popular aspirations: Chinese nationalism; freedom from foreign imperialism; security, stability, and order; and the Four Modernizations. We will then conclude Chapter 1 with a look at how the end of the Cold War has affected Beijing's future policy choices.

## CHINESE POLITICS AND IDEOLOGY

In order to understand the domestic determinants of Beijing's foreign policy choices, in Chapter 2 we will look at some of the major developments inside China to see how these enhance or limit the directions in which Beijing can move in the 1990s. We will also compare these variables with key factors affecting decisionmakers in the Soviet Union and Eastern Europe to see to what extent conditions were similar or dissimilar during the crucial period from 1989 through 1991, when communism was collapsing in those regions.

We will discuss the extent to which the CCP has been able to utilize traditional values such as the Mandate of Heaven to legitimize its rule. We will also look at challenges to party rule and how the CCP has handled these threats to its power base. In looking at the future choices of the Beijing leadership in maintaining the predominant role of the CCP, we will consider to what extent Gorbachev's policies of glasnost (freedom of expression) and perestroika (restructuring of political and economic institutions) are viable policy choices for China's leaders in the 1990s. We will ask whether the CCP can continue its control of Chinese politics. We will also discuss what policy choices might make it possible for the party to succeed.

One of the policies that the CCP used throughout the Cold War to rally popular support was to stress Chinese nationalism and the continuity of CCP policies. These policies were designed to strengthen rule in Beijing and the control of outlying areas such as Taiwan, Hong Kong, and Tibet based on the ancient appeal of the Middle Kingdom, in which the masses are unified in supporting the common values of Chinese civilization. We will ask whether in the 1990s such appeals can continue to unify the people in support of party rule.

Finally, in Chapter 2 we will look at the problem of succession. Most of the leaders of the 1990s have reached the age when they can no longer control China's destiny. Yet, like opposing chess masters, they have balanced the selection of China's future leaders (for example, at the October 1992 National Party Congress) to preserve China's future options. Some leaders are more oriented toward the Open Door policy, whereas others will seek to prevent further penetration of China's culture and traditions from the outside and at the same time preserve the dominant role of the CCP.

## THE ASCENDANCY OF
## ADAM SMITH OVER KARL MARX?

In Chapter 3, which deals with China's Open Door policy since 1978, we will look at some of the most important political, social, and economic initiatives by any major world actor in the twentieth century. Almost ten years before Gorbachev announced his new thinking in 1985, Deng Xiaoping, China's aging leader, started an economic, social, and political revolution that not only brought about basic changes in China but served as a major stimulus to revolutionary changes in other parts of the communist world.

We will look at the circumstances inside China at the time Deng assumed power after 1978, in particular the overwhelming relief of nearly all segments of Chinese society with the end of the Cultural Revolution. Then we will look at the new leadership's revolutionary decisions, which have changed the course of Chinese history. Because of the importance of these decisions, we will examine Deng Xiaoping's thinking in considerable detail. Then we will look at Deng's actual reforms at home and his new openings to the outside world, all of which were designed to raise living standards through the Four Modernizations while at the same time preserving domestic stability and the dominant role of the CCP in Chinese society.

With these changes, we will see how the outside world became fascinated with China's new image, as evidenced by exchanges of faculty, students, and tourists in unprecedented numbers, while capitalists competed with each other to take advantage of favorable investment conditions inside China and the potential market of over one billion Chinese. Thereafter, we will look at China's rethinking of its Open Door policy following the student demonstrations at Tiananmen Square in the spring of 1989. We will ask which developments since Tiananmen Square not only preserve Deng's earlier reforms but might lead to further change. We will even ask whether, in fact, Beijing's leaders have already abandoned the basic tenets of Marxist economic theory even if centralized rule from above remains, at least for now, largely intact.

## THE COLLAPSE OF THE SOVIET EMPIRE

Understanding China's choices in the post–Cold War era requires knowledge of the changing relations between the two great communist empires during a half century of confrontation between the East and the West. In Chapter 4 we will look at Sino-Soviet and then Sino-Russian relations, noting the reasons for the rise and fall of both cooperation and conflict. We will see why China has never accepted a dominant-subordinate relationship, even though until the 1990s Beijing largely reacted to policies originating in Moscow and the Soviets gave little credence to Mao's radical changes from 1949 to 1976. We will look at how Beijing viewed events as the Iron Curtain came down in Eastern Europe and the communist rulers lost power inside the Soviet Union, and we will discuss why the Chinese had to stand by helplessly as communism first collapsed in Eastern Europe and then in the Soviet heartland, with Gorbachev's resignation on Christmas Day, 1991. We will also look at the improvement in Sino-Soviet relations throughout the Gorbachev era, with the reduction in border tensions and the Soviet accommodation of Beijing's basic demands for the normalization of relations: Soviet withdrawal from Afghanistan, Soviet pressure to get Vietnamese withdrawal from Cambodia, and the reduction of Soviet military presence along its borders with China and in Vietnam.

Finally, we will look at China's relations with the newly independent republics, which are now part of the Commonwealth of Independent States, which has also been in the process of removing its communist and Marxist institutions. Both China and the former parts of the Soviet Empire have sought normalization and improvement of relations during the current era of transition, but many questions remain unanswered about the future of these relations, especially in matters of security and influence. Rather than suggest probable developments in the 1990s, after looking at current policies, we will consider a number of choices available to Beijing's leaders, with their relative risks and opportunities, especially in light of important changes taking place in the former parts of the Soviet Empire in Central Asia.

## SINO-U.S. RELATIONS

Throughout the Cold War years, U.S. policy in Asia has had a greater impact on Beijing's policy choices than that of any other state. However, as we look at Sino-U.S. relations in Chapter 5, we will see that the Soviet Union played an important role in these relations. In the latter stages of the Cold War, the Soviet Union became a greater security concern to the Chinese than the United States, especially with the withdrawal of U.S. forces from Vietnam and the buildup of Soviet military in the Far East, South Asia, and Southeast Asia during the Brezhnev era.

In discussing the different stages of Sino-U.S. relations, we will ask whether Beijing and Washington could have pursued different policies that might have avoided most of their Cold War confrontations. In any case, we will see how each side both initiated and responded to crisis situations, and that even though President Nixon and Henry Kissinger are usually given credit for the era of good feeling and peaceful coexistence in the 1970s, Mao Zedong also played a major role in the normalization of Sino-U.S. relations. With China's Open Door policies beginning in 1978, Sino-U.S. relations became more complex as Japan, Hong Kong, Taiwan, South Korea, and a number of Western European countries also became involved in China's opening to the outside world.

We will also see how economic and trade relations have largely dominated Sino-U.S. concerns in the 1980s and 1990s, accompanied by both major conflicts of interest and efforts at accommodation. We will carefully consider the events at Tiananmen Square in the spring of 1989 and the extent to which Sino-U.S. relations have been influenced by China's repression of student demonstrators.

A number of other factors, however, inside both China and the United

States, have also affected political, economic, and security relations; these factors have created cross-boundary dependencies in which different constituencies have developed inside both countries for cooperation but also for the use of threats.

## CHINA AND ITS NEIGHBORS IN THE POST–COLD WAR ERA

Although the United States probably played a greater role than any Asian state in China's Open Door policy in the 1980s, with the end of the Cold War there is a growing economic interdependence in the 1990s among China and its Asian neighbors in both investment and trade. What is lacking, with the decline of both Russian and U.S. military presence in Asia, is a stable balance-of-power system in the region. In Chapter 6 we look over the shoulders of the decisionmakers in Beijing to see how post–Cold War developments may have affected their policy choices (in terms of economics, politics, and security) in dealing with an emerging regional system that is much more advanced in economic terms than in security cooperation. In fact, although economic and security relations are interdependent and trade and investment may lessen the danger of conflict in Asia, potential power rivalries may develop in what is currently a regional power vacuum. Because of the importance of Sino-Japanese relations, we will deal with the topic separately in Chapter 7, but we will also note in Chapter 6 how Japan and China interact with their neighbors on specific issues.

All actors in Northeast Asia seem to have a common interest in defusing the long-lasting tensions and rivalry on the Korean peninsula: China, North Korea, South Korea, Japan, and Russia. Currently, Taiwan seems to be a loser as relations improve between China and South Korea, whereas the United States as well as other Western countries stand to gain by normalization of relations in the region.

As for Southeast Asia, China's policy choices involve both dangers and opportunities. Trade between China and the countries of the Association of Southeast Asian Nations (ASEAN) has been quite limited compared with trade and investment involving South Korea, Japan, Taiwan, and Hong Kong. Security arrangements in the region are almost nonexistent, with potential rivalry over control of islands in the South China Sea. The large Chinese population in all Southeast Asian countries provides both opportunities and risks in China's relations with these countries. Although China's goodwill can be demonstrated through the achievement of peace in Cambodia if the Khmer Rouge can be prevented from returning to power, the withdrawal of both U.S. and Russian influence in the region makes ASEAN countries fearful of both Japanese and Chinese influence. At the same time, the ASEAN countries seek to improve relations among all states in the region, including both Japan and China.

South Asia poses a different set of issues for Beijing's decisionmakers. With the end of the Cold War, there are fewer reasons for outside actors such as the United States, Russia, and China to back rival regional actors such as Pakistan and India. Nevertheless, in its relations with such countries, China could be a decisive factor in promoting stability in the region or the further buildup of arms (including nuclear arms).

In addition to China's influence on the regional balance-of-power system, there is also the question of rivalry or cooperation between China and India as leaders of the Third World. These are the world's two most populous states, and they are both going through a transition to modernization.

In both countries, there has been a shift in recent years from state ownership and control of the economy to marketplace incentives, but India takes pride in its claim of being the world's largest democracy, with a combination of parliamentary government, federalism, and decentralization, in which considerable autonomy is given to the different regions. As in China, however, there have been severe human rights violations as well as social, economic, and political discontent. For both China and India, the greatest stakes involve internal stability and modernization, as well as the realization that little can be accomplished without reduced population growth rates. In the 1990s, Sino-Indian relations seem to have improved, at least on the surface, but future policy choices involving the relations of these two Asian giants could be crucial to regional and global peace in the twenty-first century.

With the collapse of the Soviet Union, Beijing's leaders are faced with a new set of circumstances on their western boundaries. Currently, developments in the newly independent republics of Central Asia are potentially destabilizing, and as we will see, China's policy choices with these new republics, which are largely Islamic, all suggest caution and perhaps a wait-and-see attitude. Historically, there have been close cultural and economic ties between the peoples of Central Asia and the province of Xinjiang, which is a very large but thinly populated region of western China.

## EMERGING GLOBAL REGIMES

One of the most controversial issues in global politics is the future role of China in the emerging global regimes of the post–Cold War era. Regimes consist of the rules of behavior (or lack of rules) that seem to guide the actions of states as they become increasingly interdependent. In some types of transactions, such as international trade and finance, these rules have become systems of extensive cooperation and regularized behavior; whereas in other areas of interaction, such as regional conflicts, arms races, and arms trade, the global system in the post–Cold War era lacks effective rules for cooperation, although some states have called for more effective regimes in these areas. As evidenced by the global conference on the environment held in Brazil in July 1992, environmental agreements at the global level are also quite limited.

In all of these emerging areas of interdependence and growing interaction, the need for global cooperation is increasingly apparent. However, up to the present time, China's leaders have strongly emphasized the principle of national sovereignty, and their interactions on economic, security, or environmental issues have been more bilateral than multilateral. Yet, as we will see, there are signs that even China may be moving gradually toward more cooperation in solving these global problems, especially if there is a general consensus within the United Nations on what rules of behavior should be adopted. With respect to the emerging global regimes, Beijing's leaders must choose between following their past policies (largely refusing to take a position, actual resistance, or hesitant cooperation) and taking a greater leadership role.

### ALTERNATIVE SCENARIOS: 2000 AND BEYOND

Today, China stands at the crossroads, uncertain about its own identity in a post–Cold War world, one in which Marxist ideology has largely been discredited. Changes are taking place inside China as its leaders move more rapidly and successfully toward a marketplace economy than has been the case with former communist states throughout the Eurasian land mass. With the exception of the 1989–1990 period, China's gross national product has increased at the rate of 9 percent a year since the 1978 reforms, much more rapidly than for the Western economies (including Japan, which faces serious economic challenges in the 1990s).

In our final chapter, we will look at some of the reasons, despite its recent economic success, the Chinese people and their leaders have been unable to clarify their future role. There is a serious identity crisis inside China. The collapse of international communism has wiped away many of Beijing's views of the outside world, and Tiananmen Square has challenged the very foundations of order and the Chinese Communist Party's mandate to rule from above.

As we analyze China's current role in the international security system, we will see how Beijing's leaders remain the world's strongest supporters of the Westphalian system of power relations, which emphasizes sovereignty and noninterference in the affairs of other states. At the regional level, China has been resistant to multilateral efforts to achieve collective arrangements such as those emerging in Europe. As for its role as a model for the Third World, Tiananmen Square has seriously discredited China's image because Third World states increasingly strive for democratic societies, even if they have difficulty in achieving them. However, China's economic reforms since 1978 amount to a revolution that many Third World states might wish to emulate. In considering China's future, we will summarize Beijing's risks and opportunities in continuing its current policies, which we have examined in the previous chapters. We will also look at its choices in breaking new ground, both in its domestic policies and at the regional or global levels, and at choices that may bring China in harmony with the emerging global regimes of the twenty-first century. Beijing will have to make these choices at a time when the emerging global order seems to be increasingly supported not only by the West, but also by most of the Third World and former Second World.

# New Ideologies in the Post–Cold War Era

You, O King, live beyond the confines of many seas, nevertheless, impelled by your humble desire to partake of the benefits of our civilization, you have dispatched a mission respectfully bearing your memorial. Your Envoy has crossed the seas and paid his respects at my Court on the anniversary of my birthday. . . . As to your entreaty to send one of your nationals to be accredited to my Celestial Court and to be in control of your country's trade with China, this request is contrary to all usage of my dynasty and cannot possibly be entertained. Swaying the wide world, I have but one aim in view, namely to maintain a perfect governance and to fulfill the duties of the state. . . . Our dynasty's majestic virtue has penetrated unto every country under heaven and the kings of all nations have offered their costly tribute by land and sea. . . . It behooves you, O King, to respect my sentiments and to display even greater devotion and loyalty in future, so that by perpetual submission to our Throne, you may secure peace and prosperity for your country hereafter.

*—Excerpts from a memorial by*
*Emperor Ch'ien Lung to King George III of England*

## THE CHINESE WORLD ORDER

The Chinese people call their nation the Middle Kingdom, the center of the natural order and the world order as they knew it for centuries. From prehistory until 1911, China's emperors ruled so long as they held the Mandate of Heaven, the natural force that dictated whether a dynasty had sufficient rectitude to provide moral guidance to the people. When the mandate was lost through immoral actions, corruption, or other behavior that offended the heavens, the natural forces would show their displeasure through disasters such as floods, earthquakes, or droughts. The Chinese people then would know that a change in dynasties was imminent. Chinese leaders did not rule on the basis of a social contract with the people or on the basis of a constitutional relationship with other political entities, as did

11

leaders in Western Europe and the United States. Chinese rulers were the sons of heaven.

China was at the center of both heavenly forces and the earthly order. Surrounded for centuries by nations such as Korea and Vietnam, which sent emissaries periodically to bring presents to the Chinese emperor, the Chinese people believed that the tribute system confirmed the superiority of Chinese (Han) civilization. Relations between China and Korea or China and Vietnam were not analogous to relations between sovereign nations in an anarchic international system or even between a colonizing power and its colony; rather, the nations surrounding China were considered inferior because they were not Chinese. Only through adoption of Chinese civilization, which the neighboring elites would be exposed to during their voyages to pay tribute to the Chinese emperor, would the nations on China's borders be accepted as anything but barbarians.

Except for seven maritime voyages of exploration between 1405 and 1433, in which Chinese ships sailed as far as the Middle East and Africa, China did not seek information about the outside world. It neither fought external wars nor searched for external markets, and foreigners who came to China were welcome so long as they accepted the superiority of Chinese civilization. Those peoples such as the Mongols (1279–1367) or the Manchus (1644–1911) who dared to invade China and establish their own dynasties were quickly sinicized. The Chinese nation could easily afford to practice what today would be called an isolationist foreign policy. All under heaven could be found within the Middle Kingdom.

The Western world did not understand the Chinese concept of the Middle Kingdom. The British, the Russians, and the rest of Europe and the United States discovered China, and beginning in the eighteenth century demanded free access and free trade. China had tea, spices, silk, and porcelain, which the people in Europe and the United States wanted to buy, but the Chinese people had no particular desire to buy anything from abroad. And to Chinese emperors, the notion that emissaries from foreign monarchs should be treated as equals was even more absurd. Unless Westerners in China became sinicized, that is, accepted the superiority of Chinese civilization, the Qing dynasty court believed they should not be in China. European demands for establishment of diplomatic relations and exchange of ambassadors were therefore repeatedly denied.

The Chinese did not understand the Western system of sovereign states jockeying for power within the international system. The West did not understand the Chinese system of a political system shaped by natural forces. The result was a battle between two civilizations, each equally convinced of its own superiority. Unfortunately for the Chinese people, by the nineteenth century Western nations had become more dynamic and more powerful than China. The result of the conflict was that China was no longer in accord with the Mandate of Heaven or a sovereign state in the international system dominated by Western powers. By the early twentieth century, the foreign powers in China had as much and perhaps more political, military, and economic power than did the remnants of the Qing dynasty.

## The Unequal Treaties

The Chinese emperor Ch'ien Lung allowed a limited number of foreign merchants to establish a seasonal base near Guangzhou (formerly Canton) in the late eighteenth century, from which they were allowed to trade with thirteen authorized Chinese merchant groups (*hongs*). They quickly began to buy Chinese silks, porcelain, teas, and chinaware; the Chinese bought foreign furs, sandalwood, and ginseng. The balance of trade favored China. To redress this negative balance of trade, Great Britain began selling opium to the Chinese. By 1840 the balance of trade once again favored the West.

The Chinese emperor and his chief lieutenants, who were distressed by the negative effects of opium smoking on both the Chinese people and the Chinese economy, banned the cultivation, import, and smoking of opium. They were, however, too weak to enforce their own regulations. In 1839, after a Chinese official blockaded foreign warehouses and forced merchants to turn over 20,000 opium chests for public burning, the British military launched a punitive military expedition. The Opium Wars ensued, which were handily won by superior British military forces.

As the price for peace, the Chinese emperor was forced to sign unequal treaties that gave the island of Hong Kong to the British and established five treaty ports. The treaty ports resembled European port cities with special zones for foreigners that contained warehouses, shops, restaurants, and homes, all of which were staffed by Chinese. Foreign nationals in the foreign enclaves (and eventually in all China) were exempt from Chinese law and subject only to the laws of their home country, a doctrine known in international law as *extraterritoriality* and usually accorded only to diplomatic representatives. The treaty ports were so advantageous that all the Western powers wanted one. Eventually, more than eighty treaty ports were established.

Even the United States, which never officially had its own treaty port, demanded all the rights and privileges in China that had accrued to the other Western powers and their citizens. Thus was established the international principle of most-favored-nation (MFN) status (currently the basis of the General Agreement on Trade and Tariffs, or GATT), which is defined as agreement by consenting states to grant each other equal access to their domestic markets. China and the United States to this day spar over the terms of conditions of MFN status. Each year, members of the U.S. Congress attempt to defeat reauthorization unless China improves its human rights record.

## Free Trade

The Opium Wars, which were fought to establish who would control whether opium was exported to China, were a victory for the Western advocates of free trade. The Western powers regarded this as just, because they believed that free trade was a right rather than a privilege. President John Quincy Adams, despite his abhorrence of opium, praised England for fighting a just war for the "Christian precept" of open trade. From the 1840s onward, when the first unequal treaties were signed, the foreign powers increasingly controlled parts of coastal China and Chinese foreign trade.

Free trade, in the Chinese context, was translated into increasing foreign control. Instead of being paid tribute, the Chinese emperors had become in effect the tributaries of foreign powers that had encroached on their own land. The last Qing dynasty emperors and empresses cooperated with the foreign powers to prolong their own rule, which could easily have been ended by foreign military forces, but the dynasty had lost the Mandate of Heaven.

## Chinese Nationalism

The Chinese people chafed at the foreign presence in their country and began to develop a modern form of nationalism. Instead of viewing China's place in the world through the traditional context of the Middle Kingdom, a movement began in the late nineteenth century to develop a nation that had both wealth and power. With wealth and power, China would no longer be subject to foreign nations.

Nascent nationalist sentiments were evinced throughout all strata of Chinese society, with the "recovery of sovereign rights" as the mantra of all groups. The Boxers, a secret society with some criminal connections, joined with the rural gentry and anti-Western officials to oppose foreign influence in China. The Boxer Uprising of 1900 was put down with the assistance of foreign troops, but not before approximately 250 foreigners had been killed. A more studied approach to the problem was adopted by the urban intelligentsia and merchant classes, who sent their sons to Japan to learn how an Asian nation had beaten the West at its own game. In Tokyo in 1905 Chinese reformers established a secret revolutionary league that was the antecedent to the Nationalist Party. Even the Qing government itself favored a reform initiative, but it was a case of too little too late, and in 1911 the Qing dynasty collapsed. The mandate had passed on to a new generation.

On May 4, 1919, came the defining moment in modern Chinese nationalism. Anti-Western and anti-Japanese demonstrations erupted in China to protest the terms of the treaty that ended World War I. The

European powers, meeting in the Versailles Palace in France, had agreed that German enclaves in China would be handed over to the Japanese rather than returned to China. Inspired by the desire to force the victorious powers in World War I to redress the insults heaped on China and spearheaded by students and intellectuals, the May 4th movement spawned many political organizations dedicated to strengthening China and driving the foreigners out.

The Chinese Communist Party (CCP) was one political organization that had its roots in the May 4th movement. Founded in 1921 with some Soviet assistance, early Communist leaders actually worked together with the Kuomintang (Nationalist) Party in the interests of developing a strong nationalist movement in China. The two parties had irreconcilable visions of a strong, nationalist China, however, and their united front lasted only through the mid-1920s. From the late 1930s through the late 1940s, the Communist Party's nationalism came to be more attractive to the Chinese people than that of the ruling Nationalist Party. Under the leadership of Mao Zedong, the Communist Party used the desire for a proud and independent Chinese nation to recruit supporters throughout the fight against Japan during World War II. The perception that the Communists, and not the ruling Kuomintang Party, were truly fighting the Japanese invaders was crucial to the Communist victory over the Nationalists in the Chinese civil war from 1945 through 1949. When Mao Zedong proclaimed the establishment of the People's Republic of China (PRC) on October 1, 1949, one of his foremost goals was the establishment of a Chinese nation-state that was independent of foreign influence.

## THE COLD WAR WORLD SYSTEM

The People's Republic was established in a world unlike any other in history. Two superpowers, both armed with sufficient nuclear weapons to destroy themselves and everybody else, dominated the international system. They did so not in the interests of creating a stable, bipolar balance-of-power system to prevent a world war that would be too costly to the superpowers; rather, the superpowers added ideology to the traditional power rivalry. Communism versus capitalism became an international security issue. For the first time in history, differences over economics defined the global regime.

The stakes were high—total annihilation. Because the stakes were so high, most nation-states in the world, big or small, felt compelled to join the bloc of one superpower or the other. Belonging to one of the two alliance systems provided a security umbrella, but at the price of limiting autonomy of action. Few nation-states could maintain strong diplomatic and trade relations with their counterparts in the opposing alliance system.

The world became bifurcated, and each nation's scope of action was dictated from the center of the alliance system.

The bipolar balance of power was highly static between the United States and the Soviet Union, which prevented the Cold War from erupting into a real war, but transitions in the two alliance systems came about through competition on the fringes. Many countries in Africa and Asia bore the brunt of the Cold War as the two superpowers fought proxy wars in Vietnam, Angola, Korea, Mozambique, and countless other countries around the world. The Cold War was costly not only to the two superpowers but also to the client states they courted and sometimes fought over.

## THE PEOPLE'S REPUBLIC OF CHINA

Mao and Zhou Enlai, the Chinese prime minister and foreign minister for most of the period from 1949 through 1976, sought to maintain China's autonomy while enhancing its security within the world system created by the Cold War. China's leaders always conceived of their nation as an independent and major actor in the international system, threatened at times by the United States, at other times by the Soviet Union, and sometimes by both superpowers. But China's leaders never considered themselves to be subordinate to either major power after World War II. Mao and Zhou's foreign policy goals were as follows: "China's leaders have regularly viewed international politics as a struggle for hegemony among superpowers, have maintained an abiding concern with their security and sovereignty against threats from abroad, have sought to preserve a high degree of independence and initiative in their international conduct, and have tended to identify their country with the developing nations of the Third World, rather than with either of the two superpowers."[1]

> The Five Principles of Peaceful Coexistence, which are cited by Beijing as its standard for international contact, are as follows:
>
> 1. mutual respect for sovereignty and territorial integrity
> 2. nonaggression
> 3. noninterference in each other's internal affairs
> 4. equality and mutual benefit
> 5. peaceful coexistence.

Mao and Zhou remembered the era of the unequal treaties all too well, so much so that autonomy and a fierce defense of Chinese sovereignty became the basic tenets of the foreign policy of the People's Republic of China.

## Security

However much China's leaders may have desired autonomy, even a large regional power with nearly one-quarter of the world's population could not remain isolated from the bipolar system of the Cold War for long. Mao Zedong guided the People's Republic to "lean to one side," the Soviet side, from 1949 through 1960. Though still attempting to maintain an independent stance and ever prickly about issues relating to Chinese sovereignty, Mao believed that security imperatives and ideological similarities behoved China's friendship with the Soviet Union. When Sino-Soviet relations broke down over controversies relating to sovereignty, security, and ideology, China tried to be truly autonomous throughout the 1960s. Border clashes with the Soviet Union convinced Mao and Zhou to lean to one side again, but this time toward the United States. Throughout the 1970s, China's relations with the United States were markedly better than its relations with the Soviet Union, and Washington promoted Sino-U.S. relations as a bargaining chip with Moscow. From 1949 through 1991, Beijing leaned at times toward Moscow and at other times toward Washington, but these special relations were based on tactical interests and never amounted to anything that might be perceived as permanent alliances.[2] Rather, Mao and Zhou sought, with some success, to enhance China's security by playing off the superpowers.

## Autonomy

The constant element of Chinese foreign policy during the Cold War was the desire to participate in the bipolar international system only to the extent necessary to preserve and enhance China's autonomy. China would lean to one side and then to the other, and it would seek friends in the Third World, but its continual security imperative was the jealous preservation of its sovereignty.

To a large extent, China succeeded. Nikita Khrushchev began to acknowledge China's demands for full sovereignty in the middle 1950s when he returned territory and economic concessions wrested from Mao by Stalin. Khrushchev became nervous, however, as China worked to develop its trump card in its battle for autonomy in the international system—a nuclear capability. A sovereign communist China was acceptable to Khrushchev, even though the ideological conflicts between the two communist nations were troublesome. A nuclear neighbor on the Soviet border was not acceptable, however, and a complete rupture of relations between China and the Soviet Union ensued.

By leaning to the other side, China also achieved U.S. acceptance of the sanctity of China's borders as defined by Beijing. In the Shanghai Communique, which was signed when President Nixon visited China in

1972, the United States acknowledged that the island of Taiwan is a part of China and that unification of the island with the mainland is an internal Chinese affair. U.S. abdication of responsibility for the security of its Nationalist allies on Taiwan was deemed by the Communist Chinese as a victory. A reminder of the era of unequal treaties and foreign domination had been removed to the benefit of the People's Republic. Through a combination of obduracy and skillful diplomacy, China achieved international respect for the inviolability of its borders.

## Friendship with the Third World

Although China was constrained by the bipolar international system of the Cold War era from true independence of action, its leaders believed it could acquire friends and serve as a model to Third World nations still struggling to find their identity in the postcolonial world. Zhou Enlai therefore traveled to Bandung, Indonesia, in 1955 to join twenty-eight other nations in calling for a "nonaligned movement." In the era when China's relations with the Soviet Union were friendly if not warm and rapprochement with the United States was still in the future, promoting friendship with Third World nations was often China's only way of reaching the outside world. In some states, such as Indonesia, Chinese friendship took the form of promoting communist rebels; in other states, such as Tanzania, Chinese friendship took the form of economic aid and technical advice. Some Third World countries, such as India, came to be enemies, not friends. Yet from the late 1950s until 1972, China's attempt to define a role for itself in the international system beyond the bounds of Soviet or U.S. control was based on its relationship to the many nations that sought nonalignment in the Cold War.

Before the People's Republic of China's credentials were recognized by the United Nations in 1971, Beijing involved itself in international fora only when a Chinese security issue was on the agenda. In 1971, after the People's Republic finally assumed the Chinese seat in the United Nations Security Council, its position relative to the Third World changed. Now the People's Republic was not only a supporter of Third World aspirations. It was a powerful voice in the United Nations system, in which the non-aligned nations of the Third World exerted their power most effectively. By virtue of sheer numbers, the Third World nations could outvote the super-powers and their allies in the United Nations General Assembly. However, to make their voice heard in the United Nations Security Council, these nations had to turn to China.

The People's Republic of China had by default become a leader of the Third World movement, and Chinese statements in the United Nations have always reflected a consciousness of this position. By its inclusion in the Security Council, however, China also became a power in the international system, and its votes in the United Nations reflect a caution that belies the People's Republic's old rhetoric identifying China with revolutionary forces in the Third World.

An examination of China's changing role in the Cold War era from 1949 to 1991 reveals that the values pronounced in Beijing have often come in conflict with each other. As with every other actor in the international system, China's leaders have tried to balance changing perceptions of outside security threats with possible opportunities for increased power and influence, often with conflicting results. The demands of the Cold War system forced China to be creative in defense of its security and in seeking support from other nations. China's solution was to play the international system for all it was worth by siding with either superpower when necessary, courting the Third World when isolated, and acting as a great power when it was in Beijing's interest to do so.

## ORIGINS OF THE NEW WORLD ORDER

The end of the Cold War world order has offered China's leaders an entirely new set of foreign policy and security issues to grapple with. From 1985, when Mikhail Gorbachev became secretary-general of the Communist Party of the Soviet Union, to 1989, when the communist regimes in Eastern Europe fell, the Chinese Communist Party leaders became increasingly agitated. Gorbachev's attempts to restructure the Soviet Communist Party were considered by the Chinese to be hasty and ill-planned, a bad example to other communist regimes. When the Berlin wall fell and Germany was rapidly unified, the Chinese leaders felt at once vindicated because their reservations about Gorbachev's program had been borne out; yet they were also nervous over what it meant for the remaining communist parties in the world. Many heated discussions took place in Beijing over how China should react officially, but ultimately moderation prevailed, and the People's Republic recognized the new regimes. Ideology was not a sufficiently strong factor to motivate China's leaders to isolate themselves from the changes in Europe.

The collapse of the Soviet Union was entirely different. Not only had the progenitor of all communist regimes on earth collapsed, discrediting the ideology that still defined the political myth of the People's Republic of China, but it left in its wake a whole new international and regional security configuration. The international system was no longer bipolar. Instead, one superpower was predominant, with a number of regional powers such as the European Community and Japan becoming increasingly important. China, too, was transformed into a regional power with the potential to affect future security alignments in East Asia. As the world system is reconfigured in the post–Cold War era, a form of multipolarity may ensue.

How has China reacted? According to the *People's Daily,* "Three great trends are now evident in the world: (1) the emergence of the United States as the sole surviving superpower after the disintegration of the Soviet Union and the Gulf War; (2) the emergence of a multipolar world because of political, economic and technological changes; and (3) the resurgence of nationalism with accompanying ethnic, religious, and territorial disputes."[3] China, a nation-state with one-quarter of the world's population, an increasingly powerful military, and a rapidly growing economy, is likely to grow in power and influence as unipolarity is transformed into multipolarity. However, being surrounded by former republics of the Soviet Union, with all their ethnic and economic problems, and being emerged in several irredentist campaigns itself, China is likely to become involved in the resurgence of nationalist disputes, with the attendant external and internal security threats. Chinese involvement in military activities somewhere in central, eastern, or southern Asia is not improbable as tensions flare up on the borders with the former Soviet Union, on the Korean Peninsula, and potentially with Taiwan. In the post–Cold War era, defending China's security interests in East Asia will entail selecting from an infinitely more complex series of options than was the case during the Cold War.

## CHINA'S GOALS IN THE NEW WORLD ORDER

China will undoubtedly play an increasingly powerful role in defining East Asia's security configurations. Whether it is as a peacemaker—a "police force" that uses a combination of diplomacy and threat to prevent conflict—or as an enforcer—a military power that achieves its goals through force—will largely depend on the outcome of the succession struggle currently underway in Beijing. Statements from Beijing, however, continue to stress China's peaceful intentions and its desire to achieve a new world order that includes the following basic aspects:

1. All countries, big or small, strong or weak, rich or poor, are equal sovereign members of the international community entitled to participate on an equal footing in the consultations and settlement of world affairs, and such practices as the big bullying the small, the strong lording over the weak, and the rich oppressing the poor should be rejected.

2. Each and every country has the right to choose independently its own social, political, and economic systems and course of development in light of its specific conditions. No country should interfere in the internal affairs of other countries or seek to impose its own values, ideology, or mode of development on others.

3. In international relations, there must be mutual respect for sovereignty and territorial integrity. No country should invade or annex the terri-

tory of other countries under any pretext. International disputes should be settled in a fair and just manner through peaceful negotiations rather than the use or threat of force, let alone by means of war.

4. In order to attain common development and prosperity for all the countries in the world, the economic exchanges among countries should be carried out on the basis of equality and mutual benefit, a just international economic relationship should be established, and the assistance should be supplied without attaching any political conditions. With the world economy becoming more and more internationalized, the economies of various countries are increasingly interrelated. If the economies of the numerous Third World countries remain underdeveloped for a long time, it will neither facilitate the economic development of the developed countries nor genuinely ensure peace and stability in the world.[4]

Peace and prosperity will ensue, according to official Chinese policy, if the people of the world work together and adhere to the United Nations Charter. Yet, as with any other nation-state in the world system, China's own foreign policy goals are limited and self-serving. The drive for security, economic and military power, and influence will be the focus of the next generation of Chinese leaders. How China accommodates its broad prescriptions for the international system with the foreign policy choices it will have to make in the early twenty-first century will determine China's status. It may also affect the stability of the international system, for although China may be only a regional power, it is a large and powerful nation in the center of a regional system that will become increasingly important in the next century.

## POLICY OPTIONS IN THE POST–COLD WAR ERA

China's primary foreign policy goal for the twenty-first century is to cement political friendships and a stable international environment that will allow Beijing to develop its economy and its trade and to acquire advanced technology.[5] However, certain Chinese values and interests conflict with these goals. In the post–Cold War era, China's next generation of leaders will have to assess whether maintaining these values and interests will conflict with their primary foreign policy goal. Their decisions will have a profound effect on East Asia and the world.

### Option 1: Nationalism Versus Communism

Communist ideology has been discredited throughout the world, except in official China. Although the Chinese Communist Party continues to aver that it is leading the Chinese nation toward socialism and then communism, in reality it seems to be leading the nation toward capitalism. As a result, a large portion of the Chinese people no longer are interested in making revolution; rather, they are interested in making money. Communism has been discredited abroad and has very little credibility in China. For the Chinese Communist Party to continue its leading role, it will have to seek the support of the people through an ideology other than communism. Nationalism is the most obvious candidate, especially because an appeal to the people's sense of national pride helped Mao Zedong win control over China in the first place.

However, whipping up nationalist sentiments can be dangerous and can even redound to the detriment of those who first raise the flag. Yugoslavia is one example. Perhaps more pertinent is the revival of nationalist sentiment in Russia, which is causing great fear among Russia's neighbors and is driving them to demand stronger military ties to the North Atlantic Treaty Organization (NATO). If Eastern Europe joins NATO, even in some sort of junior status, the Russian sense of encirclement will increase. This might cause a future Russian government to react militarily.

The search by the leaders of the Chinese Communist Party to define a new political myth that justifies their continued rule is fraught with difficulties for China and its neighbors. Nationalism may be used positively by stressing the greatness of Chinese history and civilization and the Chinese Communist Party's efforts to continue that greatness. For a party that has already largely lost the support and even the interest of its people, however, the only sort of nationalism that is likely to serve as a factor to unify and motivate the Chinese people behind the banner of the CCP is the demagogic sort of nationalism. If the CCP chooses to assert itself in this manner, its neighbors will feel increasingly threatened, and security in East Asia will be endangered.

## Option 2: Nationalism Versus Irredentism

How China handles the transition in Hong Kong from British sovereignty to rule from Beijing will do a great deal to determine its international reputation in the new world order. If Hong Kong's financial markets survive intact, presumably because China honors its commitment to allow a separate economic system in the former colony for fifty years, Beijing will be credited with handling the transition gracefully. If Beijing clamps down heavily on political discourse and tries to control Hong Kong's free-wheeling financial structure, the outside world will condemn China as tyrannical. A successful transition of power will not only benefit China economically, because much of southeastern China's economy is tied into Hong Kong's economy, but it will also give the Chinese Communist leaders a boost in their political credibility at home and abroad.

This type of credibility is most important to China as it seeks finally to resolve the Taiwan issue. China has never allowed consideration of any option other than Taiwanese reunification with China. If the Hong Kong transition is smooth, Taiwanese leaders might be willing to contemplate some sort of gradual, peaceful union. If the Hong Kong transition is not successful, Taiwanese leaders will seek to maintain their independence. Chinese leaders might then be tempted to resort to the military option to effect Taiwanese reunification.

China also seeks control over groups of islands in the South China Sea, primarily because of the possibility of oil in the area. These islands are also claimed by Vietnam and the Philippines, and many believe that arguments over which nation rightfully owns the islands could easily flare up into open warfare. Alternative solutions, such as establishing joint control of the area, or dividing the islands among the contending powers, have not been discussed. The South China Sea may be an international "hot spot" in the early twenty-first century.

How China handles each of its territorial claims will have a tremendous effect on its international credibility and on its position as a regional power in East Asia. If China resorts to heavy-handed political maneuvering or, even more alarmingly, to military actions, it will harm its own economy, its international standing, and its credibility as an adjudicator of peace on the United Nations Security Council. China may, however, engage in the diplomatic maneuvering to effect expanded influence in Hong Kong, Taiwan, and the South China Sea without resorting to force or coercion. Again, the choices Beijing makes will depend on who succeeds Deng Xiaoping as China's supreme leader.

## Option 3: Leninism Versus Western Democracy and Civil Rights

Next to strong support for Chinese nationalism, perhaps the most strongly held value in the minds of China's leaders is the belief that the CCP is best able to promote not only the restoration of China as a great nation but also the people's well-being. Events in Eastern Europe and the Soviet Union, as well as the demonstrations at Tiananmen Square, have only strengthened the determination of the CCP leaders to take whatever measures are necessary to maintain the party's Mandate of Heaven. All party factions agree, ironically, that the CCP is best able to maintain Confucian values such as order, stability, and effective rule from above.

- CCP leaders, whether conservatives, moderates, or reformers, believe that the well-being of the Chinese nation and its people requires economic growth and the social rights that communist societies traditionally define as human rights, including the following: modernization; higher living standards; the right to work;

education; and the provision of life's essentials such as food, health care, shelter, and clothing.

- Although moving away from totalitarian thought control and extreme forms of suppression, the CCP firmly believes in denying practices U.S. citizens consider to be their inalienable political and civil rights, as specified in the Constitution and the Bill of Rights. These practices include freedom of speech, freedom of assembly, freedom of religion, freedom of the press, an impartial judiciary, and freedom from arbitrary arrest and cruel and unusual punishment—what most U.S. citizens consider to be essential components of a representative democracy.

China's leaders have eliminated most of the totalitarian features of Leninism while retaining authoritarian controls. The question is whether China's leaders can maintain the support of the people, which is essential to continued rule by the CCP, through authoritarianism rather than some form of democratization. If the rest of the communist world serves as a model, party leaders may discover that the Chinese people will not accept the provision of social rights as a substitute for civil and political rights over the long term.

## Option 4: Marxism Versus Capitalism

The rapid modernization and development of China's economy, with annual gross national product (GNP) growth rates averaging 9 percent or better, has been achieved through the adoption of a number of capitalist reforms, including creation of private markets, private agricultural households, rural cooperatives (largely independent of government or party control), and joint ventures with foreign corporations. China's leaders may prefer to call these developments "socialism with Chinese characteristics," but Westerners call them capitalism. At the same time, China's leaders strongly support the continuation of a public sector, which means that China in effect has a dual economy. The coexistence of both large public and private sectors creates many problems, but China's leaders support a dual economy because they hope to attain the best of both possible worlds (the good features of both socialism and capitalism without the bad features of either). Maintaining a large public sector is politically expedient for the CCP for a number of reasons, which include the following:

- Public enterprises are a major source of party power and wealth. As the private sector grows, especially at the regional and local levels, the existence of a large public sector will give the Party continued leverage because private enterprises cannot survive or prosper without access to basic commodities and services produced in the public sector.

- China, in the present and future, faces many serious economic bottlenecks, such as a lack of capital and finance, energy, transportation, and basic resources such as water, timber, and iron ore. Continued party control over key sectors such as most banking and other financial services, utilities, energy, transportation, basic industries, and water supplies gives the CCP and government leverage to deal with these bottlenecks.
- From the Chinese perspective, a dual economy, with many public enterprises and services, as well as extensive regulatory authority, can help avoid some of the severe problems and inequities found in highly individualistic and capitalist societies such as the United States.

Yet, despite the many economic successes of the past decade, China's leaders may not be able to control a dual economy over the long term. One of China's leading dissidents predicts that the Communist Party will fail:

> What will emerge in China is a mixture of these many forces, but it will not be the kind of mixture this regime wants. It will not mix economic freedom with political unfreedom. Communism and capitalism are so completely different that no one will be fooled for long that they can be joined. In the end there will be a Chinese path, but it will be a different path to freedom, a different path to democracy. The Chinese people do not speak in Western phrases and political philosophies, but they know what kind of political and economic system best serves their own welfare.[6]

## Option 5: Rural Versus Urban Interests

The Chinese communist revolution was different from all other communist revolutions throughout the world because it was in large part a peasant revolution. In the 1990s, over 800 million Chinese (over two-thirds of the population) continue to live in rural areas. China's decisionmakers must pay careful attention to the well-being and further development of rural China if they are to lead their country's emergence as a successful and powerful nation in the twenty-first century:

- If the party is to maintain its Mandate of Heaven, it must take measures to maintain the support of China's rural masses, who continue to provide most of China's party cadres, soldiers, and human resources for China's rapidly developing economy (both in rural China and in urban centers through the migration of over 100 million peasants to China's burgeoning cities).

- Even with migration to the cities (which is causing increasing urban unemployment and other problems, including crime), over 100 million working-age men and women are either unemployed or underemployed in rural areas, creating enormous hardships and human suffering.
- China's leaders must make greater efforts to overcome severe inequities both between rural and urban areas and between China's more prosperous coastal areas (which contain much of the best farmland) and interior provinces. These inequities involve educational and employment opportunities (especially for women), level of health care, quality of consumer products (which are in increasing demand throughout China), entertainment and basic human needs such as an adequate diet. These inequities are also responsible for growing disparities in rural and urban lifestyles.

To overcome these differences, especially in the creation of new services and the availability of consumer goods, China's leaders will have to provide more incentives to overseas Chinese to invest in rural China. Up to now, because of their ability to adjust to conditions inside China, including rural areas, overseas Chinese are better able than Westerners and other foreigners to move beyond China's special economic zones (SEZs) in the coastal provinces to the vast hinterlands, the development of which will determine the future of China in the twenty-first century. How Beijing treats Hong Kong and Taiwanese Chinese in the 1990s and beyond could greatly affect the future contributions of over 55 million overseas Chinese, who continue to provide a majority of China's overseas investment, especially in rural areas. How Beijing manages China's peasantry will have a profound effect on the longevity of the CCP.

## Option 6: Alignment Versus
## Nonalignment and Splendid Isolation

Some of China's most difficult policy choices in the post–Cold War era will involve efforts by China's leaders to avoid external interference in China's internal affairs. At the same time, they will try to take advantage of changing global political-security and economic structures in order not only to benefit China at home but to increase its influence abroad. China's leaders have, in fact if not in theory, followed the axioms of structural realism, the predominant theory explaining international relations in the post–Cold War era.[7] Whereas traditional realists view the intentions of states with constant suspicion, structural realists (sometimes referred to as neorealists) make no prior judgments of the intentions of other states. Instead, they believe nations constantly reassess their intentions and capabilities in a geopolitical system in which intentions and capabilities are continually changing. Each state, after assessing how these changes can affect its own vital interests, then determines which policy options can minimize dangers and maximize opportunities. This occurs through alignment, nonalignment, or isolation. Some of the following considerations may help to clarify China's future alignments in the 1990s and in the twenty-first century:

- Major external threats to China in the near future seem to have diminished, and China's continuing internal weaknesses and primary emphasis on modernization and development largely preclude any external involvements that divert major Chinese resources from domestic problems.
- At the global level, Beijing may wish to be consulted as an emerging world power; however, China's leaders expect other, more wealthy and powerful states to bear most of the burdens of dealing with international political-security, racial-ethnic, economic, and environmental problems. Logically, if China's GNP continues to grow at 9 percent or more a year, Beijing may be willing to assume more global responsibilities in the twenty-first century.
- China will seek outside help from any sources but will try to avoid dependence on any one country, especially Japan or the United States. European and overseas Chinese investors, as well as investors from other Asian countries such as Korea, help to give China greater leverage in its relationships with the outside world.
- China's Open Door policy continues to be ideologically and politically neutral, without trade or investor preference for either capitalist or former communist countries. Global economic regimes (the World Bank and the International Monetary Fund), although capitalist in nature, are also viewed as major sources of assistance.
- Global security regimes, such as the Nuclear Non-Proliferation Treaty and the Missile Technology Control Regime, are viewed pragmatically, as are Chinese arms sales. Beijing will continue to assess these security regimes and the arms sales of other countries, as well as its own, according to China's perceived interests, not according to the wishes of countries such as the United States or the majority of members in the United Nations.

Faced with external threats and limited means of dealing with external dangers throughout the twentieth century, China's leaders have at times sought alignment with one power or groups of powers and at other times have sought to avoid entangling alliances. Ideological affinities have been secondary to perceived national interests, as demonstrated by China's behavior in the early Cold War years, when it first aligned with the Soviet Union in opposing the United States, later followed a policy of isolation in its relations with both the East and the West, then aligned with the United States against the Soviets, and finally sought friendly but nondependent relations in the 1990s with all major powers. In the post–Cold War era of changing geopolitical structures, however, China's security imperative will be to work with other nations to prevent any state or group of states from dominating the international system militarily or economically, especially in Asia. China will have to learn how to become a major power broker within a multipolar international system and a fragmented power system in Asia.

## SUGGESTED READINGS

Barnett, A. Doak. *China and the Major Powers in East Asia.* Washington, D.C.: Brookings, 1977.

Choudhury, Golam W. *China in World Affairs: The Foreign Policy of the PRC Since 1970.* Boulder, Colorado: Westview Press, 1979.

Garver, John W. *Foreign Relations of the People's Republic of China.* Englewood Cliffs, New Jersey: Prentice Hall, 1993.

Harding, Harry. *China's Foreign Relations in the 1980s.* New Haven, Connecticut: Yale University Press, 1984.

Kegley, Charles W., Jr., and Gregory Raymond. *A Multipolar Peace? Great-Power Politics in the Twenty-First Century.* New York: St. Martin's Press, 1994.

Kim, Samuel S. *China, the United Nations and World Order.* Princeton, New Jersey: Princeton University Press, 1979.

———, ed. *China and the World: Chinese Foreign Relations in the Post–Cold War Era.* Boulder, Colorado: Westview Press, 1993.

Nelsen, Harvey W. *Power and Insecurity: Beijing, Moscow, and Washington: 1949–1988.* Boulder, Colorado: Lynne Rienner Publishers, 1989.

Ogden, Suzanne, ed. *China,* 5th ed. Guildford, Connecticut: The Dushkin Publishing Group, Inc., 1993.

Shih, Chih-yu. *China's Just World: The Morality of Chinese Foreign Policy.* Boulder, Colorado: Lynne Rienner Publishers, 1992.

## NOTES

1. Harry Harding, "China's Changing Roles in the Contemporary World," in *China's Foreign Relations in the 1980s,* Harry Harding, ed. (New Haven, Connecticut: Yale University Press, 1984), p. 214.

2. For a recent analysis of the emerging multipolar system in the 1990s as well as a detailed comparison of the current system with earlier geopolitical power structures, see Charles W. Kegley and Gregory Raymond, *A Multipolar Peace? Great-Power Politics in the Twenty-first Century* (New York: St. Martin's Press, 1994).

3. Wayne Bert, "Chinese Policies and U.S. Interests in Southeast Asia," *Asian Survey* 23, no. 3 (March 1993): p. 319.

4. People's Republic of China Mission to the United Nations, "China's Position on Certain International Issues," press release (January 1992): pp. 14–15.

5. Wayne Bert, "Chinese Policies and U.S. Interests in Southeast Asia."

6. Liu Binyan, "Civilization Grafting: No Culture is an Island," *Foreign Affairs* 72, no. 4 (September/October 1993): p. 21.

7. The major study of structural realism is Kenneth N. Waltz, *Theory of International Relations* (Reading, Massachusetts: Addison-Wesley, 1979). Also see Waltz's article, "Realist Thought and Neorealist Theory in the Evolution of International Relations," in *The Evolution of International Relations,* Robert L. Rothstein, ed. (Columbia: University of South Carolina Press, 1991), pp. 21–38.

# Chinese Politics
and Ideology

In the 1990s, former Cold War protagonists seem increasingly concerned with difficult problems at home. Russia and the United States, for nearly forty-five years, were unable to deal with pressing domestic issues because their resources were consumed in geopolitical and ideological struggles around the globe. But China is a different story. With Mao's triumph in 1949, the long civil war and struggle with the Japanese came to an end, only to be replaced by a struggle to revolutionize China from within, a struggle that continues to the present. With the exception of the 1950–1953 Korean War and minor border skirmishes, China's internal struggles have preoccupied the minds of its leaders and masses. Thus, foreign policy, whether political-security or economic, has always been secondary to domestic concerns. This remains true today, even though with Deng Xiaoping's Open Door policy, China has sought to use outside resources to help bolster the development of its Four Modernizations at home: agriculture, industry, science and technology, and military capability.

## CHINA'S TRADITIONAL FOREIGN RELATIONS

One can better understand China's external relations, even today, by turning back the pages of history to ancient times. For thousands of years, the Middle Kingdom has been one of the world's richest, most developed, and powerful civilizations. Supreme self-confidence and a lack of understanding of the world beyond its outer boundaries, however, poorly prepared its rulers for the colonial and imperial outreach of Western European powers, beginning with the Dutch and the Portuguese in the sixteenth century and later including the British, French, Germans, and Russians.

During periods of strong rule from Xian (China's ancient capital in the interior) and later in Beijing, China's dynasties extended their influence outward to Tibet and Central Asia to the west and the regions known today as Indochina to the southeast. During weaker periods, however, when rival regional warlords struggled with each other and with China's national dynasties, power contracted. European powers were able to take advantage of internal rivalries and weaknesses to establish colonies in China's coastal regions, such as Macao (a Portuguese colony), Hong Kong (British), and on the Shandong peninsula in eastern China (German). In the late nineteenth century, the Japanese also gained control of traditional Chinese territory, such as the island of Taiwan in the East China Sea, as well as a number of other smaller islands in the region. In the north and northeast, China's dynasties also suffered humiliation and conquest at the hands of the Russian czars as they extended their area of control across Siberia to the Pacific Ocean in the nineteenth century, exercising control over territories formerly under the influence of the Middle Kingdom in earlier times.

Unlike the European militarists who came in boats from far across the sea, China's ancient rulers extended their influence to the outer periphery of the Middle Kingdom through cultural influence and deference. During strong dynastic periods, distant rulers would send envoys to Xian and Beijing with gifts and homage, in the manner in which lords paid fealty to overlords in feudalistic societies. In Southeast Asia, Chinese influence in ancient as well as modern times has been based on the migration of overseas Chinese, who have become the backbone of business, finance, and trade in many parts of Southeast Asia.

Needless to say, twentieth-century Chinese, remembering the glories of ancient Chinese civilization in which Chinese culture, including its written language, spread throughout much of Asia have felt deeply humiliated at the hands of the Western imperialists and the Japanese invaders. These outsiders showed little respect for Chinese culture and sought to impose political, military, and economic control over China's coastal regions. Modern Chinese nationalism, which has a strong appeal to the mass ethnic-racial stock known as the Han people (over 93 percent of the population in modern China), gained its strength as a protest movement against the foreign "devils." In southern China, provinces such as Guangdong and Fujian rose up against the British in the Opium Wars of the 1840s, only to be humiliated by further British penetration of the region. The British took control of Hong Kong during this period and forced Beijing to sign a humiliating treaty at the turn of the century that gave Britain a ninety-nine-year lease over some mainland territory adjacent to Hong Kong (known as the New Territories).

Support for China's nationalist revolution of 1911, which did away with dynastic rule, came from the Chinese masses, who wished to create a strong modern China as a means of liberating the Middle Kingdom from foreign domination and humiliation. Sun Yat-sen, in the same year, was recognized as the founder of modern China when he returned from overseas to help establish a new Chinese republic. Sun pushed for three goals simultaneously, the *Three Principles of the People,* although he did not live to see them accomplished. First, he wished to instill a feeling of nationalist pride to unify the Chinese nation and free it from foreign control. Second, he sought to establish modern democratic institutions, which he believed were essential to mobilize the people to bring about his other goals. Third, he sought to bring about the modernization of China through education, technology, improvement in social well-being, and education. During his last days, Sun Yat-sen worked closely with other nationalistic leaders in China, who shared Sun's aspirations for national unity and modernization although differing with him on the political strategy (type of political mobilization) to restore China to its rightful role as a great Asian nation.

## THE MANDATE OF HEAVEN AND THE CHINESE COMMUNIST PARTY

### Early Party Days and the Long March

The Chinese Communist Party was founded in 1921, four years after the Bolshevik Revolution in Russia. On instructions from Moscow, China's fledgling Communist Party worked with the Kuomintang, led by Chiang Kai-shek, who had been trained as a revolutionary in Russia. In 1927, however, Chiang turned on his Communist partners, wiping out their urban bases and forcing the remnants of the CCP to flee to the interior countryside. Mao Zedong, who had joined the CCP in 1923, and other party stalwarts formed the first Chinese Soviet Republic in a region protected by surrounding mountains in southern China in 1931. When Chiang's forces threatened to overrun their mountain retreat, Mao and a small band of dedicated Communists retreated to Yenan in northwestern China. This difficult journey, covering thousands of miles through China's interior in 1934, became known as the *Long March,* one of the central myths of Chinese communism, showing how the Communists, supported by the people, could overcome all adversity. It was during the Long March that Mao Zedong finally assumed leadership of the CCP after defeating the more urban-oriented members of the Communist Party. Mao's strategies and tactics were unique, different in essential ways from the system of Marxism-Leninism practiced by the Bolsheviks in the Soviet Union. His unique system of politics, based on the support of the peasantry, was one of the great twentieth-century contributions to revolutionary theory and practice and contributed to the eventual triumph of the CCP over both the Kuomintang and the Japanese invaders.

### The Mass Line and Rural Revolution

Mao abandoned standard Marxist orthodoxy to favor a rural, peasant revolution out of necessity. The CCP had little choice because most of the

Communists in China's cities had been wiped out by the Kuomintang. Unlike the traditional warlords, who robbed the peasants and used them in their rival struggles for power, Mao and his followers worked with the peasants and helped them with their harvests and in their struggles to gain control of the land from ruling landlords. Mao referred to this relationship between the party cadres and the peasants as the *mass line,* in which party cadres learned from the peasants, refined the peasants' views based on party doctrine, and developed policies that reflected the people's will refracted through CCP ideology. For China's peasants, being listened to by their leaders was an unprecedented experience.

Mao and his initially small band of followers in Yenan gained strength by recruiting peasants into the CCP and the People's Liberation Army (PLA). Mao also gained strength by appealing to Chinese nationalism. Many believed that the Communist military was far more dedicated to fighting the Japanese than were the Kuomintang forces. To show their patriotism, young urban intellectuals began to journey to Yenan to join the movement.

After the defeat of the Japanese, Mao and Chiang fought for control of China, and Mao's combined appeal to the peasantry and to Chinese patriotism won the day. The Nationalists, who were holed up in the cities with little support in the countryside, were no match for Mao's rural-based revolutionary forces. Militarily, the triumphant People's Liberation Army had little in the way of modern military equipment, except for the U.S. equipment it appropriated from Nationalist forces. It triumphed instead through the support of the masses and through sheer determination.

With its final triumph on the mainland in 1949 and the retreat of the Kuomintang to the island of Taiwan in the East China Sea, Mao's Communists gained a new Mandate of Heaven from the people. The Chinese people celebrated the establishment of the People's Republic of China on October 1, 1949, as Mao's portrait was hung in triumph from the outer wall of the Forbidden City, the former home of China's emperors and empresses. China's modern unification, which began with the 1911 revolution that ended the Qing dynasty, had now come full circle. A new regime, a people's regime, had seized the Mandate of Heaven.

## The Korean War

The new government of China did not have to wait long to receive its first major test. On June 25, 1950, North Korean troops swept into South Korea. U.S. forces, under a United Nations umbrella, soon landed on the Korean peninsula and started marching northward. Mao Zedong and the other Communist leaders grew increasingly uneasy as General MacArthur, who led the U.S. effort, spoke of marching to the Yalu River. Mao, we now know, agonized over how to respond. Ultimately, however, he felt compelled to protect his nascent regime from possible invasion by committing Chinese "volunteers" to fight with the North Koreans. For the next three years, the Chinese sustained large losses, both from battle and from frostbite, but they did succeed in stalemating the Korean conflict. In the 1953 armistice, the United Nations forces agreed to stay below the thirty-eighth parallel. Mao's northeastern flank was now safe.

Even though the Korean War severely strained China's weak economy, the patriotic support of China's people (through the Resist America campaign) helped the party to consolidate its power and extend its control throughout Chinese society. Largely through its own efforts—the United States led an international commercial embargo, and the Soviet Union was miserly in its aid—the party mobilized the masses to build a new infrastructure and industrial base. What modern industry, transportation networks, communications systems, and energy utilization had existed in China before 1949 had been concentrated in the coastal areas and was destroyed during the anti-Japanese war and the civil war.

Mass mobilization was achieved in a number of ways, most importantly through land reform. The old landlord system was destroyed to allow the peasants to work under party supervision in rural collectives and workers' brigades. In addition to working the land, peasants spent slack time building roads, expanding irrigation systems, working in small-scale factories, etc. Living standards were sacrificed to provide capital for large-scale industrialization in the Soviet style of quick modernization. In return for the people's—men's and women's—sacrifices, the party promised all Chinese vastly improved medical care, sufficient food, and improved educational opportunities. These egalitarian benefits, provided by the production units in the countryside or the work units in the urban areas, became known as the *iron rice bowl*. Like in the early days of Soviet communism, the people were told that their sacrifices would create a better tomorrow for their children. Sacrifices in an era of state socialism would lead, the Chinese leaders said, to better living standards in a future era of communism.

## Let One Hundred Flowers Bloom

By 1957, Mao, who was always impatient, was dissatisfied with the pace of the party's efforts to achieve socialism. Temporarily abandoning the Leninist principle of silencing all overt criticism of the party, Mao called on the people, especially the Chinese intellectuals, to speak out about what needed to be done to improve conditions in China. Many Chinese responded to Mao's call to "let one hundred flowers bloom" by voicing criticism against existing party policies and rule. After a year of officially sanctioned criticism, Mao reversed himself and announced that there were weeds in his flower garden that needed to be pruned with a shovel. Those intellectuals who had spoken out were punished and received a black mark on their records that would come to haunt them during the Cultural Revolution.

Mao achieved two goals through the Hundred Flowers campaign. First, he exposed those who were not totally supportive of the Communist regime. Second, he was able to manipulate the people's criticisms to attack the party members who favored a rational, planned march toward socialism and communism. Fearing that he was losing ground to party members who favored development in a Soviet style, Mao sought to undermine their authority. He succeeded, but at a terrible cost. No longer would the intellectuals voice their doubts about Communist policies, and their quiescence hindered the free interchange of ideas necessary for advanced economic development and industrialization.

## The Great Leap Forward

After the collapse of the Hundred Flowers campaign, Mao sought to restore momentum to China's revolution by mobilizing the masses in new forms of social and economic efforts that would be unique to China. In 1958, collectivized farming was abandoned in favor of the creation of huge, county-size communes in which family life gave way to total sharing of resources, services, and even home chores such as cooking. To promote industrialization in the countryside, backyard steel furnaces were built all over the country, and dams and irrigation networks were built by hand. But the complete reorganization of the countryside did not suddenly produce a communist society, as Mao predicted it would. Rather, the people, who remained attached to fundamental values such as the nurturing of the traditional family, refused to accept the experiments in community living. Backyard steel was of such poor quality that the farm utensils melted down to make it would have been worth more. The irrigation networks could not withstand China's frequently adverse climatic conditions. The real results of the Great Leap Forward were economic dislocations and a drastic decline in agricultural productivity from 1958 to 1961. Widespread famine ensued. The communist government now acknowledges sixteen million deaths from malnutrition; other estimates range from twenty to fifty million deaths.[1]

The other members of the international socialist fraternity were appalled by the Great Leap Forward. The Soviet Union, in particular, resented Mao's claims that he had found the way to skip the socialist stage and immediately move into pure communism. If the first socialist country still had not advanced to Marx's second stage, how could Mao claim to have done so in an impoverished, rural society? Many CCP regulars were as appalled as the Soviets, and Mao was forced to abandon the communes in 1961 and revert to Soviet-style economic planning. The peasants were organized into workers' brigades within agricultural collectives, which were controlled by party cadres. Normal family life based on individual households was restored.

## The Cultural Revolution

After several years of ascendancy of those in the CCP whom Mao perceived to be opposed to his romantic notions of revolution, Mao came to believe that he was treated with respect but that nobody listened to him. The "Great Helmsman" became increasingly fretful that pragmatists—not idealists—pervaded the party and the state bureaucracy. Unlike Stalin, who sought to consolidate his power by using the secret police to purge his perceived enemies, Mao adopted an original approach. He called on Chinese youth to join together in groups, the Red Guards, to struggle against party cadres, government officials, enterprise managers, educators, and anyone else who may have had a blot on their revolutionary dossier.

China's youth obeyed Mao's commands with blind devotion as they traveled around the country exposing and punishing Mao's enemies. Most of China's leaders, government officials, educators, and intellectuals underwent "re-education" through cleaning latrines and pigsties in remote rural areas. They were replaced by cadres who had the requisite political ardor but mostly no other credentials, including higher education because the schools were closed. Because of international disapproval of these internal developments, China became increasingly isolated from the international community, with many countries withdrawing their ambassadors.

It did not take long before various Red Guard factions were fighting each other (with guns) for the honor of being the purest defender of Mao's beliefs. When the People's Liberation Army splintered along similar lines, China nearly disintegrated into complete chaos. Mao then decided that some sort of order had to be restored. He called in loyal units of the PLA to prevent complete disintegration of the public order. Many Red Guards were then shipped off to the countryside, where they would not be able to cause any more problems, to "learn from the peasants."

The active phase of the Cultural Revolution lasted from 1966 through 1969, but it continued in milder form until Mao's death in 1976. The Cultural Revolution changed the course of Chinese history by dismantling the existing political, social, and economic structures in China and replacing them with others that barely functioned. It was a disaster for nearly all elements of Chinese society, setting back modernization and production, disrupting education and science, and further isolating China from the outside world. Perhaps its most long-lasting effect, however, has been an increasingly pervasive cynicism among the Chinese people about the credibility of the party's leadership. Knowing that the direction of any political campaign can be reversed without warning, many Chinese now turn a deaf ear to party exhortations.

## The Rise of Deng Xiaoping

Mao Zedong, in spite of the mistakes he made in his later years, will always be remembered as the leader who created a modern, relatively classless Chinese nation that was free of imperialist interference. If he had retired before the Great Leap Forward, he would undoubtedly be remembered as one of the greatest Chinese leaders of all times. As it was, at the time of his death in 1976 China was still chaotic. The chaos continued as supporters of the Cultural Revolution struggled for power against party members who favored rational, planned economic development over revolutionary zeal. The *Gang of Four,* Mao's widow and three other supporters of the Cultural Revolution, struggled against Deng Xiaoping and his supporters for control of the nation. By 1978 Deng had won, and he began to pursue the Four Modernizations.

To modernize China, Deng introduced market incentives to the peasants and ultimately to the urban economy. To gain the support of the peasantry, Deng authorized the creation of household rural production units in which farmers leased the land they tilled. Base levels of grain production were established, and each family farm was required to sell a certain amount of grain to the government at a set price. Beyond that, farmers could produce what they wished and sell to whom they wished. At the same time, Deng encouraged the establishment of private and collective rural industries. He also established special economic zones, where joint ventures with foreign companies were allowed. More than 100 million peasants eventually migrated to work in China's burgeoning coastal industries.

Under Deng, China embarked on a new course that may ultimately be more revolutionary than anything Mao could ever have imagined. Deng stressed marketplace incentives over Mao's reliance on political consciousness. Whereas Mao stressed self-reliance and separation from the international system, Deng opened China to the outside world. He believed that modernization of the nation's economy was the most important goal for the regime. If the people's living standards rose, Deng believed the party would win back its credibility both internally and externally. Indeed, the Chinese people's living standards have risen, more dramatically than anyone could have imagined in 1979. What Deng also could not imagine at the beginning of his rule was that increased prosperity would slowly but surely erode the power and control of the party over its people.

## NATIONALISM, IRREDENTISM, AND CHINESE MINORITIES

### Restoration of the Middle Kingdom?

While Deng Xiaoping made economic development the cornerstone of his new China, the other pillar of popular appeal through which the party sought to renew its Mandate of Heaven was fulfillment of Chinese nationalism. All modern Chinese leaders have emphasized the restoration of the Middle Kingdom, which in ancient times included most of continental East and Southeast Asia. Even in the 1930s, Mao had visions of restoring China's ancient grandeur. With the end of the Cold War, the decline of the superpowers, and an emerging power vacuum in Asia, China's leaders, strongly supported by the majority Han population, have proclaimed an interest in restoring ancient boundaries that had been lost to foreign aggressors in the nineteenth and twentieth centuries.

China's leaders disagree with Westerners as to what constitutes internal restoration and consolidation versus external aspirations. Because the phenomenon of irredentism can go beyond national restoration to jingoistic expansion abroad, there is a real possibility that Chinese nationalist aspirations could threaten some of China's Asian neighbors in the twenty-first century. Legitimate nationalist goals are in the eyes of the beholder. Western nations, after practicing their own imperialism for many centuries, now question the legitimacy of Beijing's military occupation of Tibet. Chinese on both sides of the Taiwan Straits, however, agree that Tibet is an integral part of China. They also agree that parts of Indochina, the South China Sea islands, both Inner and Outer Mongolia, parts of what is now Russian Siberia, the foreign enclaves of Hong Kong and Macao, and the Japanese-controlled Ryukyu Islands were all integral parts of the Middle Kingdom and that parts of these areas should be restored to Chinese suzerainty. With the decline of party legitimacy, the CCP seems to be relying more heavily on nationalist sentiments to help legitimate its right to lead the Chinese people. If this nationalism is combined with irredentism, the results could be dangerous to China's neighbors.

## China's Minorities

China's minorities, which form less than 10 percent of the population, are either dispersed along China's periphery or located in small pockets scattered throughout China. To lessen even the minimal control China's minorities have over their governance, Beijing is encouraging a rapid migration of the Han people to areas such as Tibet, Xinjiang, and Inner Mongolia.

In Tibet, Chinese control is controversial primarily because of international awareness of the conflict between Tibetans and Han Chinese. After the People's Liberation Army rolled into Lhasa, the Tibetan capital, in 1950, the native population became increasingly unhappy with their Chinese overlords. After conditions became worse, the Tibetan spiritual leader, the Dalai Lama, fled to India with over 100,000 supporters in 1959. From there he has devoted himself to publicizing his people's cause throughout the world, for which he was eventually awarded the Nobel Peace Prize, much to the chagrin of the leaders in Beijing.

Tibetans maintain that their nation should be independent from China, or at least autonomous in domestic affairs if not foreign affairs. They accuse Beijing of using force to destroy their sense of national identity and their particular form of Buddhism. Recent drives to encourage Han migration are seen as an effort to make Tibetans strangers in their own land, and Tibetans in exile have denounced China's economic development plans for Tibet as a "smoke screen" for mass Han settlement.

The Chinese maintain that Tibet was historically a part of China and that Communist rule has resulted in increased living standards, better health care, and easier access to education. Beijing maintains that the Tibet issue is not an ethnic issue, a religious issue, or a human rights issue, but rather an issue manufactured by a handful of former Tibetan gentry and religious leaders who want to reinstitute serfdom and religious oppression.[2]

A similar process is taking place in Inner Mongolia, where Han migrants now outnumber native Mongolians by a five-to-one ratio. With the emergence of Outer Mongolia, formerly a Soviet client state, as a nonsocialist state with a resurgent Buddhist faith, Beijing is increasingly nervous. Recent reports indicate that Beijing is concerned that the regime in Ulan Bator (a city in Outer Mongolia) has become a base for supporting dissidents and separatists in Inner Mongolia. Beijing is reportedly justifying to itself the right to control all of Mongolia.[3] If it attempts to justify extending Chinese influence or control to Outer Mongolia, open conflict is possible.

China's primary goal in the minority regions is to maintain exclusive political control. The creation of new, formerly Soviet nations on its borders, many of which are populated by ethnic groups similar to China's minorities, is tremendously unsettling to Beijing. China is likely to combine a carrot-and-stick approach. Minority areas will not be allowed to break away from the Middle Kingdom or exercise any real political power, but they will be allowed limited social and cultural latitude, such as exclusion from China's one-child policy. In interior areas, this approach is likely to be successful. In areas such as Tibet and Mongolia, where international actors are involved, minority aspirations may lead to open conflict with Beijing.

## SOLUTIONS TO IRREDENTISM:
## HONG KONG AND TAIWAN

Restoration of the Middle Kingdom is also at the heart of China's policy toward Hong Kong and Taiwan. The question of the unification of Hong Kong and Taiwan with China is a political issue, not an ethnic one. Virtually all of the six million residents of Hong Kong and the twenty million residents of Taiwan are Han Chinese. Many still have close cultural and family ties to people in neighboring provinces on the mainland. In 1997 the question for Hong Kong will be how unification is to be implemented. The question for Taiwan is whether unification will ever be implemented.

When Hong Kong becomes a special administrative zone of China on July 1, 1997, the colonial era in Chinese history will finally have come to an end. Before the events at Tiananmen Square, it was hoped that the transition would proceed smoothly, following Deng's stated policy of "one country, two systems." China was set to assume control over Hong Kong's foreign and defense policy, but economic, political, and social conditions in Hong Kong would supposedly remain unchanged for fifty years.

After June 1989, however, China, the United Kingdom, and the various parties within Hong Kong began reassessing prospects for the future. After 150 years of British rule without provisions for self-rule, the new British governor of the colony proposed reforms to enhance democracy in Hong Kong. His efforts were denounced with unbelievable fury by Beijing, which also threatened to set up a shadow government. Observers believe that "Beijing could not allow this because it did not want to encourage demands for free elections in other parts of China, since that might one day lead to the demise of the Communist Party and to the loss of the current leaders' own personal power."[4] By insisting that Hong Kong is an issue of national pride, not democracy and human rights, Beijing has deftly appealed to Chinese nationalism and garnered support even from those who protested at Tiananmen Square.[5]

Disagreements over the future of Hong Kong could have wide-ranging political and economic consequences, both for Hong Kong and for China. In the 1990s, 55 percent of all external investment in China has come from Hong Kong, and the economies of Hong Kong and Guangdong province are becoming increasingly integrated. Already, over three-fourths of labor-intensive production in Hong Kong has been transferred to enterprises within China that are controlled by Hong Kong businesses. In turn, Hong Kong has become a trade transfer point and financial service center for all of southern China. With over $13 billion invested in Hong Kong, China is now the largest investor in Hong Kong. Any political disputes over the future of Hong Kong could therefore disrupt both the Hong Kong and the Chinese economies.

Should the stability and well-being of Hong Kong be threatened after 1997, China's future relations with the United States and with Taiwan could also become highly problematic. The United States has over $7 billion invested in Hong Kong. Any political or economic disruptions of the Hong Kong economy would not only affect U.S. investments, but also involve the U.S. government, particularly Congress, in efforts to sanction China, perhaps by revoking most-favored-nation status. Perhaps more important, political and economic disorder in Hong Kong would have a

negative effect on the possibility of Taiwanese unification with the mainland. Abridgement of the "one country, two systems" system would send
the wrong signal to Taipei and reverse the remarkable progress toward economic integration between Taiwan and China that has occurred in the early
1990s. The Taiwanese nationalist movement for independence would also
become stronger, which would in turn clearly alarm Beijing.

## The Future of Taiwan

From the perspective of China's leaders, it is just a matter of time until
Taiwan is reunited with the mainland. From the perspective of the Chinese
who came to Taiwan with Chiang Kai-shek in 1949, Taiwan will eventually
be reunited with the mainland but, they hope, not until a non-Communist
regime rules in Beijing. From the perspective of a growing number of
native Taiwanese, who represent 85 percent of the island's population,
Taiwan should become a democratic and independent nation with representation in the United Nations. These Taiwanese are gaining more visibility
as the ruling Kuomintang has allowed greater freedom of expression in the
1990s.

## The Case for Reunification

Since 1987, when the Kuomintang leadership allowed Taiwanese citizens
to move back and forth freely to the mainland and to trade with the mainland, interactions have grown with amazing speed. By 1990, Taiwanese
business leaders were investing $1 billion annually in mainland enterprises.
By 1993, these investments had grown to $2.5 billion annually, and over a
million Taiwanese had visited the mainland. Next to Hong Kong, Taiwan is
now the largest source of outside investment in mainland China. Eighty
percent of Taiwan's exports to China, which have been growing at a rate of
30 percent a year, involve shipping parts manufactured in Taiwan to China
for assembly into finished goods. Personal ties are also pulling Taiwan's
people closer to the mainland. Relatives and families, long separated by the
Cold War, are being reunited.

Startling developments are also taking place at the governmental
level. In 1993, for the first time in over four decades, official meetings
between Chinese and Taiwanese government officials took place. Although
there were no major breakthroughs, four limited agreements were reached:
cross delivery of registered letters; verification of official documents by the
two sides; a statement setting forth topics to be addressed at future dates;
and a schedule for future meetings between representatives, which are to be
held several times each year. Beijing has been pushing hard for even more
interactions, including official trade and movement of people directly
across the Taiwan Straits rather than through Hong Kong. Fearing that

acceding to these demands could lead to further integration with the main-land on China's terms, Taipei has been holding back. Yet, given its lack of official international status and the integration that has occurred thus far, accelerated integration with the mainland may be the only obvious route for Taiwan.

## The Case for Independence

Nevertheless, a number of factors beyond China's control may be moving Taiwan toward separation and independence from the mainland. Most important, now that the Cold War is over, the West no longer needs China as a counterweight to the Soviet Union. This has led France and the United States to break previous pledges to China by selling military equipment to Taiwan. As defense contracts shrink in Western countries, Taiwan has become one of the major markets for Western defense industries. Although Beijing denounces military sales to Taiwan with vigor, counteractions against Western trade and investment in China would hurt the Chinese economy without necessarily stopping the sales.

Political and social factors also favor continued Taiwanese separation from the mainland. With the passage of time, the Kuomintang leaders from the mainland are being succeeded by native Taiwanese and by children of mainland families who were born and raised in Taiwan. Both groups have much less attachment to the mainland and to reunification than do their elders. The notion of two Chinas is an attractive option to these groups. In January 1993, Taiwanese President Lee Teng-hui stated, "We should make good use of our overseas development fund and all other possible resources to promote more pragmatic participation in world organizations. . . . This will expedite our ultimate goal of returning to the United Nations."[6]

### HUMAN RIGHTS AND POLITICAL FREEDOMS: CHINA BEFORE AND AFTER TIANANMEN

You know the biggest surprise after 14 years (in prison) was not the new buildings, shops and highways, but the people. They are more open than before, they know more and they care about democracy, about their rights. What I have learned so far is that this economic sys-tem needs a modern political system to operate it. If China's govern-ment refuses to bring about these changes soon and fast, there is a good chance the people will push for it, that there will be unrest and turmoil, like in 1978 and 1989. And nobody wants to see that happen.[7]

These were some of the comments of Wei Jingsheng, China's most famous dissident, following his release from prison in September 1993, after serv-ing over fourteen years in prison for his activities during the democracy movement of 1979. Known as the father of Chinese democracy, Wei is convinced that the Chinese people want freedom and democracy and says that he does "not believe that they only want more money." Deng's reforms have brought new activism amongst the people. Even before Wei's dazibao, millions of China's youth became politically active during the Cultural Revolution. Having tasted power when Mao turned to them in the 1960s and 1970s, they challenged existing authorities again in the 1980s after learning that the party is not infallible and that China's youth can play a role in eliminating corruption and promoting the well-being of the people.

But it was not just the students who challenged the existing order at Tiananmen Square. College students and their instructors make up less than half of 1 percent of the population, and the million or more people who supported the students at Beijing in the spring of 1989 came from all walks of life, including blue-collar workers, government officials, intellectuals, service personnel, media people, and even some party cadres. Tiananmen Square must also be viewed as a continuation of earlier frustrations. For example, Deng Xiaoping removed his protege, Party Secretary Hu Yaobang, for his failure to put down student demonstrations in 1987 and 1988.[8]

## Why Tiananmen Square?

Hu Yaobang had become a popular symbol of reform and freedom, and his death on April 15, 1989, served as an excuse for students to gather and express their views. There was also the precedent of demonstrations and memorials in 1976 in honor of Premier Zhou Enlai, who was popular with the people. Zhou was recognized for his moderate views and his help in bringing an end to the Cultural Revolution. The 1989 spring demonstrations also came while Secretary-General Gorbachev was visiting Beijing, a major step in normalizing Sino-Soviet relations after many years of turmoil between the two communist giants. Gorbachev agreed to visit a student delegation at Tiananmen Square, and the students viewed him as a leader of economic and political reform.

At first, Party Secretary Zhao Ziyang, Deng's new heir apparent, advocated leniency with the students. The demonstration started out largely as a protest against government and party corruption, and there was considerable sympathy for the demonstrations by a broad sector of the population who felt left out of the new prosperity. Student demands for political democracy came only during the latter stages of the demonstrations, and no one, including the students themselves, seemed to have any idea what democracy would mean for China.

By the end of May, the demonstrations were diminishing, but the party leaders, divided between reformists and conservatives, were undecided as to how the demonstrations should be brought to an end and whether the students should be punished. At this point, Deng Xiaoping and the older hard-line leaders took charge, fearing that to leave the demonstrators unpunished would be a sign of party weakness and would threaten its future authority. No doubt the Old Guard was looking over its shoulders at the tumultuous events taking place simultaneously in Eastern Europe, which Deng and his cohorts blamed on weakness and basic errors in Moscow. Beijing's hard-liners were convinced that unless opposition to party rule in China was ruthlessly crushed, challenges to party authority similar to those in Eastern Europe and the Soviet Union might very well succeed in China. As for the demonstrators and their supporters, they may have had illusions resulting from economic and social reforms over the previous ten years that the party could be persuaded to accept political reforms as well. If so, they were wrong. The leaders in Beijing never intended that economic reforms should also lead to the demise of party authority.

Believing that party authority was being questioned, Deng and the Beijing leadership felt that they had no choice but to suppress the students with military force. The party leadership was also increasingly alarmed that the student demonstrators were receiving growing support from blue-collar workers, the middle class, intellectuals, and important elements within the mass media, which up to then had always been under the tight control of the Ministry of Culture. Even the military units around Beijing seemed divided as to whether they should use force to quell the student demonstrators.

## The Consequences of Tiananmen

Much of the favorable opinion of China that had been built up over the previous decade came to an end with the military crackdown on China's young people on the night of June 4, 1989. In fact, the outside world had a much better view of events in Beijing than most of China's vast population (mostly rural), which never saw all the Tiananmen events seen on Western television screens. There were also demonstrations in other cities such as Shanghai, but these were quickly crushed once the decision was made to quell the demonstrations in Beijing. Prior to June 4, China's own media services had shown some sympathy for the students, but afterward media personnel who had shown such sympathy were quickly removed, and the print and electronic media returned to the official party line. Any opposition to party authority and control of the media was suppressed, and dissenters who were not arrested went into hiding.[9]

Although the physical power of the party, with the crucial help of the military, was preserved, the legitimacy of the party, which had suffered severely from early steps such as the Great Leap Forward and the Cultural Revolution, was further undermined. In addition, as in the former Soviet Union (both in December 1991 and October 1993), the military became the key to stability and political order, a major deviation from communist doctrine. In the 1990s, a major result of developments inside China has been the increased role of the military in deciding China's future, including the future of the party itself.

## Developments Since Tiananmen

During the half decade since the student demonstrations, all of the same issues leading up to Tiananmen not only have continued to exist but in many respects have become more pressing. As the party factions maneuver for power during the succession process, the only point on which they agree is the maintenance of party power and the suppression of dissent. The dominant faction in Beijing continues to push for more economic growth, mainly through further market incentives, foreign investment, and foreign trade. But annual economic growth, as we shall see in Chapter 3, is producing social and economic contradictions. These include inequities in wealth in both rural and urban areas; further suppression of dissent by the hard-liners while de facto political participation grows at the local level; and mass consumerism and growth in Western cultural values accompanied by greed and party corruption.

## Rights of Women and Children

Continued privatization, both before and after Tiananmen, has increasingly affected the human rights and social well-being of women and children. Although Mao's socialist revolution emphasized gender equality, women are now more likely to be laid off first and hired last. Currently, 70 percent of the unemployed workers in urban areas are women. In addition, 70 percent of illiterates in China are women, and one-third of women between the ages of 15 and 45 cannot read a newspaper.[10] Similarly, the use of child labor in China's new factories is increasing.

## The Communist Party After Tiananmen

All of the contradictions leading up to the 1989 student demonstrations remain in the 1990s. As long as the dual economy exists (which we will discuss in Chapter 3), there is the temptation for party members to take advantage of dual pricing to use their position to obtain cheap public goods and sell them at high prices on the private market. Public criticism of the personal lives of high-level party officials is ruthlessly suppressed in order to try to protect the legitimacy of the party rulers. Party members themselves are now being encouraged to go into private business and make money, a practice known as "plunging into the sea." Since Tiananmen, money making seems to be the dominant ideological value in China. Some party and government officials are moonlighting to make a profit, with only a small proportion of their time dedicated to the performance of their public duties. This can occur in contemporary China because there is no effective system of accountability for party and government officials, especially when the mass media is controlled by the party and any investigation of party behavior is squashed. One of the results of Tiananmen is an even greater determination of party leaders to crush any thoughts of popular or free elections, oppose an independent judiciary and investigative corps, or permit media free of party control.

## China's Youth After Tiananmen

In the past, China's youth served as Mao's instrument for cleansing the party and bureaucracy of corruption and also as a means of renewing revolutionary fervor. Since Tiananmen, China's youth remain silent. Although they discuss their concerns privately, the price of public expression is the threat of punishment, including the loss of educational privileges or even jail. There is, however, a basic contradiction in the silencing of youth. Both the Cultural Revolution, spearheaded by millions of active youth in the Red Guards (in the 1960s and 1970s), and the student demonstrators (in the 1980s) culminating in the Tiananmen events have taught China's young people that they indeed are the wave of the future; they have learned that, sooner or later, they will be a major force in restoring Chinese idealism, as well as in achieving social and political reform. Today in China, most of the youth and intellectuals have little faith in the ability of the party to solve China's problems in the twenty-first century. Most students and intellectuals would, however, agree that breakdown of order in China, which appeared imminent in 1989, could cause great suffering, such as has occurred in other former communist lands. Those in China who question authoritarian party rule today seem more concerned with achieving economic prosperity and social well-being than with obtaining freedom of expression or political participation. Because open dissent is not allowed in China, one Western observer believes "a regime of suppression has difficulty detecting the sincerity and strength of individual loyalty. Considering its tight control of society, the PRC's claim of widespread loyalty from the people is certainly questionable."[11]

## Prisoners of Conscience

Long prison terms, reports of torture by student prisoners released from jail, and further arrests for speaking out against the government or party are a continuing reminder that the lack of freedom of expression was a Chinese legacy even before the Tiananmen demonstrations. Better-known demonstrators, at the urging of Western human rights groups, have occasionally been released as a sign that the government wishes to improve its interna-

tional human rights image. But lesser-known dissidents continue to languish in jail, refusing to renounce their dissenting beliefs.[12] Occasionally
the government shows signs of seeking a better human rights image; for
example, a white paper entitled "Human Rights in China (November
1991)" says that all Chinese benefit from social, political, and economic
rights and that these rights are protected in daily life.[13] Nevertheless, when
dissidents in exile, such as Shen Tong, returned from the United States to
test the government's intentions by speaking out publicly, they were arrested.[14]

There are signs that the rage of dissidents is diminishing with the passage of time. A Western observer who closely follows human rights issues
in China notes, "These days, especially outside Beijing, many Chinese
seem to have forgotten—not the attack itself, but at least the fury they once
felt." But he then points out:

> The great majority of Chinese intellectuals still seem to expect that the
> setback is temporary and that the official verdict on June 4 will be
> reversed. Alienation is as widespread as ever, few people believe in
> Marxism, and many Chinese and foreigners alike regard Communist
> rule as a crumbling dynasty. But outside the capital, the reason for dis-
> content has more to do with corruption and rising prices than with
> killing students.[15]

Beijing's leaders have been encouraged by the return of tourism to
pre-Tiananmen levels by 1993. And they hoped that China and the world
would be able to forget Tiananmen by bringing the Summer Olympics to
Beijing in the year 2000. Although Beijing's leaders went to great lengths
to persuade the Olympic Committee to select Beijing, including the release
of dissidents such as Wei Jingsheng just before the committee was to vote
in September 1993, their efforts were to no avail; the committee narrowly
voted for Sydney, Australia, over Beijing on the final vote. But human
rights considerations were only one of the factors affecting the vote, and
many of the selection committee members resented the U.S. Congress trying to pressure them by passing a resolution against Beijing's selection just
prior to the vote.[16] World opinion on the issue was divided, with some
Western observers believing that the choice of Beijing would have drawn
China into the mainstream of the international community and brought
pressure in the years leading up to the year 2000 to improve China's human
rights image.

## The Freedom to Study Overseas

Another test of China's human rights policies since Tiananmen has been
the government's policy with regard to Chinese students studying overseas.

Although Beijing did make it more difficult for them to leave the country after Tiananmen, the flow of students overseas has continued. In fact, the Chinese government points out that the three predominant groups of international students in the United States are all Chinese—from the mainland, Taiwan, and Hong Kong.

Though Western critics note that two-thirds of overseas Mainland Chinese students fail to return, Beijing can point out that the rate of return is even lower for Indian and Taiwanese students studying in the United States. Only 15 percent of these students return home, suggesting that the rate of return may be related more to economic considerations than questions of human rights.

> **Chinese Overseas Students**
>
> China has sent more than 190,000 people to study in over 100 countries. At present, some 120,000 are studying abroad. Of the more than 60,000 returned students, about half have assumed high-ranking professional positions, and over 20,000 have made various research achievements. Of the latter group, more than 200 have won some 500 international awards, and 1,000 of the people have won over 2,000 patents for their work.
> [*Source:* Chinese Embassy, Washington Newsletter, March 3, 1993, p. 6.]

## THE PROBLEM OF DECENTRALIZATION: EMPIRE, FEDERATION, OR ANARCHY?

> What remains in question today is how communist rule will end in China. Among the many scenarios suggested by China experts . . . [is that] the regime on the Chinese mainland may well disintegrate under the stress of increasing regionalism.[17]

One of the continuing trends before and after Tiananmen has been the movement of power away from the center to the regional and local levels. These trends, which may greatly affect China and its global role in the twenty-first century, can be observed though a number of changes taking place at the local level, especially in rural China. Some Western observers who have recently lived in a number of China's rural villages think that the party's ability to influence local farmers has declined because of the easing of social regimentation and the introduction of market reforms.[18] In prosperous areas the farmers seem interested only in cadres who have the skills to help the peasants make a profit, including the ability to run factories and market products. Although Deng's household responsibility system increased agricultural production, it also reduced the ability of the party to control the land and its farmers. Now the party competes with other groups for influence, and sometimes party cadres are viewed as an impediment rather than a benefactor in promoting the people's needs. Who are some of these competing groups?

## The Breakdown of Order and the Emergence of Local Organized Crime

With the relaxation of totalitarian central control, crime bosses have emerged, especially in southern China's rich coastal regions. Many of the social problems in contemporary Western societies, assumed to be absent during Mao's iron rule, are emerging since Deng's reforms. Criminal elements "promote prostitution and gambling, trafficking in narcotics, rural women and children, and slip hired outlaws across the border to rob Hong Kong banks."[19]

## Local Religious Revival

Up to now, Western religions have influenced only a small percentage of the Chinese population, but with the end of the Cultural Revolution, there has been a revival of Christianity. But unless local congregations have governmental approval to practice their religion, they must go underground and gather at night to worship. Government concern about growing numbers of Christians has led to a crackdown on both Protestant and Catholic groups that are not officially registered. In addition, since early 1992, there has been increased religious oppression against Muslims and Tibetan Buddhists, including beatings and forced relocations, surveillance, arrests, and property confiscation.[20]

## The Reemergence of Family Clans

One of the consequences of declining local party control has been the takeover of power in some local regions by clans, based on warlord-type rivalries prevalent in ancient times. Local leaders, supported by extended family connections, may assume actual power at the village level, control local government, and allocate privileges. Rivalries between clans within or between villages can lead to violence. In the western part of Yunnan province, China's paramilitary police were called in to the remote town of Pingyuan in 1992, where they battled local criminal elements for nearly three months before restoring order. Two thousand police confiscated over a ton of drugs, and eight hundred people were arrested.

## Economic Decentralization

The significance of Deng Xiaoping's economic reforms will be discussed in detail in Chapter 3. But it is important to note here that much of China's economic miracle (9 percent annual growth rate since 1978 and 12 percent in 1992) has been due in large part to economic decentralization, especially in rural areas, where over 100 million peasants now work in local service industries and factories that are locally controlled.

The redistribution of power has been magnified by the continuing losses of state enterprises, one of the major sources of power of the party and central government in Beijing. Although the party continues to proclaim the values of socialism with Chinese characteristics, state enterprises are hamstrung by a growing national debt, much of which results from the inefficiencies of the public sector. At the same time, decentralization of power is growing because of the ability of rich coastal provinces to increase their taxation of local enterprises, both domestic and foreign owned. Beijing's choice seems to be either to allow regional and local taxation and investment to increase, which risks an increase in inflation and loss of central power, or to risk instability and political challenge by trying to restrict the actions of local authority. The latter choice is becoming increasingly difficult because these authorities no longer depend on Beijing for finance, which can be obtained directly from foreign investors or through the reinvestment of local profits.

The problem of decentralization is compounded by the uneven economic growth in different provinces with growing discontent in poorer interior provinces, while the southern and eastern coastal provinces get rich. Table 2.1 shows how growth rates in different regions increase the power of coastal provinces while others in the interior languish. These disparities will be discussed in greater detail in Chapter 3, but it is important to note here how decentralization is redistributing both economic and political authority, while at the same time economically integrating the rich coastal provinces with other Asian economies such as Taiwan, Hong Kong, South Korea, Japan, Indonesia, and Singapore, through both trade and investment. Not only are their economies becoming more similar and interdependent, but cultural lifestyles are also converging based on mass consumerism. Life is more relaxed in Guangdong province (next to Hong Kong) and Fujian province (across the straits from Taiwan). In many respects, coastal cities such as Shenzhen and Xiamen seem to have more in common with Hong Kong and Taipei than with Beijing, one thousand miles to the north, where living standards are much lower and people's lives seem more controlled by public authority.[21]

**Table 2.1    Provincial Growth Rates in 1992: It's Better by the Ocean**

| Four Coastal Provinces | | Two Middle Region Provinces | | Two Far-Western Interior Provinces | |
|---|---|---|---|---|---|
| Shandong | 19.5% | Shanxi | 11.0% | Guizhou | 7.5% |
| Jiangsu | 27.0% | Henan | 13.6% | Yunnan | 9.0% |
| Fujian | 21.7% | | | | |
| Guangdong | 19.5% | | | | |

*Source:* Based on Sheila Tefft, "Chinese Reforms Widen the Gap Between Haves and Have Nots," *Christian Science Monitor,* April 2, 1993, p. 1.

## Military Decentralization?

One of Mao's greatest accomplishments was the unification of military power throughout the Middle Kingdom, which even made it possible to extend the party's control quickly to far-western regions such as Tibet and Xinjiang soon after Mao came to power in 1949. Although the military has always backed the central party leadership, which was crucial to the party's retention of power at the time of the Tiananmen demonstrations, recent developments inside the military raise important questions about the future role of China's military forces, which now number approximately 3.2 million, perhaps the largest military force in the world, depending on developments inside Russia.

As a result of the army's decisive role at Tiananmen Square, there was a reemphasis on ideology and party discipline. But since June 4, 1989, Deng and his followers, at least for the time being, have regained control of the military leadership from the conservative wing of the party and reestablished professionalism as its primary mission. The recent purchase of modern military aircraft from Russia, the buildup of the navy, and increased wages for soldiers would all suggest that China's military will perform the traditional functions of military forces of other major powers in modern times.

There is, however, another Chinese military that is largely unknown to the outside world. After the Cultural Revolution, the authorities in Beijing cut back on funding of the military as the government's resources shifted to building China's infrastructure and revitalizing the economy. Interestingly, military units were told to create their own economic enterprises and convert many of their military factories to civilian production. China's military has always been largely self-reliant, producing much of its own food supply. Through encouragement from Beijing, 65 percent of production from military-owned factories now goes to civilian goods. Many of these products, such as motorcycles, refrigerators, and color televisions, are in great demand. Factories still producing military products sell their goods on the world market. Sometimes high-level government and party officials are involved in these transactions, which is a major source of independent income for the military establishment as well as for high-level party officials and many of their children, who are involved in overseas sales. One of the more interesting examples of these capitalist-type military sales operations is the setting up of import companies inside the United States, controlled by China's military. They have sold over $1 billion of light weapons to the private arms market in the United States, including highly sought after AK-47 automatic weapons.

The sale of both civilian and military products has not only made the military partially independent of central funding, but has also helped make a major proportion of the armed forces avowed capitalists who are strongly dedicated to Deng's market reforms and strongly supportive of a market economy. Dependence on Beijing has been further diluted by growing ties between local military units and local officials. These relationships have been mutually beneficial. Local military units have provided work brigades to perform essential functions such bridge and road repair, maintenance of irrigation ditches, and other needed services that local authorities do not have the money to pay for. Local authorities, in turn, provide the military education, housing, and other essential needs.

Local military units produce over 50 percent of their own food, such as meat, vegetables, and eggs, and they also provide much of their own chickens, grain, and fruit. Military food production and factory units have become an important part of the local economy, working with private and cooperative farms, factories, and retail services at the local level. In effect, China now has two military forces: the professionalized forces that are being rearmed with modern equipment, especially naval and air units; and the local economic production units, which are to a considerable extent self-reliant and tied in to local community services and market operations, both as consumers and providers.

In order to further improve relations between the military and the civilian population, which had been badly damaged by the military's role in quelling student demonstrations, the party has increased the role of paramilitary units, independent of the army. These units now have prime responsibility for putting down future demonstrations, disturbances or challenges to authority, whether in Beijing or at the regional or local level. The future role of the military may become more problematic, however, as local authorities and economic units take more initiative, based on their own resources and bargaining power, in speeding up economic development as well as bargaining overseas for more trade and investment. Significantly, local military-controlled businesses are heavily involved in setting up their own sales and investment arrangements, often in cooperation with parallel private and local public enterprises.

## Implications of Decentralization

Historically, large empires have been held together by highly authoritarian regimes, such as in ancient Rome or the Russian Empire. When the central authorities of Western colonial empires such as Great Britain turned to democracy at home in the twentieth century, overseas colonies demanded the same rights, and today traditional Western imperialism is largely relegated to history books. As for the unification of large territories into single governmental units, the preferred way of achieving the advantages of large markets and economies of scale has been through the creation of democratic federal systems, with the people directly electing and controlling governing bodies at the local, regional, and national levels. The United States led the way in 1789, followed by Canada in 1867 and Australia in 1900. Other large former colonies of Western countries, such as Brazil, Mexico, and India, which are now formally democracies, have all adopted federal systems with varying degrees of democratically controlled national, regional, and local units of government.

But what about China? Federalism, with a real division of power between different levels of government—based on experience going back to Rome, Sparta, and Athens—seems to be incompatible with highly authoritarian forms of government. Under authoritarian systems, power is either highly controlled from the center or else the system breaks up into parts, as in the case of the Roman Empire or what was formerly the Soviet Union. Whether Russia, with its difficulties in the 1990s, will be able to hold together or to join together in a federal system with other parts of the former Soviet Union is highly problematic. As for the Middle Kingdom, outsiders may hope there will be a peaceful evolution to a more democratic society, which might in time lead to effective popular control at the local, regional, and national levels. But inside China, the problem of decentralization, which is becoming an increasing reality as economic power devolves from the center, seems to pose one of the greatest Chinese enigmas of the late twentieth century.

No one seriously wishes to see the breakup of China into rival regions, which would probably undermine the remarkable economic development and stability that has enabled China to become increasingly economically and politically integrated into the global system, something that benefits both China and the world community. Western social scientists like neat explanations of social, economic, and political power structures, but perhaps future relationships inside China may confound the outside critics. Could it be that the party and central control will continue in varying degrees far into the twenty-first century, with an informal type of bargaining system allowing considerable devolution of power in response to local needs? In reality, the process may have already begun, as well as the pluralization of Chinese society at different levels. Few, either inside or outside China, seem to feel that there is any advantage in pointing out the loss of party power and central authority. In fact, based on the Russian experience beginning with Gorbachev, Deng Xiaoping may be much wiser than his critics give him credit for. If, in his final campaign to build a successful China, he has succeeded in avoiding the monumental problems of contemporary Russia, then he may have ensured his place alongside Mao as one of China's two greatest leaders of the twentieth century.

## THE PROBLEM OF SUCCESSION AND CHINA'S POLITICAL FUTURE

Deng's efforts to ensure a smooth process of succession following his departure from the political scene are highly problematic. Most observers feel that despite his efforts to avoid a struggle for power within the higher levels of the party by placing reformers in key positions at the time of the Fourteenth Party Congress in October 1992 and the National People's Congress in March 1993, a struggle for leadership of the party and the country is likely to take place following his death. One of the major weaknesses of communist political systems, including the People's Republic of China, is the lack of any orderly process for selection of new leaders. In China, following Mao's death, a number of heir apparents failed to consolidate their power, and it was nearly two years before Deng Xiaoping, who was not one of Mao's favorites, was able to establish his power base and institute major economic reforms.

In the 1980s, two of Deng's proposed successors, Hu Yaobang and Zhao Ziyang, were both removed from power, and his current heir apparent, Jiang Zemin, is generally viewed as an interim figure in spite of his appointment as party general secretary, president of China (following the National People's Congress in March 1993), and head of the Military Advisory Commission (a structure set up to give the senior brass an honorable place to retire).

## *Deng's Strategy for Ensuring the Future of the Party and the Nation*

The events of Tiananmen Square failed to solve the basic contradictions inside China in the post–Cold War era. In fact, the use of force to put down the student demonstrations strengthened the hands of the conservative wing of the party, which wished not only to crush any opposition to party rule, but to strengthen hard-liner control of the media, reaffirm Leninist principles of authoritarian rule by the party, place stronger limits and controls on the private sector, and maintain the public sector as the dominant economic force in the Chinese economy.

Even though he had given up all public office in the 1990s and spent most of his time playing bridge with octogenarian comrades from the days of the Long March, Deng temporarily reemerged on the political scene in order to revitalize the reformist wing of the party and set the stage for its reemergence at the Fourteenth Party Congress in October 1992 and the National People's Congress in March 1993. After Tiananmen, the reformist wing had suffered setbacks, including hard-liner control of the military and the Ministry of Culture, which was responsible for controlling not only the mass media but also the circulation of published material. In China, over 80 percent of published information originates with the government, which is also the primary consumer of published information, generating 95 percent of the demand.[22]

In his last political campaign to revitalize and ensure continued market reform after he was gone, Deng Xiaoping toured Guangdong province in southern China in January 1992, where he visited the special economic zones in Shenzhen and Zhuhai. He noted the tremendous economic development and prosperity that had occurred since his previous visit in 1984. With an eye to the mass media, he announced to the world that he had now seen the future and it worked. Deng's purpose was to mobilize mass support for further market reforms, which he said would ensure China's place in history and provide for the well-being of the people, as well as the legitimization of the party.

Deng was convinced that further and even faster development, based on market reforms, was the key to the future. This could best be accomplished by combining economic reform with the four cardinal principles that he said were essential to the achievement of socialism with Chinese characteristics: (1) party leadership; (2) socialism; (3) proletarian dictatorship; (4) and Marxism-Leninism-socialism. The conservative wing of the party, which still controlled the mass media, saw that Deng was trying to mobilize overwhelming support for the speeding up of market reforms, so that after he was gone no one would be able to reverse the process.[23]

Evidence of party conservative control of the media and Deng's difficulties in publicizing his campaigns was confirmed by the immediate refusal of the Chinese mass media to publicize Deng's last campaign in southern China. Although the Hong Kong press told the world about Deng's last hurrah, giving immediate coverage to his campaign across the border from Hong Kong in Shenzhen, it was over two months before anything appeared in the conservative-controlled Chinese mass media, including any story in the *People's Daily,* the leading party-controlled daily, published in Beijing. The Leninist antireformers in the party had good reason to be concerned. Once the news of Deng's last campaign to reaffirm and gain support for market reforms did reach the public, there was a groundswell for Deng's policies, and the reformists within the party rallied to Deng's efforts to weed out the conservatives and put reformers in key positions of leadership at the 1992 Fourteenth Party Congress and the 1993

National People's Congress. Building on his momentum of support from his campaign in the south, even though he was eighty-eight and unable to attend events, Deng worked behind the scenes through his cohorts to remove his opponents and place his supporters in key positions in the party and government.

## Eliminating the Old Guard

In China, because there is no democratic process for the selection and removal of leaders, political selection takes place through intraparty struggles behind the scenes. The process involves key leaders seeking to place their own cliques in power positions while countering the maneuvers of rival leaders and their followers. Although the hard-line conservatives reasserted themselves after Tiananmen Square, especially through control of the military, the Politburo, the mass media, and the paramilitary police, Deng and his reformists reemerged as the dominant force during the struggle for leadership in 1993. The hard-line conservatives, however, continue to hold considerable power, and the struggle for leadership will no doubt continue during the transition after Deng's demise.

The appointment of key people during the 1992 Fourteenth Party Congress and the 1993 National People's Congress should be examined in some detail. These appointments probably represent Deng's last will and testament, the last political hurrah of a remarkable man who ranks second to Mao Zedong in China's leadership hierarchy since the Communists came to power in 1949. The importance that Deng gives both to military appointments and to the Standing Committee of the Party Politburo is worth noting. Because none of the party leaders talk about democracy or political change, the issue of political reform is masked behind the struggle for selection of economic reformists or hard-liners, those who wish to speed up or slow down (or even reverse) the transition from a statist economy to a private market system. The party hard-liners at the national, regional, and local levels are well aware that privatization may undermine their power base because most of their influence and wealth come directly from their control of state enterprises and services. The struggle between economic reformers and conservatives extends even into the military, which has a major stake in both the public and private economic sectors.

One of Deng's key opponents to further privatization of the economy was Chen Yun. Chen was a key person in helping to put down the student demonstrations at Tiananmen Square. He was chairman of the Central Advisory Committee (CAC), a group made up of over 160 older members of the party, which was responsible for making recommendations to the leadership on important issues. Chen was convinced that further promotion of market capitalism would undermine socialism and the power of the Chinese Communist Party. Though a limited advocate of the private market, he sought to maintain the public sector as the dominant part of the economy, using party central planning to keep the private sector within closely supervised limits, like a bird in a cage. At the Fourteenth Party Congress, Deng eliminated the CAC, thereby lessening the power of Chen Yun.

In order to reduce the temptations of the military to become actively involved in the succession process, Deng arranged a major overhaul of the leadership, removing or transferring key officers who had become politically involved in putting down the student demonstrations on June 4, 1989. Those who advocated ideological fervor and communist indoctrination were replaced by those who strongly supported a professionalized army. At the Fourteenth Party Congress, Yang Baibing was removed from the Military Affairs Commission, the key body controlling China's military. Yang Baibing, with his older brother, Yang Shangkun, had built up a personal network of high-level supporters within the military before and after Tiananmen Square. As compensation for his removal, Yang Baibing was made a member of the Politburo but not a member of its seven-member Standing Committee, the key decisionmaking body. An old-line professional military man, Admiral Liu Huaqing (born in 1917), was then made a member of the Politburo and its political Standing Committee. Liu Huaqing was expected to keep the military out of any power struggles during the succession process and to support Deng's objective of maintaining a low-key professional military service. Yang Shangkun, who was in much better health than Deng Xiaoping, was then removed as president of China when the National People's Congress convened in March 1993.[24]

In order to stem criticism of party nepotism, in which the children of prominent party members (known as *tazi,* children of the leaders) have been given prominent positions and accused of corruption, Deng Xiaoping deliberately removed tazi from key positions in the party, government, and business community. None of his own five children were allowed to hold important positions, although some of them had gained prominence since his rise to power in 1978.

Deng, in his last hurrah, also sought to strengthen the position of the economic reformists in the Party Central Committee, the ruling Politburo, and the seven-member Standing Committee of the Politburo. As a result of changes made at the Fourteenth Party Congress, the Old Guard leftists were substantially weakened. But China's most prominent hard-liner, Premier Li Peng, who had been the point man in the suppression of Tiananmen demonstrators, kept his position as a member of the Party Standing Committee within the Politburo. Then, at the National Party Congress in March 1993, he was reappointed for another five-year term as premier of China. Deng wished to keep Li Peng within the top power structure of the party and the government as a warning to intellectuals, students, and others that any revived attempts to criticize and challenge the party would not be tolerated. Reaffirming his basic philosophy after assuming power in 1978, Deng hoped to ensure the future role of the party and the well-being of the country by creating a power structure that would continue economic reform but prevent the rise of Western-type political processes that could lead to power struggles and instability. Deng's greatest fear was that without firm party leadership, based on Leninist rule from above, China would go the way of the former Soviet Union. Other members appointed or reappointed to the Party Standing Committee of the Politburo in October 1992 reinforced Deng's attempt to ensure a smooth succession after his departure through a balance of economic reformists, moderates, and the hard-liner Li Peng.[25]

## Members of the Politburo's Standing Committee

*Jiang Zemin (born in 1927).* Viewed as a moderate and a balance between different factions, Jiang was summoned to Beijing after the Tiananmen demonstrations of 1989. At that time he was appointed general secretary of the party. He was also appointed chairman of the Central Military Commission and then made president of China, replacing Yang Shangkun, at the National Party Congress in March 1993. Jiang is the heir apparent to Deng Xiaoping, who hoped that Jiang's simultaneous holding of three of the key leadership positions would enable him to survive the struggles of succession. In the past, however, Jiang has not been viewed as a strong leader. He may turn out to be an interim figure during the transition to the post-Deng era.

*Li Peng (born in 1929).* He is the conservative hard-liner on the Party Standing Committee. One of the adopted sons of former prime minister and party leader Zhou Enlai, who played an important role in Li's rise to power, he has moderated his hard-line speeches in the past year and represented China at key global conferences such as the meeting of the leaders of the five permanent UN Security Council members held at the United Nations in January 1992. In addition to his opposition to student demonstrators, he has strongly criticized Hong Kong governor Christopher Patten's proposed reforms aimed at creating a democratic political system in Hong Kong prior to the Chinese takeover in 1997. He has also advocated slower economic investment, arguing that a heated-up economy would bring dangerous inflation, discontent, and instability. He advocated a 6 percent growth rate in 1992, but China's 12 percent growth rate conformed to Deng's proposals for even more rapid development, which, if continued, might indeed lead to the conditions that Li Peng fears.

*Qiao Shi (born in 1925).* Viewed as a moderate, Qiao heads up China's internal security and police apparatuses. He could be a key person in the leadership struggle following Deng's demise. At first resisting the use of police force against the Tiananmen demonstrators, he later supported martial law and the military crackdown on the demonstrators. Qiao Shi could potentially emerge as the key Chinese leader in the 1990s.

*Li Ruihuan (born in 1935).*   A supporter of economic reform, Li became a member of the Politburo Standing Committee after the Tiananmen crackdown, with responsibility for the ideology portfolio. Previously he was mayor of Tianjin. Without a university education, Li is sometimes looked down upon by intellectuals, but he is recognized for his pragmatic approach to economic reform and his support for change.

*Zhu Rongji (born in 1930).*   Zhu is recognized as a strong advocate of economic reform. Appointed mayor of Shanghai in 1987, he refused to call out the army to quell student demonstrators in Shanghai in 1989. Appointed to the Standing Committee of the Politburo in 1992, he is also director of the Economic and Trade Office and is recognized for cutting through bureaucratic red tape to get things done. Zhu could be one of the people to watch during the succession struggle. There seems to be a mutual feeling of respect between Zhu and China's young people, something that is lacking with most other high-level party officials.

*Liu Huaqing (born in 1917).*   Having spent over sixty years of his life in the military, Liu is known as a professional soldier who has no known desire to mix politics with the professional military. Rather, he wishes to modernize and upgrade the military. Liu's appointment to the Politburo Standing Committee and as deputy chairman (next in rank to Jiang Zemin) of the Central Military Commission appears designed to prevent more ambitious officials with military connections from filling these positions. Deng Xiaoping apparently wishes to structure the political and military command posts to prevent the military from becoming involved as allies of different rivals for power. Admiral Liu Huaqing would be expected to play a neutral role, with no ambitions of his own.

*Hu Jintao (born in 1944).*   Viewed as a strong supporter of economic reform, Hu is a rising star in the party hierarchy. Prior to his 1992 appointment to the Politburo Standing Committee, he was Communist Party secretary in Tibet. Originally viewed as a hard-liner early in his career, he later became a protégé of Hu Yaobang, who counted on him to promote major economic reform.

## Will Deng Xiaoping's Final Campaign to Promote a Smooth Succession Succeed?

Could it be that all of Deng's efforts to avoid a dangerous struggle for power, breakdown of order, revival of democratic protests, or a reversal of the economic reform process will be to no avail? Based on past struggles in

China, a smooth succession would appear to be less likely than a troubled one. The party lost legitimacy as a result of both the Cultural Revolution and the crackdown at Tiananmen Square. Having lost the support of the students, who became energized in efforts to reform the party during the Cultural Revolution and again in Beijing in 1989, it may be only a matter of time before the younger generation, supported by intellectuals and others who have lost faith in the party, again seek to take matters into their own hands. Nevertheless, China's youth and its intellectuals are leery of promoting instability, which could lead to developments such as those that destroyed the Soviet Union. Such developments are something that practically everyone in China, both inside and outside the party, abhors.

Most observers are skeptical about Deng Xiaoping's efforts to work out a careful balance between the different factions as a means of heading off a power struggle after he is gone. The hard-liners are convinced that if the reform process is not slowed down or reversed, Leninist-type party rule is doomed. The reformists, however, agree with Deng Xiaoping that party rule and "socialism with Chinese characteristics" can be saved only by speeding up the process of development and modernization. They believe that by supporting such a policy, the party can regain legitimacy in the eyes of the people, thereby enabling it to restore its Mandate of Heaven and also revive support based on nationalist aspirations. Because the People's Liberation Army has always been a decisive factor in China's power struggles, going back to Mao's assumption of party leadership in 1935, it is hard to imagine how the military can avoid becoming involved in the struggle for succession, especially if rival leadership factions develop supporters within the military itself or demonstrations occur that risk the breakdown of order. The international community could also be an important factor in any power struggles inside China. With China's rapid rate of development, increased foreign investment, and growing trade (especially with the developed countries), it is in the interest of the outside world to help dampen forces that might lead to breakdown and disorder inside China.[26]

## POLICY OPTIONS

China's decisionmakers, like those in other large contemporary societies, are greatly limited in their domestic policy choices by the availability of resources and the complex structures that restrict their ability to change existing policies. In China, governmental, economic, and social groups at the national, regional, and local levels, by their very existence, place severe constraints on policy choices. Compared with the limited options available in many Third World countries and former communist states, however, China's leaders may have many more opportunities and choices.

The following analysis of options is based on the assumption that the CCP leadership seeks to retain its power and influence to control events inside China and maintain its ability to conduct relations with other states. If this is the case, then all party factions would logically support the continuation of the following policies:

1. Maintain a monopoly of political power by trying to prevent the formation of any groups dedicated to questioning or overthrowing the party's authority.
2. Maintain party control over public security forces, the military, and the police.
3. Maintain control over the mass media so that the party can frame the parameters within which public debate takes place.
4. Keep the struggle for power among the various party factions an internal affair, outside of the public arena.

If the contract between the party and the Chinese people becomes unglued after the death of Deng Xiaoping, internecine struggle within the party as well as external opposition to continued party rule, in whichever form it may take, is possible.

## Option 1: Promote Nationalism

Creating pride in the unity of the Chinese nation, along with accompanying policies, can help achieve the overall objective of promoting nationalism. China is more fortunate than most large contemporary states in that its ethnic, racial, and religious minorities are limited to relatively small groups, mostly in peripheral areas. Beijing's current policy, which is likely to continue, of sending large numbers of the Han majority ethnic group to outlying regions will in time make minority groups strangers within their own land. If Beijing wishes to ameliorate outside criticism of human rights conditions in these outlying regions, however, it would be logical to combine population migration with protection of personal freedoms, social well-being, and cultural rights of minority groups, so long as these do not lead to challenges to political authority. In addition, virtually no Chinese want to see their country follow the same course as the Soviet Union, where "Balkanization" was the direct result of the collapse of Communist rule. Promotion of Chinese nationhood is a policy the party can use to rally the people. Appealing to the past grandeur of China's Middle Kingdom strikes a responsive chord among the Chinese people.

## Option 2: Use Persuasion Rather Than Force in Creating a Greater China

How the party chooses to pursue its goal of unifying the Chinese nation by resuming political control over Hong Kong, Macao, and Taiwan will also help determine its future credibility. Successful integration of Hong Kong would create a better environment for Taiwanese reunification with China. Rather than pressing for political reunification or threatening military measures to achieve reunification, as has been the official policy since 1949, the party could continue to allow the de facto economic integration that is already occurring to continue and strengthen. Growing Taiwanese nationalism or political protests against Chinese rule in Hong Kong could, however, so threaten the Chinese leaders that they choose to intervene politically or militarily. In that case, the upheaval could be extremely dangerous because both sides have been making great efforts to upgrade their military forces.

## Option 3:
## Combine Nationalism with Military Modernization

China's leaders could choose to emphasize combining nationalism with military modernization, stressing the military's role in guarding China from foreign enemies. This might involve taking limited steps to restore China's ancient sphere of influence in neighboring regions. Although China's involvement in external conflict may strengthen nationalist feelings and rally support to the regime, Beijing will have to orchestrate patriotic desires carefully for the restoration of Chinese influence in areas such as the South China Sea. Any major increase of Chinese military activities in such regions could trigger regional arms races in Asia. This could threaten China's relations with neighboring Asian nations and with the international community.

## Option 4: Speed Up Economic Reform

Deng Xiaoping and his supporters have sought to ensure the future well-being of China and the legitimacy of party rule by rapidly modernizing and reforming the economy. They believe that rising living standards and increased production will legitimize the role of the party leadership and that achievement of social and economic well-being will lessen demands for political rights. In opposition to socialism with Chinese characteristics, party hard-liners appreciate the need for market reform but wish to slow down the process. They argue that China's weak infrastructure—its limited transportation, energy, and natural resources—will be unable to sustain more rapid development. Instability, inflation, and dislocation could result as the center loses its ability to control the economy. Deng's opponents fear that his reforms will in time fatally undermine the power of the CCP. The succession struggle that is bound to occur after the death of Deng Xiaoping is likely to solve this controversy.

## Option 5: Restore Party Legitimacy

Reformist leaders in China recognize that the party can survive only if it restores its credibility among the people. This is predicated on a positive perception of the party and its cadres, particularly among the peasantry. To achieve this credibility, the party will have to change its own ethical standards, which increasingly seem to be based on personal enrichment and corruption rather than service to the people and society. Development of a just society, many argue, also depends on establishment of a legal system that administers justice on an equitable basis to peasant and cadre, merchant and scholar. The party cannot put itself above the law.

## Option 6: Promote Greater Cooperation Between Different Levels of Government and Regions

As greater decentralization takes place, economic disparities have increased between the "have" provinces and the "have not" provinces. Deng Xiaoping to date has adopted the "trickle down" theory that the poorer, interior provinces will be pulled into the orbit of their richer neighbors eventually. Many argue, however, that wealth does not automatically migrate and that the regime will have to force the richer provinces to contribute to infrastructure development in the poorer provinces. Unless the party can develop ways through which local, regional, and national officials can interact and bargain to promote the national well-being, then the bottlenecks and inequities created by further disparities in economic growth may in time overwhelm China's existing social, economic, and political structure, including the party itself.

## DISCUSSION QUESTIONS

1. To what extent do the Chinese people and their leaders believe in the teachings of Karl Marx, Lenin, and Mao?
2. How do the Chinese people view Mao Zedong and his accomplishments today? How is the Chinese Communist Party seeking to continue its "Mandate of Heaven" to rule China in the future?
3. Are Deng Xiaoping's efforts likely to be successful in achieving a peaceful transition of power after he is gone? With the passage of time, how are the people of China likely to view Deng Xiaoping's contributions to China?
4. Compare and contrast how the Cultural Revolution and the events at Tiananmen Square have affected the relationship between the Chinese people and the CCP?
5. What changes are likely to occur in Hong Kong after 1997?
6. What are the prospects for Tibet becoming an independent nation-state?
7. Discuss the alternative scenarios for Chinese-Taiwanese relations in the future.
8. In what ways are feelings associated with cultural identity and the idea of the Middle Kingdom a source of unity or disunity inside contemporary China?
9. Would Western-type democratic reforms be more beneficial or harmful to the well-being of China and its people as the twenty-first century begins? Is it feasible to create a legal system in China that guarantees the basic rights of individuals and corporate entities while at the same time maintaining the leading role of the CCP?
10. What problems facing China may be associated with its rapid rate of economic development (8 to 9 percent) over the past ten years?
11. What forces inside China might eventually lead to one of the following forms of political structure in the twenty-first century: empire, federation, or decentralization?
12. What is the relationship between the PLA and the CCP? What role might the PLA play as the nature of CCP control over the nation adapts to the future?
13. How are developments within China in the 1990s likely to affect its foreign relations?

## SUGGESTED READINGS

Bachman, David. *Bureaucracy, Economy, and Leadership in China: The Institutional Origins of the Great Leap Forward.* New York: Cambridge University Press, 1991.

Baldinger, Pamela. "The Birth of Greater China." *China Business Review* 19 (May–June 1991): pp. 13–22.

Barnett, A. Doak. *China's Far West: Four Decades of Change.* Boulder, Colorado: Westview Press, 1993.

Barnouin, Barbara, and Yu Changgen, *Ten Years of Turbulence: The Chinese Cultural Revolution.* New York: K. Paul, International, 1993.

Bian, Yanjie. *Work and Inequality in Urban China.* Albany, New York: State University of New York Press, 1994.

Black, George, and Robin Munro. *Black Hand of Beijing: Lives of Defiance in China's Democracy Movement.* New York: John Wiley, 1993.

Brook, Timothy. *Quelling the People: The Military Suppression of the Beijing Democracy Movement.* New York: Oxford University Press, 1992.

Carlson, Jude. "Tibet in the News." *Bulletin of Concerned Asian Scholars* 24, no. 2 (1992): pp. 25–49.

Chang, Maria Hsia. "China's Future: Regionalism, Federation or Disintegration." *Studies in Comparative Communism* 25 (September 1992): pp. 211–227.

———, "Taiwan and the Mainland: A Shifting Competition." *Global Affairs* 7 (Summer 1992): pp. 14–28.

Chang, Parris, and Martin L. Lasater. *If China Crosses the Taiwan Strait: The International Response.* Lanham, Maryland: University Press of America, 1993.

Chen, Te-sheng, "Conditions Are Not Yet Ripe for the Establishment of a Greater Chinese Economic Sphere." *Issues and Studies* 28 (February 1992): pp. 131–133.

Cheng, Tun-jen, Chi Huang, and Samuel S. G. Wu, eds. *Inherited Rivalry: Conflicts Across the Taiwan Strait.* Boulder, Colorado: Lynne Rienner Publishers, 1995.

Cheng, Tun-jen, and Stephen Haggard, eds., *Political Change in Taiwan.* Boulder, Colorado: Lynne Rienner Publishers, 1992.

Ch'i Hsi-sheng. *Politics of Disillusionment: The Chinese Communist Party under Deng Xiaoping, 1978–1989.* Armonk, New York: M.E. Sharpe, 1991.

Chi, Wen-shen. *Ideological Conflicts in Modern China: Democracy and Authoritarianism.* New Brunswick, New Jersey: Transaction Publishers, 1992.

Chiang Chen-ch'ang. "The Influence of the 'Old Guard' in Mainland Chinese Politics." *Issues and Studies* 28 (February 1992): pp. 25–34.

Clough, Ralph N. *Reaching Across the Taiwan Strait: People-to-People Diplomacy.* Boulder, Colorado: Westview Press, 1993.

Des Forges, Roger V., Luo Ning, and Wu Yen-bo. *Chinese Democracy and the Crisis of 1989: Chinese and American Reflections.* Albany, New York: State University of New York Press, 1993.

Dikotter, Frank. *The Discourse of Race in Modern China.* Stanford, California: Stanford University Press, 1992.

Dittmer, Lowell, and Samuel S. Kim, eds. *China's Quest for National Identity.* Ithaca, New York: Cornell University Press, 1993.

Dreyer, June Teufel. *China's Political System: Modernization and Tradition.* New York: Paragon Press, 1993.

Drinan, Robert F., and Teresa Kuo. "The 1991 Battle for Human Rights in China." *Human Rights Quarterly* 14 (February 1992): pp. 21–42.

Dutton, Michael Robert. *Policing and Punishment in China: From Patriarchy to the People.* New York: Cambridge University Press, 1992.

Emerson, M.S. Niou. "Taiwanese Investment in Mainland China As a Policy Tool," *Issues and Studies* 28 (August 1992): pp. 14–31.

Folsom, Ralph H., John H. Minan, and Lee Ann Otto. *Law and Politics in the People's Republic of China in a Nutshell.* St. Paul, Minnesota: West Publishing Company, 1992.

Folta, Paul Humes. *From Swords to Plowshares? Defense Industry Reform in the PRC.* Boulder, Colorado: Westview Press, 1992.

Friedman, Edward. "China's North-South Split and the Faces of Disintegration." *Current History* (September 1993): pp. 270–274.

———. *National Identity and Democratic Prospects in Socialist China.* Armonk, New York: M.E. Sharpe, 1994.

Fu, Feng-cheng. "The Decentralization of Peking's Economic Management and its Impact on Foreign Investment." *Issues and Studies* 28 (February 1992): pp. 67–83.

Gladney, Deru C. "The Muslim Face of China." *Current History* (September 1993), pp. 275–280.

Han Minzhu, ed. *Cries for Democracy: Writings and Speeches from the 1989 Chinese Democracy Movement.* Princeton, New Jersey: Princeton University Press, 1990.

Han, Theodore, and John Li. *Tiananmen Square, Spring 1989: A Chronology of the Chinese Democracy Movement.* Berkeley, California: Center for Chinese Studies, 1992.

Harding, Harry. "The Emergence of Greater China." *American Enterprise* 3 (May–June 1992): pp. 46–55.

Heberer, Thomas. *China and its National Minorities: Autonomy or Assimilation?* Armonk, New York: M.E. Sharpe, 1990.

Kau, Michael Ying-Mao, and John K. Leung, eds. *The Writings of Mao Zedong, 1949–1976,* Vol. II. Armonk, New York: M.E. Sharpe, 1993.

Kau, Michael Ying-Mao, and Susan H. Marsh, eds. *China in the Era of Deng Xiaoping: A Decade of Reform.* Armonk, New York: M.E. Sharpe, 1993.

Kent, Ann E. *China and Human Rights.* New York: Oxford University Press, 1992.

Kim, Ilpyong, and June Teufel Dreyer, eds. *Chinese Defense and Foreign Policy.* New York: Paragon House, 1988.

Kim, Samuel S., ed. *New Directions in Chinese Foreign Relations.* Boulder, Colorado: Westview Press, 1989.

Korzec, Michael. *Labor and the Failure of Reform in China.* New York: St. Martin's Press, 1992.

Lambert, Anthony. "Post-Tiananmen Chinese Communist Party Religious Policy." *Religion, State and Society* 20, nos. 3–4 (1992): pp. 391–397.

Lee, Wei-Chin. "Crimes of the Heart: Political Loyalty in Socialist China." *Studies in Comparative Communism* 25 (September 1992): pp. 228–241.

Lin, Bih-jaw, et al. *The Aftermath of the 1989 Crisis in Mainland China.* Boulder, Colorado: Westview Press, 1992.

Lin, Chong-Pin. "The Coming Chinese Earthquake." *International Economy* 6 (May–June 1992): pp. 50–57.

Lin, Nan. *The Struggle for Tiananmen: Anatomy of the 1989 Mass Movement.* Westport, Connecticut: Praeger, 1992.

Liu Binyan. "The Long March from Mao: China's De-Communization." *Current History* (September 1993): pp. 241–244.

MacFarquhar, Roderick. "Deng's Last Campaign." *The New York Review of Books* (November 19, 1992): pp. 22–26.

McCormick, Barrett L., Su Shaozhi, and Xiao Siamong. "The 1989 Chinese Democracy Movement: A Review of the Prospects for Civil Society in China." *Pacific Affairs* 65 (Summer 1992): pp. 182–202.

Metzger, Thomas A. *The Unification of China and the Problem of Public Opinion in the Republic of China in Taiwan.* Stanford, California: Hoover Institution, 1992.

Muskat, Miron. *The Economic Future of Hong Kong.* Boulder, Colorado: Lynne Rienner Publishers, 1990.

Ogden, Suzanne. *China's Search for Democracy: The Student and the Mass Movement of 1989.* Armonk, New York: M.E. Sharpe, 1992.

————. *China's Unresolved Issues: Politics, Development and Culture.* 2d ed. Englewood Cliffs, New Jersey: Prentice Hall, 1992.

Oksenberg, Michael, Marc Lambert, and Lawrence H. Sullivan, eds. *Beijing Spring, 1989, Confrontation and Conflict: The Basic Documents.* Armonk, New York: M.E. Sharpe, 1992.

Saich, Tony, ed. *The Rise to Power of the Chinese Communist Party: Documents and Analysis.* Armonk, New York: M.E. Sharpe, 1993.

Schram, Stuart R., ed. *Mao's Road to Power: Revolutionary Writings, 1912–1949,* Vol. I. Armonk, New York: M.E. Sharpe, 1993.

Scobell, Andrew. "Why the People's Army Fired on the People: The Chinese Military and Tiananmen." *Armed Forces and Society* 18 (Winter 1992): pp. 192–213.

Shambaugh, David. "Losing Control: The Erosion of State Authority in China." *Current History* (September 1993): pp. 253–269.

Unger, Jonathan, ed. *The Pro-Democracy Protests in China: Reports from the Provinces.* Armonk, New York: M.E. Sharpe, 1991.

Wachman, Alan M. *Taiwan: National Identity and the Democratization.* Armonk, New York: M.E. Sharpe, 1994.

Wai, Ting. "Hong Kong's Changing Political Order and Its Relations with Taiwan." *Issues and Studies* 28 (August 1992): pp. 46–72.

————. "The Regional and International Implications of the South China Economic Zone." *Issues and Studies* 28 (December 1992): pp. 46–72.

Yeung Yue-man, and Xu-wei Hu. *China's Coastal Cities: Catalysts for Modernization.* Honolulu: University of Hawaii Press, 1992.

Yu, George T., ed. *China in Transition: Economic, Political, and Social Developments.* Lanham, Maryland: University Press of America, 1993.

## NOTES

1. Perry Link, *Evening Chats in Beijing* (New York: W. W. Norton, 1992), p. 299.

2. For the Chinese viewpoint on Tibet, see Dai Yannian, Edna Driscoll, Yen Qinghong, and Zhu Yuan, eds., *China in Focus—Tibet: Myth and Reality* (Beijing: Beijing Review Publications, 1988) and *Tibetans on Tibet* (Beijing: China Reconstruction Press, 1988).

3. Bradford Trebach, *New York Times,* May 19, 1992, p. A14.

4. T.L. Tsim, "Hong Kong: The Middle of the Journey," *The Yale China Association China Update,* 2, no. 3 (Fall 1991): p. 4.

5. Sheila Tefft, "Even Chinese Who Liked British Rule Are Irked Over Hong Kong," *Christian Science Monitor,* April 21, 1993, p. 2.

6. United Press International, Taipei, January 1, 1993.

7. Wei Jingsheng, quoted in Uli Schmetzer, "Chinese Dissident Optimistic," *Chicago Tribune,* October 10, 1993, section 1, p. 12.

8. For an analysis of the Chinese democracy movement and the events leading up to Tiananmen Square, see George Black and Robin Munro, *Black Hands of Beijing: Lives of Defiance in China's Democracy Movement* (New York: John Wiley, 1993). Susan Ogden, et al., eds., *China's Search for Democracy: The Student and Mass Movement* (Armonk, New York: M.E. Sharpe, 1992). Roger V. Des Forges, Luo Ning, and Wu Yen-bo, eds., *Chinese Democracy and the Crisis of 1989: Chinese and American Reflections* (Albany, New York: State University of New York Press, 1993). Theodore Han and John Li, *Tiananmen Square Spring 1989: A Chronology of the Chinese Democracy Movement* (Berkeley, California: Institute of East Asian Studies, 1992).

9. For the significance of the events at Tiananmen Square and their consequences, see Bin-Jaw Lin, et al., eds., *The Aftermath of the 1989 Tiananmen Crisis in Mainland China* (Boulder, Colorado: Westview Press, 1992). Timothy Brooks, *Quelling the People: The Military Suppression of the Beijing Democracy Movement* (New York: Oxford University Press, 1992). Lee Wei-chin, "Read My Lips or Watch My Feet: The State and Chinese Dissident Intellectuals," *Issues and Studies,* 28 (May 1992): pp. 29–48. "China's Sort of Freedom," *Economist,* October 17, 1992, pp. 39–41. Richard A. Hartness and Guilian Wang, "The Problem of Culture: The Clash between Gerentocrats and Paedocrats in the 1989 Spring Uprising in China," *Asian Profile,* 20 (April 1992): pp. 97–107. Anthony P.B. Lambert, "Post-Tiananmen Chinese Communist Party Religious Policy," *Religion, State and Society,* 20, nos. 3–4 (1992): pp. 391–397 (in this article the author notes that "the downfall of Marxist regimes in Eastern Europe . . . aroused fears of a similar mass movement taking hold among China's working class, and suspicions that both the Catholic and Protestant churches in China could become bases for political subversion"). Andrew Scobell, "Why the People's Army Fired on the People: The Chinese Military and Tiananmen," *Armed Forces and Society,* 18 (Winter 1992): pp. 193–213. Martin King White, "Prospects for Democratization in China," *Problems of Communism,* 41 (May–June 1992): pp. 58–70.

10. See Sheryl WuDunn, "Focus on Profits, China Reviews Bias Against Women," *New York Times,* July 28, 1992, pp. A1, A5. Lena H. Sun, "The Feminization of Poverty In China: Mao's Promises of Equality Are Giving Way to the Bad Old Days," *Washington Post National Weekly Edition,* April 5–11, 1993, p. 9.

11. See Lee Wei-chin, "Crimes of the Heart: Political Loyalty in Socialist China", *Studies in Comparative Communism* 25 (September 25, 1992): pp. 228–241.

12. See Sheila Tefft, "Prison Letters Reveal Plight of Chinese Dissidents," *Christian Science Monitor,* March 4, 1993, p. 1.

13. Hou Xiaotian, "A Start on Human Rights in China," *New York Times,* June 17, 1992, p. A17.

14. Sheryl WuDunn, "China Arrests a Student Leader Back from Exile in the United States," *New York Times,* September 2, 1992, p. A8.

15. Nicholas D. Kristof, "Beijing Journal: Three Years After Tiananmen Protests, Who Among Chinese Remembers," *New York Times International,* June 5, 1992, p. A4.

16. Several months prior to the Olympic vote on selecting the site, International Olympic Committee president Juan Antonio Samaranch said that China's record on human rights would be an important factor in the site selection. [Associated Press Release from Beijing reported in the *Charleston Illinois Times Courier,* May 26, 1993, p. A2.]

17. Maria Hsia Chang, "China's Future: Regionalism, Federation or

Disintegration," *Studies in Comparative Communism* 25 (September 1992): pp. 211–227.

18. See Ann Scott Tyson and James L. Tyson, "As Party Declines, Who Is in Charge?" *Christian Science Monitor,* August 12, 1992, pp. 9–12.

19. Tyson and Tyson, "As Party Declines, Who Is in Charge?" p. 9.

20. These developments were reported in a survey by Asian Watch, "Continuing Religious Repression in China," which was released on May 28, 1993, and is discussed in the *Chicago Tribune,* May 30, 1993, section 1, p. 14.

21. See Luc Chartrand, "Hong Kong's Reverse Takeover," *World Press Review* 39 (September 1992): p. 42. Cindy Fan, "Regional Impacts of Foreign Trade in China 1984–1989," *Growth and Change* 23 (Spring 1992): pp. 129–159. James L. Tyson and Ann Scott Tyson, "Chinese Reforms Widen Gap Between Coast and Hinterland," *Christian Science Monitor,* July 22, 1992, pp. 9–12. Ting Wai, "The Regional and International Implications of the South China Economic Zone," *Issues and Studies* 28 (December 1992): pp. 46–72. Chris Bramall, *Legacies of Maoist Economic Development in Sichuan* (New York: Oxford University Press, 1993).

22. National Committee on U.S.China Relations, "Delegation Examines Management of the Information Age," *Notes From the National Committee* 21, no. 2 (Spring/Summer 1992): p. 7.

23. See Roderick MacFarquhar, "Deng's Final Campaign," *New York Review,* November 19, 1992. Chiang Chenchiang, "The Influence of the Old Guard in Mainland Chinese Politics," *Issues and Studies* 28 (July 1992): pp. 25–34. Chenpang Chang, "A New Round of Power Struggle in Peking," *Issues and Studies* 28 (April 1992): pp. 109–111. Chong-Pin Lin, "The Coming Chinese Earthquake," *International Economy* 6 (May–June 1992): pp. 50–57. David Shambaugh, "Regaining Momentum Deng Strikes Back," *Current History* 91 (September 1992): pp. 257–261. Ross Terrill, "Rocking the Old Guard," *World Monitor* 5 (May 1992): pp. 24, 26–28. Nicholas D. Kristof, "Chinese Shake Up Top Party Group; Free Market Gains," *New York Times,* October 20, 1992, pp. A1, A6. Lena H. Sun, "A Last Hurrah for China's Old Guard," *Washington Post Weekly Edition,* September 21–27, 1992, p. 18.

24. For a detailed analysis of the role of the military in China's political process and how this might affect the succession struggle, see Michael P. Swaine, *The Military and Political Succession in China: Leadership Institution Beliefs.* (Santa Monica, California: Rand Corporation, 1992).

25. See "New Party Leadership," *Beijing Review* (November 2–8, 1992): pp. 13–17. Nicholas D. Kristof, "Chinese Shake Up Top Party Group; Free Market Gains," *New York Times,* October 20, 1992, pp. A1, A6.

26. For a presentation of how China might avoid the "Russia syndrome," see "Reform and Soviet Collapse Spur Discussion Between American and Chinese Specialists," *Notes from the National Committee* 21, no. 2 (Spring/Summer 1993): pp. 6, 12.

# The Ascendancy of
# Adam Smith over Karl Marx

> We have in the past dozen years implemented the policy of reform and
> opening to the outside world which was initiated by Comrade Deng
> Xiaoping, and have carried out a structural economic reform with great
> success. This reform first succeeded in the rural areas. Reform and
> opening have brought China great economic growth, social prosperity,
> higher standard of living and a great change in the mental outlook of
> the people.
>
> —*Premier Li Peng*

Li Peng's comments at the 1992 World Economic Forum in Davos,
Switzerland, confirm Chinese satisfaction with the tremendous economic
changes that have taken place inside China in the past fifteen years. Li, recognized as a conservative and a hard-liner, nevertheless eulogizes the
sweeping reforms introduced by Deng Xiaoping, confirming the approval
of the fundamental economic changes that are the basis of China's remarkable economic development. To bring about these reforms within China, its
leaders have turned to the outside world for investment, aid, trade, and
technology. Although the formal decisionmaking process on the surface
seems as totalitarian as in the past, beneath the surface several different
policymaking processes are evolving that have helped make these economic reforms possible, reaching down from the leaders in Beijing to the local
village and township governments in China's vast rural hinterland. In reality, decentralization of economic decisionmaking is affecting the way in
which political decisions are being made at all levels of Chinese society.
Current economic policy, in turn, is based on remarkable changes in
Chinese economic thought, which has gone through a number of dramatic
stages in the twentieth century.

Chapter 2 examined China's economic and political developments up
to the time of the 1978 economic reforms. This chapter will look at the
remarkable economic changes brought about by Deng Xiaoping and his followers, which have occurred at all levels of society, and it will note the
relationship between changing economic practices and the evolution of the

71

decisionmaking process, especially at the local level and in rural areas. Although the trappings of Leninism and totalitarianism remain in place, under the surface there has already been substantial movement toward different decisionmaking processes, as we will see when we look at the results of Deng's Open Door policy: new models in technology, markets, and education; economic revolution in rural China; joint ventures and special economic zones; trade and tourism; and finally the relationship between economic liberalism, political freedom, and human rights.[1] Deng Xiaoping himself used a modified rational actor approach in which, after weighing the costs and benefits of different economic practices beyond China's shores, he announced and then implemented radical changes in Chinese economic practice; he did this years before Gorbachev and his followers began to think about such changes toward economic liberalism, which have yet to be carried out effectively in the former parts of the Soviet Union.

## THE NEW ECONOMICS:
## DENG XIAOPING AND THE OPEN DOOR

Deng Xiaoping, after defeating a number of rivals to succeed Mao, faced the unenviable task of saving China's communist system and the power of the Chinese Communist Party, both of which had been damaged almost beyond repair by the Cultural Revolution. Deng sought pragmatic solutions to China's problems. In principle, Deng supported Marxist theory. In practice, he modified many of Mao's policies, especially in the production and distribution of goods and in China's economic relations abroad. As Deng reportedly said, he did not care if the cat was black or white, so long as it caught mice.

The evolution of Marxist, neo-Marxist, and Leninist principles within China may be divided into three periods. The 1920s up to 1949 saw the following:

- emphasis on nationalism
- anti-imperialism
- rural class struggle and revolutionism

The period from 1949 to 1977 saw a shift toward

- Leninist principles of revolution and rule
- emphasis on nationalism and anticapitalism
- anti-imperialism
- rural revolution and communes
- the Great Leap Forward
- the Cultural Revolution

- neo-Marxism
- autarky
- Leninist and Stalinist rule

From 1978 to the present, China has witnessed

- nationalism
- dual economy
- empowerment of the rural population
- Open Door policy
- entry into the global economic system
- partial shift from Leninist to authoritarian rule
- emphasis on basic economic and social, but not political, rights

The Cultural Revolution had damaged China's infrastructure and educational system, as well as the country's ability to advance science and technology. By 1978, Deng and his followers realized that drastic changes were needed. Stagnation and disillusionment, brought about by the Cultural Revolution, needed to be replaced by new approaches that would allow the people to work together toward a brighter future.

Deng, no supporter of capitalism, was a pragmatist. He observed the successes of China's neighbors such as Japan and the Four Little Tigers (South Korea, Taiwan, Hong Kong, and Singapore), three of which had Chinese populations. Though Deng may have believed that the capitalists of the West sought to exploit Third World countries, he also recognized that even in protesting this exploitation, Third World countries, acting through the United Nations, were no longer rejecting the global capitalist system but seeking to make it more equitable and fair to the poor countries of the world.[2] Beginning in 1978, Beijing took a similar approach. Whereas Mao had practiced economic autarky, Deng believed that China's future depended not only on its joining the international economic system, which is based on marketplace capitalism, but also on actively participating in the different economic regimes that make up the global system, such as the World Bank, the International Monetary Fund, and the General Agreement on Trade and Tariffs. Thus, Deng and his followers abandoned self-reliance in favor of the Open Door policy, which Deng introduced in late 1978. Instead of isolating China from the international system, Deng sought to use the capitalist system and its market incentives to bring about immediate improvement in China's economy by introducing capitalist practices and trade with the West.

In fact, Deng and his followers took advantage of China's disillusionment with Maoist policies to introduce new approaches that the people would welcome. He first carried out reform in the countryside, releasing the energies of the peasants by allowing them to farm their own land and create rural industries. Private production and distribution of goods was first allowed in the countryside and then gradually extended to the cities. At the same time, a dual economic system was maintained. New enterprises created new jobs, greatly expanding China's economy, but the old public sectors were also maintained to avoid the displacement of existing jobs, with their socialist benefits. Thus, part of the iron rice bowl was retained. Only gradually has the Beijing leadership cut back on subsidies to the public sector in the 1990s; it has done so in order to give the public sector time to adjust to market incentives, including the possibility of bankruptcy.

In effect, the public production and service sectors increasingly have to compete with the more efficient private sectors, which have to face bankruptcy and reorganization if they are unable to compete with both the public sector and other private competitors. However, a Western diplomat has observed that the problem of reforming the state enterprises is that they are "more like enormous feudal villages than modern corporations. They have to provide housing, recreation, hospitals, parks, and all manner of services, sometimes for hundreds of thousands of employees and their families."[3]

In spite of all the difficulties, the proof of Deng Xiaoping's success in moving China towards an economy of global importance is visible through the results. According to the World Bank, conditions in the Chinese countryside have improved remarkably, especially in comparison with Third World countries like India (see Table 3.1).

**Table 3.1**    **A Comparison of Chinese and Indian Development: Annual Growth Rates (in percentages)**

| China | 1970–1980 | 1980–1991 | India | 1970–1980 | 1980–1991 |
|---|---|---|---|---|---|
| Growth in domestic product | 5.2 | 9.4 | Growth in domestic product | 3.4 | 5.4 |
| Manufacturing | 9.5 | 11.1 | Manufacturing | 4.6 | 6.7 |
| Exports | 8.7 | 11.5 | Exports | 4.3 | 7.4 |
| Agriculture | 2.6 | 5.7 | Agriculture | 1.8 | 3.2 |

*Source:* Compiled from World Bank data, *World Development Report 1993: Investing in Health* (New York: Oxford University Press, 1993), pp. 240, 244, 264.

Although productivity has increased in both China and India in the last fifteen years, growth rates in China have been much higher than in India, especially in agriculture. China's increase in (GNP) of over 12 percent in 1992 and an estimated 13 percent in 1993 is even more remarkable, considering low growth rates in the Western world, including North America, Western Europe and Japan, which are the primary markets for Chinese exports.

Should China be able to continue these economic growth rates in the twenty-first century, its rate of growth could exceed those in most other countries and match the economic miracles that occurred in Japan in an earlier era, followed by similar miracles in recent years in South Korea, Taiwan, Hong Kong, and Singapore. In the twenty-first century, barring unforeseen circumstances, China, with its huge population, could have markets and production rivaling not only Japan, but North America and Europe. These are big ifs, however. First, China will need to maintain stability and order during an era when popular aspirations are even greater than the opportunity to fulfill these demands. Second, because the population continues to grow at a rate of over 15 million a year, ways must be found to provide more jobs outside of traditional agriculture, especially through the creation of light industrial and service jobs in China's rural hinterland. Third, China's strained infrastructure and energy supply must be improved. Transportation and electricity are inadequate to meet current demand, much less support an economy that has been growing at the rate of over 9 percent during the past fifteen years. Finally, support from the global economy must continue, including increased investment and Chinese exports at a time when other regions either are in recession or are experiencing very low growth rates. For example, in 1993, Japan, a major market for Chinese commodities and a major source of investment funds, was growing at a rate of less than 2 percent, in contrast to Japanese growth rates in GNP exceeding 10 percent in recent decades.

## TECHNOLOGY, MARKETS, AND EDUCATION: THE JAPANESE OR THE WESTERN MODEL?

China's post-Mao reformers knew that the existing system was not working. But there were a number of other different possibilities based on the experience of other countries and regions, all of which, from the Chinese perspective, had both advantages and disadvantages. In the end, Deng and his followers adopted some practices while rejecting others based on the U.S., European, Japanese, and other Asian systems.

### The U.S. Model

Beijing's reformers admired U.S. technology, which in 1978 was still more advanced than in most other parts of the world. Beginning with Deng's Open Door policy, thousands of Chinese students were sent to the United States, many with Chinese government assistance, to learn about science and technology as well as new business and administration techniques. Ideally, they would then bring this knowledge back to China and help China catch up with the West. Because the United States in 1978 was an informal Chinese ally in resisting Soviet influence in Asia, Beijing also hoped to get help from the United States in modernizing China, including the military.

Furthermore, Beijing sought both technology and capital from the United States by encouraging U.S. corporations to invest in China, both through joint ventures and by creating U.S. subsidiaries in China. Ideally, these investors would then export their goods back to the United States and other Western countries and provide hard currency through the sale of labor-intensive products such as shoes, textiles, clothes, Christmas tree light bulbs, greeting cards (including the musical kind), toys, and glassware. These measures succeeded beyond anyone's imagination. By the 1990s, China was providing one-third of all U.S. toys and one-sixth of all U.S. clothing in a highly competitive market. In 1991, China had a $12 billion trade surplus with the United States, which grew to over $20 billion in 1993.

But other parts of the U.S. model have had little appeal to Beijing. The U.S. government has practiced a hands-off policy in regard to the economy, whereas Beijing's reformers continue to support a dual economic system. The Chinese central government owns and subsidizes large industries, and the private market and system of production has been allowed to grow alongside the public economy. Beijing's leaders also dislike the extreme disparity of wealth in the United States. Although they want to increase the well-being of the people, they also have held on to their socialist egalitarian values, in which government is supposed to use its power to enhance the well-being of all segments of society. In practice, however, Chinese economic reforms have substantially undermined China's social services. The burden of education, health care, pensions, disability, and unemployment benefits have been increasingly shifted to the local government level. In the past, agricultural collectives and state enterprises provided these services, but in the 1990s, most of the growing private sector does not provide them, and local government is hard-pressed to find revenues to meet these needs.

Beijing was also concerned with the role of special interests and the public in the U.S. political system. Deng and his followers did not believe that marketplace reforms would have to be followed by political reforms in which the people and organized economic interests would replace the dominant role of the CCP. Deng and his supporters believed that the Chinese Communist Party could orchestrate the creation of a private sector while at the same time maintaining a large public sector, something that is almost totally absent in the U.S. economy. Furthermore, Deng and his economic reformers were convinced that the energy of the people could be utilized in supporting these new private enterprises, in which the appeal would be enrichment and a better life; at the same time, the party and government would continue to manage the changing economy by using the party-controlled media and its monopoly of power to prevent any organized opposition to party policies.

## The Western European Model

Deng sought to diversify China's relations with the West in order to gain more investment capital and trade, but also to avoid too much dependence on any single country, such as the United States. Beijing, however, has been less successful in opening up the European Community market to Chinese goods than in increasing its sales to the U.S. market. Still, the European model, with greater government assistance and regulation of the economy, appeals to Beijing's leaders, especially the government planning and assistance aimed at increasing production and the distribution of wealth. With privatization in the countryside, however, China's governmental units provide much less in the way of socialist services such as health care, educational benefits (especially at the higher level), unemployment benefits, and old age benefits. Larger state enterprises in China continue to provide such benefits, based on the principle of the iron rice bowl, but employees in the private sector are largely on their own unless they can persuade local enterprises and governments to help take care of these needs. As production has increased in China's coastal provinces and economic export zones, tax resources have gravitated to the regional and local levels.

One thing that China's leaders are now considering is Europe's value-added tax (VAT), in which both European governments and the European Community place an indirect tax on the production and distribution of goods and services rather than imposing a sales tax on goods when they are finally sold to the consumer. But Beijing's authority to impose new taxes seems to be eroding as the power to tax increasingly shifts to the regional and local levels. This, in turn, means less provision of services by the central government. A VAT-type tax could mean an increase in Beijing's ability to raise revenue and distribute benefits. This is happening in European Community headquarters in Brussels, where the European Community is taking over increasing responsibilities, but the trend inside China since 1978 has been in the opposite direction.

## The Japanese Model

The Japanese model has both virtues and dangers from the Chinese perspective. Beijing is quite aware of how Japan's authoritarian leaders were able to impose reform from above beginning in the 1860s. The Meiji reforms were directed by a transformed Japanese aristocracy, which shifted its rural power base to the new capitalist economy based on industry, finance, and trade. In sending hundreds of thousands of students overseas since 1978, mainly to Western countries, Beijing has emulated the Japanese practice of sending its sons and daughters to Western Europe and the United States to learn the latest Western technology. However, approximately 70 percent of Chinese students, especially since Tiananmen Square, have avoided returning to the Chinese mainland. Like the Meiji reformers, China offers incentives and good positions to get the students to come back and assume key jobs in the economy, government, elite structure, research, and the educational system, but with limited success.

A major difference between the Japanese and the Chinese models relates to investment. Japan's ruling elite, from the time of the Meiji reforms to the present, has severely restricted overseas investment. Unlike in China, nearly all Japanese capital has been generated within Japan or through overseas trade in other countries, not through outside investment or loans. Today, Beijing's leaders have mixed feelings about Japanese investment in China and other parts of Asia. They want the technology and the capital, but they are concerned about Japanese domination of the Chinese and other Asian economies, more so than the danger of domination by investors from North America and Europe. They remember Japan's desire for a "coprosperity sphere" in Asia during World War II all too well. In the future, China and Japan may be competitors for Asian resources. On the other hand, China needs Japanese investment to develop its own resources, especially energy, including oil, natural gas, and new solar technologies. Japan's low technology investments in China and its refusal to transfer its more advanced technology, especially technology that could be used to modernize China's military, raises suspicions in Beijing that Japan wishes to exploit China's resources, cheap labor, and markets while preventing the upgrading of its military capability.

## The Four Little Tigers and the Overseas Chinese

In China's search for development models as well as capital investment, the greatest source of help has come from the 55 million Chinese living outside mainland China (see Table 3.2) and, more recently, in South Korea.

In both Taiwan and South Korea, land reform was successfully introduced in the 1950s, resulting in the breakup of large estates into small private farms, which were then assisted by the government. Cheap loans, availability of inputs (such as low-priced fertilizer), hybrid seeds (part of the green revolution), market transport, and market structures based on competition all contributed to a revolution in the countryside. Increased agricultural production then provided capital to help industrialize Taiwan and South Korea. Beijing's leaders could look to the Korean model as an example of how to build large capitalist corporate operations, such as shipbuilding and heavy industry, and they could look to the Taiwanese model as an example of how to create small light industries based on intensive

**Table 3.2     Ethnic Chinese Outside Mainland China (in millions)**

| | |
|---|---|
| Taiwan | 21.0 |
| Indonesia | 7.2 |
| Hong Kong | 6.0 |
| Thailand | 5.8 |
| Malaysia | 5.2 |
| Singapore | 2.0 |
| Myanmar (Burma) | 1.5 |
| Vietnam | 0.8 |
| The Philippines | 0.8 |
| Rest of Asia and Australia | 1.8 |
| United States | 1.8 |
| Canada | 0.6 |
| Latin America | 1.0 |
| Europe | 0.6 |
| Africa | 0.1 |

*Source: Economist,* July 18, 1992, p. 2. The data come from the *Overseas Chinese Economy Yearbook.*

labor.[4] Deng and his followers first carried out their post-1978 land reforms based in part on the South Korean and Taiwanese models. Then they introduced small factories in the countryside, based on light industry and cheap labor, patterned after the Taiwanese model.

China's utilization of overseas Chinese, who number over 55 million (if Taiwan and Hong Kong are included), may be China's secret weapon in making it one of the world's leading economies in the twenty-first century. Since Deng and his followers adopted their Open Door policy in 1978, two-thirds of direct outside investment has come from Hong Kong and Taiwan, with another 10 percent coming from overseas Chinese in other parts of the world.[5] Hong Kong Chinese have provided the largest single source of capital for mainland China. By 1992, Hong Kong business leaders were employing four times as many workers in manufacturing operations inside China as in Hong Kong itself, where wages are at least ten times as high as on the mainland. But investment has also come from overseas Chinese in other parts of Asia as well as North America.

Ethnic Chinese throughout Southeast Asia (see Table 3.2) are a key part of the business community, conducting family businesses that make up a major portion of manufacturing, marketing, trade, and finance in countries such as Thailand, Malaysia, Vietnam, Singapore (which is three-quarters Chinese), the Philippines, and Indonesia. Along with Chinese from Hong Kong and Taiwan, they are accustomed to avoiding politics while at the same time working with authoritarian systems, in which business relationships are conducted on the basis of personal contact and influence (*guanxi*). Because overseas Chinese have many family ties and personal relationships with Chinese mainlanders and they also understand the culture and requirements of doing business back home, they have many advantages over other outside investors, such as those from Japan, Europe, and non-Chinese from North America. Although Japan has been considered the leading investor in Asian countries, the combination of Chinese ties throughout Asia, North America, and inside China is creating an interdependent Chinese economy without borders. Hong Kong is the chief service center for these activities, with the largest amount of capital coming from Hong Kong and Taiwan. However, the network of Chinese contacts is creating interdependency and informal relations in which business transactions are conducted on a highly personal basis, with mainland China becoming the chief location for manufacturing operations. With Deng's Open Door policy, overseas Chinese have flooded into the mainland as tourists and on business. They have established contacts through relatives and friends, as well as with local government and party officials, all of whom have worked closely with them in setting up a growing number of business operations. Already, in the areas of Guangdong province in southern China adjacent to Hong Kong and Macao, living standards have risen dramatically as the countryside becomes integrated with the Hong Kong economy.

As for Chinese mainlanders, through both government and private investors, they have in turn invested over $11 billion in the economy of Hong Kong, which along with Shenzhen, a border city of two million next to Hong Kong, has become the financial and service center for economic activities throughout southern China. Operations involving overseas Chinese investment extend beyond China's special economic zones in Guangdong and Fujian provinces (the latter is adjacent to Taiwan) and are now reaching into China's hinterland and rural areas. There, the use of personal family ties and cooperation, with local officials willing to make deals, are resulting in the integration of most of southern and southeastern China into a single international market network. Investment comes from overseas Chinese, light manufactured goods are produced with cheap mainland labor, and the goods are then trucked to Hong Kong or other ports for shipment to overseas markets.

## ECONOMIC REVOLUTION IN RURAL CHINA:
## LIFE IN THE CHINESE VILLAGE

The township and village enterprises were a great invention of the Chinese farmers made in the reform process. In the 1980s, these enterprises of different types mushroomed rapidly, giving employment to various townships and preventing a rush of surplus rural labor to the cities. Now, in the total value of rural production, the output value of the township and village enterprises and tertiary industry has exceeded that of agriculture. This is of major significance to the improvement of the farmer's livelihood and the stability of the rural areas and the society as a whole.[6]

Probably Deng Xiaoping's greatest contribution to the future development of China was his radical agrarian reform beginning in late 1978. Mao's farm collectives and communes were largely a failure because China's farmers were unable to reap the fruits of their own labor through lack of incentive and reward. Rural populations felt exploited and longed to have control over their own land and to make the decisions that would enable them to receive the benefits of their efforts. Deng Xiaoping correctly observed how returning the land to the peasants in South Korea and Taiwan helped to initiate the economic miracles in those countries, providing both capital and labor for later industrial development. Today in China, household production units can lease their land, and these leases can be inherited.

Realizing that the breakup of the communes and increased efficiency in farm production would also release millions of peasants who would then become surplus labor, Deng and his reformers also carried out a second rural revolution, creating the incentives and opportunities for the establishment of millions of rural industrial and service enterprises. These would be created through the efforts of the rural people themselves, who under the new township and village rules would be allowed to create private and collective enterprises; these enterprises would then sell their products and services in the marketplace and use most of the profits for improvement in living standards or reinvestment.

Local Communist Party cadres directly benefitted from both increased agricultural and rural industrial production. Because they controlled power structures at the lowest level of government, they were able in many cases to have household farmland assigned to themselves and to participate in the ownership and management of rural industries and services. The newly created wealth resulting from a dramatic increase in production could then be either taxed through local governmental structures, allegedly to provide locally needed social services, or siphoned off through corrupt deals, in which the rural entrepreneurs gave rewards and favors to party cadres for contracts and necessary arrangements in order to produce and market their products.

The overall results of these reforms have been truly astounding, creating growth rates exceeding those in most other regions of the world, in either developed or less developed regions. By 1992, according to World Bank data and Chinese officials, 18.5 million new rural enterprises employed 96 million people and accounted for one-fourth of China's GNP.[7] This was in addition to agricultural production, which reached 441 million metric tons of grain in 1992, enough to feed nearly all of China's people and provide certain types of surpluses for export. By 1992, China had become a major exporter of corn and oilseeds, even though it continued to be a major importer of wheat. Although these increases in both rural enterprises and farm production were highly uneven, occurring mainly in

China's more fertile and highly populated coastal and central regions, the overall standard of living has clearly improved dramatically for most of China's people. National growth rates in GNP of 8 to 9 percent after 1978 came mainly from the market sectors, especially in the rural areas, but also in China's new special economic zones. Since 1978, a third of state enterprises, mostly huge industrial complexes, continue to lose money, and they are much less efficient than the rural enterprises, which have spearheaded a Chinese economic revolution largely unmatched in any other region of the world during the past fifteen years.

If current rates of growth continue, China's rural enterprises could provide as many as 150 million jobs and up to 50 percent of the GNP. From 1985 to 1990, rural industry expanded production at twice the rate of state-run factories. By the 1990s, they accounted for a third of all Chinese industrial production.

### China's Rural Development

"The output of township and village enterprises grew nearly 27 percent a year between 1978 and 1990, and by 1990 comprised 55 percent of total rural output value. Whereas rural industry provided work for only nine percent of the rural labor force in 1978, by 1990 it employed 22 percent. During this period rural income rose from 133 yuan to 629 yuan per capita." [Tyrene White, "Reforming the Countryside," *Current History* (September 1992): p. 273.]

The rapid growth of both agricultural and industrial production in rural China has also been accompanied by a number of political and economic problems that will need to be resolved if China's rural economic miracle is to continue. Politically, the self-sufficient communes of the Mao era have been replaced by the township, which now is the basic unit of government throughout rural China. Depending on population density, a typical township may have as many as 50,000 people, with greater numbers in China's rich coastal provinces, such as Guangdong and Fujian. Typically, there are now elective councils at the township level, with both party cadres and local dignitaries, who are often successful in business, serving for three-year terms. Throughout most of rural China, however, most of these elective positions remain uncontested. Local party cadres in effect both control the bureaucratic structures and have decisionmaking power with regard to authorizing the creation of economic enterprises, controlling tax revenues of the townships, and providing channels for obtaining needed resources that often are not available to local enterprises through the free market system. In China's dual economy, prices and resources through the state structure are much cheaper, but party officials down to the local level are able to decide who gets these materials, giving them guanxi (personal influence) with local enterprises that are dependent on their favors.

Villages, which are below the townships, have developed a certain amount of autonomy in local decisionmaking parallel to decentralization of economic decisionmaking since Deng's rural reform began in 1978. In the past, the local party secretary at the village level was they key decision-maker, but with the growing desire of the local population to control local government decisions, the party secretary has become vulnerable to outside influence in the local village. In the village council, two or three persons now frequently run for office. Even if party cadres are elected, they must take into consideration the needs of local enterprises, which are the source of wealth for the cadres, local bureaucracy, and everyone else. Increasingly, townships and villages are dependent on local financial resources, not only for providing the capital for new agricultural or industrial undertakings, but also for local services such as education, health care, and infrastructure for road maintenance, irrigation, and water supplies. Because local party cadres are also farmers and participate in local enterprises, if they do not have the support of the people, they might receive unfavorable treatment after they have completed their term of office on village councils.[8]

Several different types of economic structures coexist at the village and township levels. In addition to the household land leases for agricultural production, there are private enterprises, collectives, and public enterprises. Most private enterprises tend to be rather small, often initiated by individual families and friends. Collectives, on the other hand, are composed of community businesses in which the participants are shareholders. Because party rules give a number of privileges to collectives that are not always available to private enterprises (for example, tax breaks and sometimes the availability of resources at cheaper prices from the controlled public sector), these economic units have expanded very rapidly in rural areas. In fact, many collectives are in reality private undertakings that are structured as collectives to take advantage of their special privileges. Public enterprises are often able to compete only because they receive even more privileges from government, such as access to loans from government and state-controlled financial institutions that are unavailable to the private sector. The maintenance of public sector enterprises, however, is frequently very important as a major source of employment in rural regions where there may be little opportunity to develop other types of successful enterprises. China's rural areas are very uneven in resources, infrastructure, and market opportunities, and the local party cadres and rural population have to rely largely on their own initiatives and alternate forms of economic structures to provide a livelihood and basic needs. As can be seen in Table 3.3, however, since Deng's Xiaoping's economic reforms, the most rapidly

**Table 3.3    Ownership Structure of Chinese Industry, 1971-1989 (percentages of total industrial output value)**

| Year | State | Urban Collective | Urban Individual | Urban Other | Rural Nonstate | Town Portion | Village and Below |
|------|-------|------------------|------------------|-------------|----------------|--------------|-------------------|
| 1971 | 85.5 | 10.9 | | | 3.2 | 1.6 | 1.6 |
| 1975 | 81.2 | 13.7 | | | 5.1 | 2.6 | 2.5 |
| 1978 | 77.6 | 13.7 | | | 8.7 | 4.8 | 3.9 |
| 1980 | 75.1 | 14.4 | | 0.5 | 10.0 | 5.4 | 4.6 |
| 1981 | 74.3 | 14.1 | | 0.6 | 11.0 | 5.9 | 5.1 |
| 1982 | 73.8 | 14.3 | 0.1 | 0.7 | 11.2 | 6.0 | 5.2 |
| 1983 | 72.6 | 14.4 | 0.1 | 0.8 | 12.1 | 6.3 | 5.8 |
| 1984 | 67.6 | 15.9 | 0.2 | 1.1 | 15.2 | 7.7 | 7.5 |
| 1985 | 64.9 | 15.9 | 0.3 | 1.2 | 17.7 | 7.8 | 9.9 |
| 1986 | 62.3 | 15.0 | 0.3 | 1.5 | 21.0 | 8.8 | 12.2 |
| 1987 | 59.7 | 14.6 | 0.4 | 2.0 | 23.3 | 9.3 | 13.0 |
| 1988 | 56.8 | 14.3 | 0.4 | 2.7 | 25.9 | 10.1 | 15.7 |
| 1989 | 56.1 | 13.9 | 0.4 | 3.4 | 26.2 | 10.0 | 16.2 |

*Source:* William Byrd, "Rural Collective and Private Industry," *The Sectoral Foundations of China's Development, World Bank Discussion Paper No. 148,* Javed Burki and Shahid Yusuf, eds. (Washington, D.C.: The World Bank, 1992), Table 1.2, p. 5.

growing sector of industrial production has been that of nonstate enterprises at the township and village levels.

Although China's rural revolution has produced remarkable results, there has been controversy within the CCP over what role party and government should play in rural China at the local level. In 1988, even prior to the Tiananmen protests, the party conservatives sought to slow down the transition to private control, fearing that the party would lose its influence in China's townships and villages. Then, with the student demonstrations at Tiananmen Square, where students complained about party corruption throughout China, the conservatives seized the initiative. For the next three years, they sought not only to slow down privatization in the countryside, but to reverse the process by taking over the more successful private enterprises and converting them to state ownership. According to one local official, "Officials seize rural enterprises in order to squash the supposed threat to communism from industries flourishing outside the direct control of bureaucrats and party officials." However, "they were driven by nothing more than bureaucratic gluttony."[9] The people would again be dependent on favors from local party officials, since they would no longer have control over the production and distribution of wealth. The reformist wing in Beijing, however, was opposed to these conservative efforts, even though the Tiananmen events tilted the balance of power temporarily in favor of those who wanted to resist privatization. Deng Xiaoping's famous January 1992 visit to the Gold Coast in southern China signaled a resurgence of the reformists in Beijing and a renewal of economic reform and support for the "socialist economic market," an expression used to identify socialism with marketplace reforms. Though the Gold Coast SEZs received new approval from Deng and his supporters, his public relations trip to the South also signaled full support for market and investment reforms throughout China, and China's rural reforms at the township and village levels were the heart of these reforms. In October 1992, the reform wing further strengthened its party leadership at the Fourteenth Party Congress, and the conservative wing seemed to be in retreat.

Strengthening of the household farm, private, and collective enterprises (collectives really operate much like private factories) did not mean smooth sailing for the private sector. But the party cadres would now have to take into account the wishes of the rural population. By the twenty-first century, contested elections could lead to a grass-roots democracy. The party could then work with the people and accept more democracy, which would be rooted in China's own Confucian traditions as well as in the social, economic, and political structures that are already transforming life in the townships and villages.

Another problem, also involving the future role of the party cadres in rural China, needs to be resolved if the harmony and well-being of the people are to be ensured. In the past, party cadres have often been above the law at the township and village levels. With the new contracts creating private, collective, and other enterprises, as well as inheritable household leases on farmland, a new legal system is needed in rural China. Contracts should not be subject to the personal whims of political and bureaucratic officials, whether party cadres or others. A new system of law and order is needed in which contracts and rights are enforceable in courts of law, which in turn render impartial justice not subject to party interference. Because over two-thirds of China's population continues to live in rural China and their loyalty and well-being depend on fair treatment and protection of hard-earned wealth from corrupt officials, an independent court system capable of impartially providing due process of law is urgently needed.

## JOINT VENTURES AND SPECIAL ECONOMIC ZONES

The inner face of China's economic reforms since 1978 has been the remarkable level of change in the Chinese village. The outer face has been China's dramatic opening to outside investment and trade, keyed by joint venture investments in China's special economic zones. The first zones were created in the province of Guangdong, which borders Hong Kong. Shenzhen, the most famous SEZ, is located next to Hong Kong on the Zhu River Delta. Other SEZs are Zhuhai, adjacent to Macao; Shantou, in Guangdong; and Xiamen, in Fujian province. China's SEZs are patterned after Taiwan's SEZs, in which foreign investors were given special privileges, including special rights to import resources and export finished prod-

ucts with a minimum of regulations and taxes. Joint ventures, in which foreign investors enter into contracts with Chinese counterparts, have been the
principal form of corporate structures, but other arrangements have also
been made available. The Deng reformists sought to attract new technology, capital, and production of goods, which then could be exported for hard
currency. These resources, in turn, could be used to speed up modernization and development. Initially, China's SEZs were not designed to serve
the domestic market, and restrictions were placed on how much of a joint
venture's production could be sold inside China. The phenomenal growth
of the Shenzhen SEZ typifies the success of Deng's outward reach for new
investment and capital, which have been attracted by China's cheap and
disciplined labor. From a population of 70,000 in 1980, Shenzhen has
grown to over two million, with another half-million migrants living illegally inside Shenzhen in a shadowy existence. Wages in the city are three
times as high as in surrounding regions. However, by the 1990s, regions
surrounding Shenzhen were also creating their own light industries, and
combined with other SEZs and adjacent territories they are now providing
100 million additional jobs for the Chinese people, mostly migrants from
rural China.

Shenzhen, the center of these developments in southern China, is
rapidly becoming another Hong Kong as it shifts from light industry to
finance and other service industries. A visitor to Shenzhen and the other
SEZs is overwhelmed by the sound of jackhammers, accompanied by end-
less construction sites with bamboo scaffolding. New factories, highways,
sewer and water lines, and apartment complexes are being built as far as the
eye can see. Traffic jams seem to be everywhere as bicycles, trucks, and
buses (but few cars) patiently wait their turn to weave through the construction bottlenecks.[10] To speed up transport between Guangzhou and Hong
Kong (almost 100 miles to the south), a new four-lane superhighway is
being built that will cut travel time in half.

Following the student demonstrations at Tiananmen, Western investment in China temporarily slowed down. But investments from overseas
Chinese, as well as from South Korea and Japan, did not slow down at all.
Another SEZ has been established on Hainan Island in the South China Sea
(especially to attract investment from Southeast Asia), and Beijing is creating SEZs in other regions. By 1992, China was strongly encouraging further
overseas investment. Additional provinces opened up new special industrial zones, in some cases providing even more advantages than those created
in southern China. Shenzhen expanded its free trade zones, and new ones
were created along China's eastern coast at Shanghai and Tianjin.
Investment was at the same time further encouraged by allowing more foreign currency exchange, the lack of which has been a major bottleneck limiting new investment. Beginning in 1991, foreign corporations were also
permitted direct leasing of land. Additional Yangtze River ports located at

Wuhan, Jiujiang, and Wuhu were opened up to foreign ships, and foreign banks were allowed to open branch banks in a number of China's major cities. Previously, this had been permitted only in Shenzhen. A future project could have far-reaching effects on foreign investment and trade in northeastern China: proposals for a free port and development zone at the mouth of the Tumen River located at the border between Russia, China, and North Korea.

China's additional investment agreements with foreign firms reached "a total of $17.8 billion in 1991, an increase of 47 percent over the previous year; $11.3 billion of this was spent."[11] Because of increased investment in both rural and urban regions from both domestic and international sources, the Chinese economy grew at a rate of 12 percent in 1992. Although Beijing's leaders wished to slow this rate down in order to prevent an overheated economy, they were nevertheless interested in seeking large overseas investments that would bring in new types of technology and balance the light industry in China's rural economy and special economic zones. Beijing wishes to avoid too much dependence on any one source of capital, whether from Asia, North America, or Europe. In the first half of 1991, Germany was the second largest source of new capital, at least temporarily exceeding new investment from Taiwan or Japan. In 1992 there were also new investment commitments with U.S. corporations. IBM agreed to build a new plant in Beijing, Motorola agreed to build the largest single foreign project in Tianjin, and GM entered into a joint venture to build trucks.

From the point of view of the West, the resurgence of Beijing's commitment to the Open Door policy may be reassuring, but China's growing interdependence with the outside world poses serious problems for Beijing. In the SEZs and in the coastal areas, lifestyles are rapidly changing. In Shenzhen, with its many discotheques, lifestyles are closer to Hong Kong than Beijing or even Shanghai. In Macao, Chinese gamble using Hong Kong dollars. This has brought new ills, which the Communists had claimed to have eradicated from China, such as crime, prostitution, etc. All of these things are disturbing to the party, which fears cultural pollution from the West but realizes the impossibility of returning to the past.

### TRADE AND TOURISM:
### HOW MUCH EXPOSURE TO INTERDEPENDENCE?

The early resumption of China's lawful status as a contracting party to GATT will facilitate China's efforts to further develop her trade relations of equality and mutual benefit with other countries in the world. To enjoy the rights provided by GATT, it is only natural that China will fulfill all the obligations thereunder.[12]

China's readmission to the GATT, which was pending in 1994, is a major step in its acceptance and integration into the global trade system. Premier Li Peng's comments suggest that China claims it is ready to assume full responsibility in meeting GATT obligations, by which members agree to abide by all the multilateral rules that have been accepted in GATT negotiations since 1947. With its membership, Beijing will be obligated to restructure its regulations for importing many types of goods into China. But there will be new opportunities for China to use its comparative advantage in labor-intensive goods by exporting to Western markets, as well as other states that fully meet their GATT obligations to provide reciprocity and most-favored-nation trade privileges.

Since the initiation of Deng's Open Door policy, even without GATT membership, China's trade performance has been truly remarkable. "Between 1980 and 1987 the value of Chinese trade tripled; over the 1987–1990 period the trade doubled. With this remarkable trade expansion China became the third largest developing country exporter of manufactures. When China's trade is combined with those areas over which it has territorial claims (Hong Kong and Taiwan), its manufactured exports are twice those of Canada and about one-quarter larger than those of the United Kingdom."[13] However, if China is to continue its remarkable increase in exports, it will need to broaden the number of products for which it has a comparative advantage, gain greater access to overseas markets, and open up its own markets to international competition based on both bilateral and multilateral agreements with other states.

## China's Comparative Advantage

There are many industrial products in which other Asian countries have a clear comparative advantage over China. Because China's economy is expanding at a rapid rate, with greater maturity it could gain comparative advantage in other products. However, this would require much greater efficiency in the production of a wide range of products. China would also need to overcome a number of basic problems relating to energy shortages, transportation bottlenecks, state and party interference in the running of enterprises, excessive and unpredictable regulations, excessive taxes, employment of unneeded workers, lack of incentive to make a profit, and the presence of a dual economy in which many products are unavailable at reasonable prices or are available only through bribery of party cadres or government officials. Other problems that may greatly hinder China's future development and ability to compete on world markets relate to extreme variations in living standards and economic development and the immature nature of the market system. In addition, planning at the national, provincial, or local level is often inconsistent or may even work at cross purposes. There is also a shortage of capital available to the national government to overcome the many bottlenecks as China's overall economy continues to grow.

## External Trade Barriers

Although China's overall trade has grown at a rapid rate since 1978, in the future it could be severely hindered by trade barriers imposed by other states, especially Japan, the United States, and the European Community. Bilateral and multilateral agreements have reduced or eliminated many trade restrictions since World War II, but many states have actually increased restrictions on imports. Currently, Japan, the United States, and the European Community all place nontariff barriers on at least some Chinese products. With a worldwide recession, trade barriers are likely to be strengthened, even if they violate the principles of free trade.

## Tourism

Tourism has been a major source of hard currency for China. Visitors from the United States and Europe came to see the exotic East in vastly increasing numbers during the 1980s until Tiananmen scared them away. Overseas Chinese continued to visit, as did tourists from other parts of Asia, however, and 1993 was a record tourism year. To keep a high profile, Beijing campaigned unsuccessfully for the 2000 Summer Olympics. If China wants to host the 2004 Olympics and thereby improve its image, it may have to consider rectifying rights abuses first and hosting the games second.[14]

### ECONOMIC LIBERALISM, POLITICAL FREEDOM, AND HUMAN RIGHTS: WHAT RELATIONSHIP?

Beijing's leaders, after the death of Mao, were well aware of some of the dangers of opening China to interdependence with the global system by opening markets at home. The other alternative looked worse, however, and few in the party leadership were willing to defend the economic policies of the past. The example of the Soviet Union precluded any defense of stringent central planning.

China's leaders have adopted an incremental approach to economic change, combined with a negative approach to political change. Yet China's future economic development and its role as a leading member of the global community in the next decades may depend not on incremental changes but on a rational, systematic political and economic restructuring guided by a vigorous leadership. Incremental change may well lead eventually to economic and political instability that could undermine China's global position. These structural problems include the following:

- China's dual economic system: inefficient state versus efficient private industry
- party and government Officials: increasing personnel costs and rising corruption
- growing disparity in wealth and income: the poorer interior regions versus the richer coastal regions
- iron rice bowl: the need to provide a mechanism to give social benefits formerly provided by the state

These problems were a major complaint of student demonstrators at Tiananmen Square, who were also joined by workers from many other sectors of society. Following the demonstrations, party leaders sought to improve living conditions but to no avail. Underemployment and unemployment continue to be problems. Disparities in wealth and social benefits are increasing, even as the annual GNP continues to rise at an annual rate of over 9 percent. The national government is running a large deficit, and there are no funds available to help the poorer provinces and local communities, even as the national military budget is being increased. Without solutions to these problems, the Communist Party leadership may have great difficulty in holding on to power in the 1990s. But what are the alternatives? What kind of political, economic, and social reforms are required, and how can they be implemented?[15] From the Chinese perspective, an authoritarian political system based on party leadership seems essential to ensure China's rapid transition to a "socialist market economy" while at the same time maintaining order and stability. China's leaders seem convinced that overseas investors, as well as tourists, will go where there is political stability, regardless of whether the regime is authoritarian or democratic. In fact, China's leaders probably believe that Western investors, given a choice, might prefer investing where there is political stability with an authoritarian government, so long as there is legal protection and a guarantee of the investor's contracts entered into in good faith with Chinese officials and coinvestors. Some of these Western investors may in fact, from the Chinese perspective, see greater opportunity to make a profit in an authoritarian society such as China than in a democratic society such as the United States.

During China's current leadership transition, China's political factions may prefer to avoid political infighting over the future nature of China's economic and political systems, which might only complicate the problem of leadership succession. China may wish to continue Deng's policy of avoiding discussion or considering implementation of major political reforms. For example, at both the Fourteenth Party Congress in October 1992 and the National People's Congress in March 1993, there were major pronouncements about economic reform but almost no comment about reform of the political system. China's leaders might, however, consider allowing the media to discuss economic and social change while prohibiting it from discussing basic change in the political system. But the lack of discussion does not mean that political change is not taking place. Even with a reemphasis on central political control following the 1989 demonstrations, a certain amount of grass-roots democracy has been emerging in the 1990s, especially in China's rural areas, including both villages and townships. In local rural communities, party cadres are actively involved in interacting with nonparty interest groups, increasingly on a cooperative basis rather than through a dominant-subordinate relationship. In addition, with the growing number of small businesses in rural areas, party cadres are often partners in these operations in which they share in the profit making. Although there has been little publicity about grass-roots democracy in rural China, party cadres and non-Communist local dignitaries are increasingly running against each other in competitive elections for council seats in villages and townships. By supporting grass-roots democracy in rural China, the CCP may in the future be an important part of the emerging political system. By helping to support, on an incremental basis, greater meaningful participation of the people in electing and removing political leaders at the local level based on popular appeal, the Chinese Communists might avoid the fate of their counterparts in Eastern Europe and the former Soviet Union.

Though China's leaders have important economic, social, and legal choices involving political considerations, most changes are likely to be incremental and gradual. If so, power may remain in the hands of the CCP, especially at the provincial and national levels. Whether Adam Smith in the 1990s will finally triumph over Karl Marx remains problematic, even though China seems committed to moving further in the direction of marketplace capitalism. On the other hand, both the reformist and conservative party wings seem unconvinced that Western-style democracy is necessary, or even desirable, as China seeks development of its "social market economy," increasingly based on government by law rather than by people, but not based on representative democracy.

## POLICY OPTIONS

Only if we steadily deepen the reform and open wider to the world can we resolve deep-seated contradictions in our social and economic activities and promote economic development.[16]

Premier Li Peng in the past has been one of Beijing's hard-liners favoring a slow-down in market reforms. By the time he addressed the 1993 People's Congress, as cited above, Li endorsed Deng Xiaoping's call for speeding up efforts to open China further to the global market system and carry out further steps to solidify market reform at home. Beijing's leaders are aware of the contradictions in their dual economic system, which will cause increasing difficulties in furthering development. But they are also worried about inflation and overheating of the economy, with Li Peng first calling for a growth rate in 1993 of only 6 percent, but later agreeing to the 8 or 9 percent rate recommended by Deng's followers.

## Option 1: Maintaining China's Current High Rate of Economic Development

Although the majority of China's leaders support rapid economic development at home and an Open Door policy abroad, there are growing contradictions resulting from this rapid development that pose serious problems, even threatening China's social and political stability. In order to continue China's rapid economic growth, it will also be necessary to deal with the following developments, which are closely related to China's economic reforms since 1978:

- China needs more effective legal protection for property and investors. Traditionally, Chinese prefer to settle disagreements through personal negotiation or mediation, which often means rewarding those who are in a position to help protect your interests. Growing corruption and danger of confiscation can no longer be handled effectively through these traditional procedures, and there is a growing need for impartial commercial law dealing with individual and corporate property rights. However, there is little Chinese tradition for this type of formal legal system. Under Confucianism as well as in contemporary China, justice relies more on the ethical behavior of people in positions of responsibility than on legal restraints on those in power.
- In order to increase economic efficiency and eliminate corruption, China may need to either phase out its dual economic system (both a large public and private sector) or else make the public sector subject to marketplace discipline (elimination of double pricing and unlimited ability of public enterprises to borrow without worrying about going bankrupt). But the public sector is a major source of party wealth. By controlling goods from the public sector, priced much lower than the open market, party officials can personally sell these goods at open market prices and pocket the markup. Further, because of the shortage of certain resources available only through the public sector, party officials are in a position to channel these resources to purchasers who are willing to make the highest side payments.
- China needs to eliminate crime and corruption through greater

appeal to community pride and public morality. Since 1978, the emphasis on getting rich has spurred new efforts to produce wealth, but it has also brought corruption both in and outside government as people seem more concerned about personal enrichment than the well-being of society. Renewed efforts at Marxist indoctrination, which were reinstituted after Tiananmen Square, have been a failure. If China's future is to be ensured, then ways must be found to balance the desire for personal gain with dedication to the well-being of the community.

- Ways must be found to meet the basic needs of hundreds of millions of Chinese who seem to have fallen through the cracks since the implementation of Deng's economic reforms. In the Maoist era, the iron rice bowl provided the basic needs of the people, such as food, clothing, employment, disability payments, old age benefits, education, housing, and health care, all of which were the responsibility of one's public work unit, whether rural or urban. With increasing privatization, millions of people may be better off, but millions of others no longer have access to these social and economic benefits. Because the central government has no funds to provide these services, logically, local authorities should provide them through taxation. But it is very difficult to raise taxes, especially in interior provinces that have not experienced the rapid growth of the coastal regions.

- China must more fully utilize human resources. With privatization and increased pressures on families to have only one child, there appears to be an increase in discrimination against women in both education and job opportunities. Preference is given to males, who have opportunities for better education and jobs, whereas women work long hours at low wages in China's newly established labor-intensive light industries. But if China is to continue its rapid economic development, ways must be found to train and utilize the talents of Chinese women fully.

- Ways must also be found to provide more energy and better transportation, as well as obtain needed resources such as timber and iron ore, which are in short supply inside China. China also needs more food production just to keep up with its 15 million new mouths each year. However, reliance on coal for energy, continued rapid cutting of China's forests (with only partial replacement of trees), and more intensive cultivation of China's limited cropland all place further stress on the environment. One solution may be greater imports of cleaner energy as well as timber, food, and other crucial commodities. But this will require greater exports or risk an unfavorable balance of payments.

## Option 2: Slowing Down China's
## Rate of Economic Growth in the 1990s

High growth rates create inflation if there are shortages of goods and services such as transportation and electricity. High growth rates also create greater inequities and discontent because many people and regions do not share in the newly created wealth. Discontent can bring instability and protest. Two of the major causes of the Tiananmen demonstrations were inflation and corruption, both stimulated by China's rapid economic change. Party hard-liners also believe that corruption, crime, breakdown in morality, and decreasing social responsibility can all be traced to China's rapid economic change since 1978, especially changes associated with Western cultural and materialistic consumer values. Slowing down growth rates (which was Premier Li Peng's preference until it was clear that the reformists were again becoming dominant in 1993) may solve some of China's growing problems.

- Slower growth rates may lessen pressure for basic structural reforms, which are creating serious bottlenecks, for example, in transportation and energy. Less demand for these resources makes it easier to correct these deficiencies on a long-term basis.
- Slower growth rates will mean less pressure on the dual economy. China's leaders need time to make adjustments in the public sector to make it more efficient and responsive to the marketplace. Virtually all party leaders seem dedicated to pragmatic adjustments within the dual economy rather than elimination of the public sector (the latter might further undermine party authority and power). There is also fear that without central regulation and control of key industries and services such as finance, communications, and transportation, China could become divided into economic regions without sufficient central authority to hold them together.
- Slower growth rates may reduce temptations for a further buildup of China's military at a time when China faces fewer external threats than at any time in the modern era. Economic necessity was a major factor inducing the superpowers to bring the Cold War to an end. If China grows more rapidly than its neighbors, Beijing may be tempted to use military buildup as an instrument of foreign policy. This could stimulate an arms race in East and Southeast Asia. Rapid growth could also speed up China's efforts to find new oil reserves in the South China Sea to alleviate its growing energy shortages, even though countries in Southeast Asia may take measures to counter Chinese military domination of these territories, which they also claim.

- Slower growth rates may help create an atmosphere in which China's people are less addicted to get-rich schemes and more willing to seek careers based on service to community needs. With 1.2 billion people, there is a limit to consumerism patterned on countries such as the United States and those in Western Europe.
- Slower growth rates may help China avoid vulnerabilities in the global economy that might undermine Chinese stability and well-being. Should recession continue in most regions during the 1990s, many countries may face overwhelming pressures to practice protectionism in trade and jobs. Slower growth inside China could give its leaders greater flexibility in avoiding outside leverage to extract concessions from China as a condition of trade and investment.

## Option 3: Working More Closely Together

China's leaders at the national, regional, and local levels need to work closely together to share and more effectively divide responsibilities if domestic trade wars and inefficient use of resources are to be avoided. Already, provincial authorities are husbanding scarce resources and protecting their own industries at the expense of interregional trade and the economic benefits of comparative advantage. In the past, the Chinese Communist Party has been able to use its party unity to carry out economic policies made in Beijing, but increasingly ways must be found to promote cooperation based on the mutual self-interest of the different regions, especially if the resources of China's vast interior are to be utilized effectively.

- Because the central government is losing its power to extract revenue while the richer provinces are gaining increased revenue, basic social services must largely be provided by local government. Richer provinces must be persuaded to share their newfound wealth with their poorer neighbors, or else they will be inundated with hundreds of millions of Chinese seeking better services and opportunity by migrating to coastal provinces such as Shandong, Fujian, and Guangdong.
- With its limited resources, the central government must concentrate on what it can do best, such as conducting foreign policy and opening up greater opportunities for trade and investment. However, even these efforts will require greater cooperation with regional and local authorities.
- The central government should also concentrate on ways to speed up the development of the interior and eliminate internal trade barriers that, if not corrected, could lead to economic disintegration and regional trade blocs inside China.

## DISCUSSION QUESTIONS

1.  Is China fully committed to creating a capitalist-type market economy?
2.  Are making money and improving living standards much more important to the Chinese than attaining Western-type political rights?
3.  Do capitalists prefer to invest in a society with a Western-type political system rather than one with an authoritarian-type political system?
4.  To what extent is the protection of human rights essential to attracting tourists to China and increasing Chinese exports to Western democracies?
5.  In the 1990s, what are the prospects for improving political rights inside China?
6.  Is a Western-type legal system essential to the development of a capitalist market system?
7.  To what extent is China committed to creating a legal system based on government by law, rather than government by people who are above the law?
8.  What is the relationship between economic liberalism, political freedom, and human rights?
9.  To what extent has Adam Smith triumphed over Karl Marx in China?
10. How have Hong Kong, Taiwan, Japan, and South Korea each made special contributions to the economic development of China?
11. How has economic development since 1978 changed life in China's rural villages and townships?
12. What are the advantages and disadvantages of maintaining a dual economy in China?
13. What can be done to promote economic development in China's interior provinces?
14. How have Deng Xiaoping's economic reforms changed the relationship among national, regional, and local government in China?
15. Would China be better off by trying to maintain or slow down its current rate of economic development?
16. How is the question of women's rights related to China's future economic development?
17. How have Deng Xiaoping's economic reforms affected Chinese social values concerning such issues as crime and dedication to community service?

## SUGGESTED READINGS

Burki, Shahid Javed, and Shahid Yusuf, eds. *The Sectoral Foundations of China's Development.* Washington, D.C.: World Bank, 1992.

Conable, Barber B., Jr., and David N. Lampton. "China: The Coming Power." *Foreign Affairs* (Winter 1992/1993): pp. 133–149.

Foxsom, Ralph H., John H. Minan, and Lee Ann Otto. *Law and Politics in the People's Republic of China.* St. Paul, Minnesota: West Publishing Company, 1992.

Goodman, David S. G., and Gerald Segal, eds. *China in the Nineties: Crisis Management and Beyond.* New York: Oxford University Press, 1991.

Howell, Jude. *China Opens Its Doors: The Politics of Economic Transition.* Boulder, Colorado: Lynne Rienner Publishers, 1993.

Karaosmanoglu, Attila. "Challenge of Sustaining Growth and Equity in Asia." *Finance and Development* (September 1991).

Kraar, Louis. "A New China Without Borders." *Fortune* (October 5, 1992): pp. 124–128.

———, "Asia 2000." *Fortune* (October 5, 1992): pp. 111–113.

Lardy, Nicholas R. *Foreign Trade and Economic Reform in China: 1978–1990.* New York: Cambridge University Press, 1992.

Prime, Penelope B. "The Economy in Overdrive: Will It Crash?" *Current History* (September 1993): pp. 260–264.

Prybyla, Jan. "China's Economic Dynamos." *Current History* (September 1992): pp. 262–267.

Schlender, Brenton. "China Really Is on the Move." *Fortune* (October 5, 1992): pp. 114–123.

Shambaugh, David. "Regaining Political Momentum: Deng Strikes Back." *Current History* (September 1992): pp. 257–261.

Singh, Inderjit. *China: Industrial Policies for an Economy in Transition.* Washington, D.C.: The World Bank, 1992.

Smil, Vaclav. "How Rich Is China?" *Current History* (September 1993): pp. 265–269.

Solinger, Dorothy J. *China's Transition from Socialism.* Armonk, New York: M.E. Sharpe: 1993.

Wall, David. "Special Economic Zones in China: The Administrative and Regulatory Framework." *The Journal of East Asian Affairs* 7, no. 1 (Winter/Spring, 1993): pp. 226–260.

White, Gordon, ed. *The Chinese State in the Era of Economic Reform.* Armonk, New York: M.E. Sharpe, 1992.

White, Tyrene. "Reforming the Countryside." *Current History* (September 1992): pp. 273–277.

World Bank, *World Development Report 1992: Development and the Environment,* New York: Oxford University Press, 1992.

Yeats, Alexander J. *China's Foreign Trade and Comparative Advantage,* Washington, D.C.: The World Bank, 1991.

## NOTES

1. See Suzanne Ogden, "The Changing Content of China's Democratic Socialist Institutions," *In Depth: A Journal for Values and Public Policy* 3, no. 1 (Winter 1993): pp. 237–256. She describes the growth of pluralistic decisionmaking processes at the local level. The struggle for succession in the 1990s creates caution and hesitancy to use the rational actor decisionmaking model. This reinforces the bureaucratic-organizational model, which preserves the privileges of both the new private sectors and also the remaining public sectors of the economy. Ogden, how-

ever, points out that there is clearly a growth in grass-roots democracy, and these developments indicate the growing importance of a pluralistic decisionmaking process in the 1990s. She also notes that China's people now feel that they have more personal freedom than at any time in their memory.

2. Third World countries proposed that a New International Economic Order (NIEO) be established in the 1970s. Third World economic issues are dealt with through the United Nations Conference on Trade and Development.

3. Quoted in Brenton Schlender, "China Really Is on the Move," *Fortune* (October 5, 1992): p. 118.

4. For an analysis of the contrasting South Korean and Taiwanese industrial models, see Tun-jen Cheng, "Distinctions Between the Taiwanese and Korean Approaches to Economic Development," *The Journal of East Asian Affairs* 7, no. 1 (Winter/Spring 1993): pp. 116–136.

5. See Louis Kraar, "A New China without Borders," *Fortune* (October 5, 1992): pp. 124–128. Jan Prbyla, "China's Economic Dynamos," *Current History* (September 1992): pp. 262–267. Joel Kotkin, "China Dawn: A Rising Economic Power Is on the Horizon," *Washington Post National Weekly Edition,* October 13–18, 1992, p. 23. "The Overseas Chinese," *The Economist* (July 18, 1992): pp. 21–24.

6. Premier Li Peng, January 31, 1992.

7. Ann Scott Tyson and James L. Tyson, "China's Villages, Part 2: Rural Entrepreneurs Take Root," *Christian Science Monitor,* July 29, 1992, pp. 9–12.

8. For an analysis of changing political relations at the village level, see Tyrene White, "Reforming the Countryside," *Current History* (September 1992): pp. 273–277.

9. Anne Scott Tyson and James L. Tyson, "China's villages, Part 2," p. 12.

10. David Wall suggests that because of imports of duty-free resources into the SEZs as an incentive for investment, as well as a diversion of a large proportion of production in the SEZs to the domestic market (which is highly profitable and carried out through guanxi-type deals in which officials allow the diversion of production from intended overseas markets), China's SEZs may in fact be a net drain on China's hard currency reserves. [David Wall, "SEZs in China: The Administrative and Regulatory Framework," *The Journal of East Asian Affairs* 7, no. 1 (Winter/Spring 1993): pp. 226–260.]

11. David Wall, "SEZs in China," p. 269.

12. Premier Li Peng, January 31, 1992.

13. Alexander J. Yeats, *China's Foreign Trade and Comparative Advantage,* Washington, D.C.: The World Bank, 1992, p. v.

14. Sheryl WuDunn, "Beijing Goes All Out to Get Olympics in 2000," *The New York Times,* March 11, 1993, p. A5.

15. Most Western observers are convinced that China's leaders will continue economic reform, but they also believe that Adam Smith's laissez-faire economics will in time lead to greater civil and political rights, not just social and economic rights. [In David S. G. Goodman and Gerald Segal, eds., *China in the Nineties: Crisis Management and Beyond* (New York: Oxford University Press, 1991) see David Kelly, "Chinese Marxism Since Tiananmen: Between Evaporation and Dismemberment," pp. 30–34; Anita Chan, "The Social Origins and Consequences of the Tiananmen Crisis," pp. 64–86; and Ann Kent, "Human Rights: The Changing Balance Sheet," pp. 105–130.] In analyzing the evolution of Marxist values since Tiananmen, some argue that there has not been a mass movement toward popular democracy. Instead, critics inside China have shown more interest in party reform, as well as greater individual opportunity to engage in meaningful dialogue, on the

basis of political interaction amongst the articulate elements of Chinese society, not on the basis of mass participation by the peasants, who currently make up about 70 percent of China's population. Furthermore, even many of the Tiananmen demonstrators were and are strong supporters of political order.

16. Premier Li Peng, speaking at the opening session of the National People's Congress in March 1993, quoted in Sheila Tefft, "Legislature to Solidify China's Move to Market: Leaderships's Desire to Join World Trade Body Drives Reform Measures," *Christian Science Monitor,* March 16, 1993, p. 8.

# The Collapse of
# the Soviet Empire

Observe developments soberly, maintain our position, meet challenges
calmly, hide our capacities, bide our time, remain free of ambitions, and
never claim leadership.
                              —*Deng Xiaoping on the CCP's response*
                              *to the mounting crisis of world socialism*

## TRADITIONAL RIVALRIES:
## QING CHINA AND ROMANOV RUSSIA

China and Russia have one of the longest common borders in the world.
Since the seventeenth century this border, which extends from Afghanistan
in the west to Korea in the east, has been the cause of conflict and of diplomatic contact and negotiation. How to determine where Russia meets China
has been the theme of Sino-Russian relations for 300 years as an ascendent
Russia steadily expanded its sphere of influence into areas claimed by Qing,
Nationalist, or Communist China. Even after the establishment of the
People's Republic of China in 1949, during the era of fraternal relations
among communist countries, Chinese fears of Soviet encroachment both
into its territory and into its affairs undermined the relationship and led
directly to the Sino-Soviet split in 1960. In the 1990s, long after arguments
over communist ideology have become obsolete, Russian and Chinese diplomats are still meeting to settle acrimonious border issues.

China, in effect, entered into the international system because of its
border with Russia. The Treaty of Nerchinsk, signed by Russia and China in
1689, was China's first formal border treaty. Relations were to some degree
formalized by this treaty and later agreements, so much so that by 1850 trade
had expanded to the point where almost half of Russia's exports of manufactured goods were going to China.[1] At the same time, however, the Qing
dynasty was quickly losing its mandate to rule, allowing England, France,
and other Western nations to encroach on Chinese sovereignty. Russia also
took advantage of Chinese weakness to expand its political and economic

influence in the border areas and particularly in Manchuria. Although the Qing dynasty was increasingly apprehensive of Russian expansion into areas it considered to be part of the Chinese Empire, by the mid-nineteenth century it had too many enemies to fight the Russians vigorously. The Sino-Russian Treaty of Peking, signed in November 1860, opened the entire northern frontier to Russia's political and commercial influence.[2] Inexorably, the czars acquired tracts of land that the Qing Empire also claimed. Russia had succeeded in its quest—not dissimilar from that of Europe and the United States in southern China—of creating its own enclaves within China's border areas.

## REVOLUTIONARY RELATIONS:
## THE BOLSHEVIKS AND THE CHINESE COMMUNISTS

The Chinese Revolution in 1911 caused hardly a stir in Russia, which had its own political problems. A world war and a revolution similarly prevented Russian interference in Chinese politics. But a Soviet Union led by the Bolshevik Party was dedicated to world revolution against the capitalist powers, whether in their home territories or in their colonies. China, which in the early 1920s was ruled by a jumble of rival military leaders and by foreign powers, seemed to the Bolsheviks to be ripe for revolution.

Lenin and the Third Communist International therefore sought to help China throw off the influence of the imperialist powers and thereby advance international communism. In 1920, the Soviet Union announced that it would relinquish the special privileges, including extraterritoriality, that czarist Russia had acquired through its "unequal" treaties with Qing China. This voluntary abrogation of its special status aroused much admiration for Lenin and the Soviet Union among the growing numbers of nationalist Chinese who sought to end foreign penetration of their country.

Even Sun Yat-sen, the "George Washington of China," was willing to accept help from Moscow. By 1923, the Soviet Union had engineered an uneasy alliance with Sun Yat-sen and his Nationalist (Kuomintang) Party. The Soviets believed that Sun was the most likely to succeed in reunifying China and ridding it of foreign influence. To that end, Moscow sent money, advisers, and military equipment. A Nationalist army was organized for the first time, with the assistance of Soviet advisers, and the Nationalist Party was reorganized on the principles of democratic centralism, which guided it well into the 1980s.

The formation of the Chinese Communist Party in 1921 did not alter Soviet strategy, which was to ally itself with the group most likely to gain control of China and drive out the capitalist nations. Communist ideology was far less important to Moscow than was the ability to damage the imperialist system and to attack the weak links in the imperialist chain that controlled the world's economy. Chinese Communist Party members were therefore required to become members of the Nationalist Party and to submit to its discipline. Zhou Enlai even taught at the Nationalist Party military academy headed by Chiang Kai-shek. The first united front between the Nationalists and Communists barely outlived Sun's death in 1925, however, and the rise of Stalin in Russia and Chiang Kai-shek in China ensured its quick demise.

Chiang began to take control of the Nationalist Party in the mid-1920s and to rid it of Communists. Through a series of bloody purges he succeeded, and the Chinese Communists were driven into the interior mountains in the late 1920s. Stalin had advocated a policy of promoting urban revolution through Communist Party activities in China's urban areas. Chiang's victories showed that this policy had been a dismal failure, and by the mid-1930s Mao Zedong had taken control over the Chinese Communist Party on a platform that advocated fomenting agrarian revolution through organizing the peasants first before moving into the cities. Mao's theory of revolution was the antithesis of Stalin's, and until their dying days each resented the other's claim to know how best to implement a communist revolution in China.

By the late 1930s, the Communists had survived the Long March and were a political power in Yenan. They had succeeded in evading Chiang's troops and were winning plaudits for their campaigns against the Japanese invaders. Stalin was presented with a quandary that he initially tried to solve by urging (with the United States) another KMT-CCP united front, this time to fight the Japanese. The second united front ended in another split, and the Chinese Communists began to gain strength on their own without any substantial aid from the Soviet Union. In any case, the Soviet Union was desperately fighting the Nazis and therefore unable to help either the Nationalist Party or the CCP in any substantive way. At the end of World War II, after Stalin finally declared war on Japan, Soviet armies moved into Manchuria to drive out the Japanese. Arms confiscated by the Soviets from the Japanese were given to the Chinese Communists, Stalin's only major contribution to the CCP war effort; yet Stalin's order that Manchuria's industrial facilities be dismantled and shipped back to the Soviet Union enraged the Chinese, Communists and Nationalists alike.

"Before and after the campaign for the liberation of Nanking, there were some well-meaning friends, both within and without the country, who said that we should be content with separate regimes in North and South China and should not provoke the intervention of imperialism, especially of American imperialism." [Written by Kuo Mo-jo. The term *friends* refers to Stalin. *Source:* Stuart Schram, *Mao Tse-Tung.* Baltimore: Penguin, 1975, p. 245.]

Stalin's ineptness in managing Soviet relations with China from the late 1920s through the end of World War II actually strengthened, rather than weakened, Mao Zedong and the Chinese Communists. Mao Zedong had carefully cultivated a Communist Party that was beholden to him rather than Stalin, thereby making it more attractive to nationalist Chinese who would support any group whose charter called for expelling all foreign powers from China. Of course, Stalin did not appreciate such independence. During the civil war that followed the end of World War II, as Mao's troops fought the Nationalists for control over all China, some observers came to believe that Stalin preferred a Nationalist China or a China split between Nationalists and Communists to a China controlled by Mao's independent, nationalist Communist Party. A divided China was a weak China, and Stalin's preference for weak neighbors was well known.

Even Stalin, therefore, may have greeted the establishment of the People's Republic of China with mixed emotions. Whereas the outside world was unnerved by the world's most populous nation joining the international communist movement, Stalin feared that so potentially powerful an ally as the Chinese Communists could upset the movement's balance. The People's Republic of China was established in the same year that Yugoslavia consolidated its maverick status in the international communist movement in an almost cocky manner: "The Communist chieftain of a primitive Balkan country with a population of only 16 million said no to Stalin, chased out Soviet minions, imprisoned Soviet partisans, and dared the Soviet bloc to do its worst."[3] Mao's Chinese Communist Party likewise was beholden to none and was not likely to follow Stalin's every order. The Chinese Communists had achieved the victory hoped for by Lenin and the Bolshevik Party, but at what cost to the international communist movement?

## TWO COMMUNIST SUPERPOWERS

After the establishment of the People's Republic of China, Mao chose to "lean to one side," that of the Soviet Union. Washington's anticommunist rhetoric and a common Marxist-Leninist ideology made an alliance between China and the Soviet Union more attractive to Mao than any sort of entente between the United States and China. Mao also hoped a Sino-Soviet alliance would provide some security for his infant regime, especially against Japan, which the Chinese still feared.

So Mao traveled to Moscow in late 1949, and after enduring Stalin's disrespectful treatment, the Sino-Soviet Treaty of Friendship, Alliance, and Mutual Assistance was signed in February 1950. Stalin, according to Mao, "was not willing to sign a treaty. . . . After two months of negotiations he at last signed."[4] The terms of the Sino-Soviet alliance bear out Stalin's reluctance to accord the People's Republic of China equal status, rather than the satellite status accorded to the Eastern European nations. China was given the equivalent of $300 million in credits for five years, which it would have to pay back with raw materials at a 1 percent interest rate. Poland received more aid from the Soviet Union than China! In addition, Mao had to accept Soviet control over two major ports in Manchuria and over the Chinese Eastern Railway. Soviet-Chinese joint stock companies were created to exploit mineral deposits in western China and thereby to ensure Soviet economic penetration into China.[5] Mao had achieved an alliance with the Soviet Union, but at great cost to his personal pride and the pride of the Chinese state. Once again, the traditional Russian goal of expanding its control in the border regions and of controlling its neighbors was more important than a common ideology.

Relations between China and the Soviet Union continued to be difficult, especially after the outbreak of the Korean War in June 1950. Although Mao was probably informed—most likely by the Soviets—of the North Korean decision to invade South Korea prior to the beginning of the campaign, he probably had little input into the decision. Neither Mao nor Stalin expected the commitment of U.S. troops (under the United Nations umbrella) to fight the North Koreans, and when General Douglas MacArthur began to march north toward the Chinese border, Mao made the agonizing decision to send the China People's Volunteers to North Korea.[6] Three years of bitter fighting led to a stalemate, and not until after Stalin died in 1953 was an armistice finally signed. Mao and Chinese military leaders would not forget, however, that Stalin did not commit Soviet troops to the struggle. Their bitterness at bearing the burdens of the Korean War would not be easily overcome.

To the outward world, however, Sino-Soviet ties appeared to be flourishing. The Soviets provided additional economic aid to China in the form of loans, credits, technical assistance, and training. By 1960, about $2 billion worth of Soviet credits had been extended to China.[7] The Soviets also made some efforts to equalize the political relationship. Nikita Khrushchev visited China in 1954, and he agreed to return to Chinese control the ports, railroad, and joint stock companies that were included in the Sino-Soviet Friendship Treaty. Just as important to the Chinese was the 1957 Sino-Soviet treaty for nuclear technology cooperation, under which the Soviet Union was to provide China with a sample atomic bomb and technical data on its manufacture.[8] After the death of Stalin, the Soviet leaders appeared to be treating Mao and the People's Republic as their equals rather than as another satellite regime.

However, by the summer of 1960, the Soviet advisers in China—nearly 10,000 people—were called home. To add insult to injury, they were ordered to bring all blueprints, plans, etc., home with them. The Chinese were left with Soviet-designed factories and military equipment for which they had no design information. This withdrawal of advisers signaled to the world that the two Communist giants were no longer partners. Although many in Washington came late to an acceptance that the Sino-Soviet split was not a hoax, relations between the two nations deteriorated markedly throughout the decade, to the point where they engaged in border skirmishes in the late 1960s.

The reasons for this deterioration in relations were numerous. Some ascribe the origins of Sino-Soviet distrust to the traditional Russian distrust of the Chinese.[9] Others look to historical resentments that turned the Chinese against the Soviets, especially Stalin's lukewarm support for the Chinese Communist Party in its early days. In addition, the Soviet economic aid of $2 billion to the People's Republic sounds impressive until one realizes that it was only 40 percent of the aid the United States gave to Taiwan during the same period.[10] Ideological differences also created tensions. Although Mao resented Stalin's treatment, he did not approve of Khrushchev's denunciation of Stalin in 1956 or of his de-Stalinization campaign. In particular, Khrushchev's condemnation of the cult of personality hit too close to home for Mao Zedong. The Soviets, for their part, condemned Mao's Great Leap Forward, especially its claim to lead China into pure communism at an accelerated rate. The Soviet Union, after all, was the birthplace of communism and would, Moscow believed, be the first nation to pass through Marx's dictatorship of the proletariat into communism. Foreign relations also played a part in the Sino-Soviet split. China's claims of Third World leadership were bound to annoy the Soviets, as were Khrushchev's attempts to improve relations with the United States in the late 1950s. Khrushchev's handling of the Cuban Missile Crisis, during which the Chinese believed he caved in to the United States, and Soviet support for India during the Sino-Indian border war—both in 1962—only inflamed the already uneasy relationship.

By the time that the Soviet Union signed the Atmospheric Limited Test Ban Treaty in 1963 (which prohibited nuclear testing in the atmosphere, in outer space, and underwater), after reneging on its promise to aid China's nuclear development, relations were irreparably ruptured. Some even claim that the Soviet Union and the United States considered a joint strike against China's nuclear facilities before China completed work on its own nuclear bomb.[11] A preemptive strike never happened, however, and in October 1964 the People's Republic of China exploded its first nuclear bomb. What had been a falling out over historical and ideological issues now became a potentially devastating security threat for the Soviet Union, China, and the world.

Why did the Sino-Soviet alliance degenerate into the Sino-Soviet split in little more than a decade? Instead of being considered a limited economic and security partnership, as exists in most alliance systems, the Sino-Soviet alliance was conceived in broad terms based on a common ideology. Because of the presumed congruence of interests, no mechanism was established to resolve disputes. Neither the Soviets nor the Chinese could admit that serious problems mights arise. Disagreements therefore escalated into personal power struggles.[12] Neither Khrushchev's successors nor Mao would compromise. The Sino-Soviet split continued through more dangerous and more passive phases until 1989, when the Soviet Union was on the verge of disintegration.

## THE BREZHNEV DOCTRINE

Leonid Brezhnev, Khrushchev's successor, consolidated his power as China was descending into the chaos of the Cultural Revolution. Soviet horror at Mao's deliberate decimation of the Communist Party apparatus, offices, and personnel was acute. That the chaos could be curbed only by army control of several provinces exacerbated the Soviet reaction. In Marxist-Leninist societies, the Communist Party was supposed to be the

Winter clouds are heavy with snow, which flies like willow catkins,
The myriad blossoms have all faded, and flowers are rare for the moment,
High in the heavens frozen currents whirl imperceptibly,
Only the hero dares pursue the tiger,
Still less does any brave fellow fear the bear,
The plum blossoms rejoice in the snow that fills the sky,
Small wonder that the cold should kill the flies.
[In this poem by Mao Zedong, the tiger is U.S. imperialism and the bear is the Soviet Union. *Source:* Stuart Schram, *Mao Tse-Tung,* p. 306.]

vanguard, leading the masses and controlling the military. That the People's Liberation Army had to be called in to rescue the Chinese regime was anathema to communist doctrine. The Soviet Union, a society that had come to value order and stasis above all else, could not comprehend Mao's ultimately self-destructive drive for a complete revolution in the party and in society.

Brezhnev, of course, had problems closer to home. Czechoslovakia, too, was experimenting with forms of communism that deviated from the Soviet model. The consequences were disastrous for the Czechs and Slovaks, as Soviet tanks rolled into Prague in 1968. The proclamation of the Brezhnev Doctrine, which averred that the Soviet Union had the right to invade any fraternal communist state that did not meet Moscow's expectations, sent a chill through not only Eastern Europe but also the Asian communist nations. By 1969, the Soviet Union could not get even five of the fourteen ruling communist parties in the world to attend an international conference of the world's communist parties in Moscow. China, North Korea, North Vietnam, Albania, and Yugoslavia boycotted the proceedings. The conference communiqué illustrated the weakness of international com-

## The Brezhnev Doctrine

There is no doubt that the peoples of the socialist countries and the Communist Parties have and must have freedom to determine their country's path of development. However, any decision of theirs must damage neither socialism in their own country nor the fundamental interest of the other socialist countries nor the worldwide workers movement, which is waging a struggle for socialism. This means that every Communist Party is responsible not only to its own people but also to all the socialist countries and to the entire Communist movement. Whoever forgets this in placing sole emphasis on the autonomy and independence of Communist Parties lapses into onesideness, shirking his internationalist obligations."

[Joseph L. Nogee and Robert H. Donaldson, *Soviet Foreign Policy Since World War II,* 3nd ed. Elmsford, New York: Pergamon Press, 1984, p. 247.]

munism. It did not censure the Chinese Communists, as the Soviets had hoped it would, and it observed that there was "no leading center of the international communist movement."[13]

This was further proven later in 1969 when Soviet and Chinese armed forces fought in the border areas. Some, notably Henry Kissinger, then the U.S. national security adviser, believed the Soviets were responsible for the confrontations.[14] Most believed, however, that forces loyal to Lin Biao, China's defense minister, initiated hostilities as part of the struggle for leadership going on in Beijing and throughout China during the Cultural Revolution. Tensions continued to mount in the 1970s, especially after the Vietnamese, who were Soviet allies, invaded Cambodia and, after the Soviets, invaded Afghanistan. Indeed, despite military needs on the southern and western borders of the Soviet Union, U.S. intelligence experts estimated that nearly one-quarter of all Soviet military forces were aligned against China in the 1970s.[15] The Soviet Union obviously felt the need to contain the Chinese, a tremendous drain on its military and economic resources that became insupportable within a decade.

Indisputably, the greatest impact of the Sino-Soviet border clashes, coming so soon after Soviet tanks rolled into Prague, was that they illustrated to all communist nations and to the entire world that international communism was a chimera. From 1969 on, it was evident that only military force, and not ideology, bound the nations of Eastern Europe to the Soviet Union. For China, the Soviet Union's military strength became a source of great fear, so much so that rapprochement with the United States, the capitalist enemy, seemed preferable to nonalignment with either side in the Cold War. The progression of the Sino-Soviet split into open hostilities was seen as irrefutable proof by many that traditional power relations continued to be overriding determinants of state-to-state relations, never to be superseded by ideological beliefs or other "low" politics factors.

Even the world's greatest military powers cannot afford to practice broad-scale containment for an extended period of time, however, and by the early 1980s both Soviet and Chinese leaders were issuing statements calling for a lessening of tensions. In 1979, the Chinese announced their conditions for a normalization of relations: reduction of Soviet troops in the border areas; Soviet withdrawal from Afghanistan and Mongolia; and an end to Soviet support for Vietnam's invasion of Cambodia.[16] Leonid Brezhnev responded in his Tashkent speech of March 1982 by calling for normalization of relations. The Soviet quagmire in Afghanistan, its economic problems, and its isolation from the Third World combined to make it less of a threat to the Chinese. In addition, with President Reagan assuming office in the United States after an election campaign in which he promised to review U.S. relations with Taiwan, Beijing became nervous about U.S. intentions and therefore more willing to explore ways to reduce tensions with the Soviets.[17] At the same time, the Soviets became more and more anxious to reallocate their resources from the border with China to other, more pressing areas. Full Sino-Soviet normalization of relations would not come quickly, however, because old antagonisms were not easy to overcome and because of the stasis in the Soviet political system as one leader after another died in office.

## GORBACHEV AND SINO-SOVIET RELATIONS

Finally, in 1986, a new Soviet leader called for a new China policy. Mikhail Gorbachev, the new secretary-general of the Soviet Communist Party, was eager to reduce Sino-Soviet tensions so he could reduce military spending. He was also eager to find economic partners, particularly to furnish the consumer goods in such short supply in the Soviet Union. In a speech in Vladivostok, which is in the Soviet Far East and abuts China, Gorbachev called for an end to a China encirclement policy. As a direct result of Gorbachev's Vladivostok speech, talks between the Soviets and the Chinese on issues including demarcation of the frontier began in 1987. Sino-Soviet economic interactions also expanded dramatically. Trade between Heilongjiang province and the Soviet Union increased 95 percent between 1986 and 1987, and trade between Xinjiang province and the Soviet Union increased 75 percent during the same period. Even more startling, the Chinese Communist Party sent a delegation to Moscow to attend the celebration of the seventieth anniversary of the Bolshevik Revolution, and Chinese officials in Beijing held a reception to honor the occasion.[18]

Mikhail Gorbachev's thoughts extended beyond Soviet relations with China alone to a conceptualization of an East Asian security system. In a 1988 speech in Krasnoyarsk, in central Asia, Gorbachev included a seven-point proposal that he reiterated throughout his rule. Gorbachev called for the following steps to reduce tensions in East Asia: discussions relating to a freeze on nuclear weapons in the region; balanced reduction of naval and air forces in the area and limits on their activities; further actions to reduce the risk of incidents at sea and in the air; and opening of security talks including the Soviet Union, the United States, and the People's Republic.[19] Gorbachev could not achieve an East Asian security system, or even a multilateral security conference, but he did convince the Chinese that a Soviet Union that practiced glasnost and perestroika was a less threatening neighbor than a Soviet Union that espoused the Brezhnev Doctrine.

Gorbachev's efforts to fulfill China's three prerequisites for a normalization of relations bore fruit. On May 15, 1989, Gorbachev arrived in Beijing for a summit meeting, the first visit by a Soviet leader since Khrushchev visited China in the 1950s. Ironically, Gorbachev arrived in Beijing just as China was being riven by demonstrations in Tiananmen Square against corruption in the Chinese Communist Party and for more openness in society. The students and workers who took to the streets knew that the world press would be in Beijing for the summit meeting and planned their protests for maximum coverage from foreign television networks. No real decisions could be made at the summit—when Deng Xiaoping did not even control the streets of Beijing and Gorbachev had to enter the Great Hall of the People through a back door—but the point had been made. China and the Soviet Union had finally opened a dialogue after nearly thirty years of unremitting hostility.

Over the next two years Soviet and Chinese delegations met fre-

> The still uneasy nature of Sino-Soviet relations in 1989 was illustrated in Foreign Minister Qian Qichen's review of the People's Republic's foreign relations. Qian wrote of "Soviet big-power chauvinist performances . . . breaching contracts, withdrawing experts, pressing for the repayment of debts, deploying heavy concentrations of troops along the border and provoking clashes. In the following decades [1960–1980], not once did the Soviet Union abandon its military threat against China."
> [Allen S. Whiting, "China's Foreign Relations After 40 Years," in Anthony J. Kane, ed., *China Briefing, 1990* (Boulder, Colorado: Westview Press, 1990), pp. 70–71.]

quently and increasingly profitably, although the Chinese leaders were not happy with the Soviet decision not to interfere with the revolutions in Eastern Europe in late 1989. Paradoxically, China had been a leading critic of the Brezhnev Doctrine in 1968. In 1989, when Gorbachev decided to let Eastern Europe go its own way, the Chinese leaders were equally as discomforted by the wholesale rush to abandon communism. Although Deng Xiaoping offered a cautious response—the implications for the remaining communist regimes in the world were obvious and unsettling. Nevertheless, realist politics and economic imperatives again triumphed over ideological differences. As Li Peng told a German magazine, "This normalization does not apply to the ties between the two communist parties; only the relations between the two sides have again returned to normal."[20] In other words, China and the Soviet Union were moving toward state-to-state relations that would be considered normal between a superpower and a large regional power. Issues of Communist Party relations, ideological differences, etc., were not a part of the equation.

This was best illustrated by the series of moves to improve military relations that ensued. Gorbachev had demobilized 200,000 troops, reduced the Soviet Pacific fleet by one-third, withdrawn Soviet troops from Mongolia and Afghanistan, and destroyed the intermediate-range ballistic missile force east of the Urals.[21] By May 1990, Chinese fears of the Soviet military had abated to the point that Central Military Commission Vice-Chairman Liu Huaqing visited Moscow to discuss Chinese purchase of Soviet weapon systems and technology.[22] On May 16, 1991, Party Secretary Jiang Zemin visited Moscow to witness the signing of an agreement on border issues by the foreign ministers of the Soviet Union and the People's Republic, nearly three hundred years after the first Russo-Chinese border treaty. China even extended $1 billion in commodity credits to Russia.

Ironically, a rift that began at least partially over interpretations of communist ideology outlived the birthplace of communism itself. The border agreement, which was initially agreed to by the Soviet Union and China, was ratified by the Russian Supreme Soviet in February 1992. In March 1992, the foreign ministers of Russia and the People's Republic exchanged the instruments of ratification.[23] Not only had the Sino-Soviet split officially ended, but the Soviet Union had also officially ended. Relations between Russia and China would henceforth be based on the same political, military, and economic factors that govern relations between most nation-states in the post–Cold War international system.

## THE END OF COMMUNISM

The unthinkable occurred in August 1991. After the coup attempt against Gorbachev failed, he was forced to dissolve the Soviet Communist Party and, by December, to announce the end of the Soviet Union. China had become the largest and (with the exception of small nations such as Cuba, North Korea, and Vietnam) virtually the only communist nation left in the world. Understandably, the Chinese Communist leaders were nonplussed. With the rest of the world, they had watched Gorbachev's moves with a mixture of fascination and dread, and they were as surprised as everyone else by the precipitate collapse of the entire Soviet political and economic apparatus.

Chinese preferences in the battle over Soviet reform were never expressed openly, but it is clear that most leaders in Beijing preferred Soviet hard-liners to the reformers. In 1989, Chinese leaders regarded Gorbachev as a class traitor who let Eastern Europe succumb to capitalist encroachment. By 1991, however, with the rise of Boris Yeltsin, the Chinese Communist Party supported Gorbachev, especially because Gorbachev was increasingly forced to rely on more hard-line supporters.[24] Gorbachev had become the lesser of two evils.

The coup attempt therefore seemed to the Chinese leaders to be a godsend, an opportunity for orthodox Communists to restore the Communist Party of the Soviet Union to its correct role. Indeed, the coup leaders, realizing that they would have a sympathetic audience in Beijing, may have warned China's leaders of their plans beforehand. Army Chief of Staff Chi Haotian met with Soviet defense minister Dimitri Yazov in Moscow on August 12, and when Chi returned to Beijing he reported to an enlarged Politburo meeting on August 18, the day before the coup attempt. When the coup began, the Chinese press carried many articles, mostly favorable, that were perhaps prepared ahead of time.[25] Chinese disappointment at the failure of the coup attempt was acute, although in accordance with Deng Xiaoping's guidance regarding the CCP response to the crisis of world socialism, the public response was muted.

Within party circles, however, the mood was bitter. The official line was that the Soviet Union collapsed because glasnost was carried out too far and perestroika not far enough. Gorbachev, according to this school of thought, erred in managing the reform process rather than dealing with the structural defects of the Soviet system. He also erred in his precipitate introduction of political and economic reforms in a nation suffering from "excessive centralization of political and economic power [that] fostered bureaucratism, personal arbitrariness, patriarchy, lifelong official tenure and all sorts of privileges and corruption."[26] Gorbachev's reforms undermined the Communist Party of the Soviet Union, leaving him no base of support.[27]

Others attributed the collapse of the Soviet Union to a more sinister motive: a U.S. policy of peaceful evolution. The United States, according to this school of analysis, seeks to undermine the values of socialism through economic, political, and cultural penetration of socialist states accompanied by Western assistance and commerce.[28] Gorbachev, by opening up the

Soviet Union to Western influences, some Chinese leaders believed, allowed a pernicious anticommunism to invade and destroy the Soviet Union.

Whichever theory they espouse to explain the collapse the Soviet Union, all of Beijing's leaders were badly frightened by the events in Eastern Europe and the former parts of the Soviet Union. China's leaders are now even more convinced that they were right in suppressing the student demonstrations in light of the mass demonstrations that led to the collapse of communist regimes in Eastern Europe. At the same time, they congratulate themselves on China's successes in avoiding Soviet economic mistakes, which they attribute largely to the reforms introduced by Deng Xiaoping and his followers.

Since 1989, any opposition in China has been crushed; therefore, Chinese civil society today has no organized forces capable of challenging the ruling Chinese Communist Party. Deng and his followers are also convinced that the retention of party rule and authoritarian government is also essential for the development, well-being, and stability of the Chinese nation, as well as the avoidance of all the political turmoil and splitting apart of states that has occurred in the former communist world. Perestroika without glasnost has therefore become the modus operandi of the Chinese leaders.

## THE FOUR MODERNIZATIONS
## VERSUS GLASNOST AND PERESTROIKA

The end of Soviet communism gave rise to a debate that will undoubtedly last for generations. What did Deng Xiaoping do right in his attempts to reform Chinese communism? What did Mikhail Gorbachev do wrong? Why did Deng's reforms bring China to the verge of economic "takeoff," whereas Gorbachev's reforms only deepened the Soviet economic crisis? How did Deng Xiaoping manage to survive the massive demonstrations at Tiananmen Square, whereas Gorbachev's Soviet Union could not outlast a bumbling coup attempt? What were the critical differences?

When analyzing what was wrong with their systems, Deng Xiaoping and Mikhail Gorbachev came to completely opposite conclusions. Deng Xiaoping concluded that communism would be preserved in China only if the living standards of the people improved, and he concluded that this could happen only if the economy was liberalized and private enterprises were encouraged. Because Deng's purpose was preservation of the communist system he had wrested from the ashes of the Cultural Revolution, political reform was not his goal; rather, he sought to preserve power for those he had appointed to office since returning from political exile. A combination of an open economy and a strong Communist Party was, Deng believed, the best insurance of a wealthier and more powerful China.

Mikhail Gorbachev approached the Soviet Union's problems from a diametrically opposed perspective. He viewed the Communist Party apparatus, which had not been shaken up since the horrors of Stalin's purges, as the cause of the Soviet Union's problems. The apparatchiki were, Gorbachev believed, interested only in preserving their own perquisites and were unalterably opposed to any changes, even if these changes would benefit the Soviet people. So Gorbachev tried to restructure the Communist Party apparatus first through allowing public criticism of its defects and by replacing Khrushchev- and Brezhnev-era cadres with his own appointments. No overarching plan for economic change was ever developed, and the proposals for economic restructuring that Gorbachev put forth were either extremely limited in scope, proposed but never implemented, or implemented in such a half-hearted fashion that they were bound to fail.

Deng and Gorbachev, of course, faced different obstacles. Deng had to restructure a political system that had collapsed. Gorbachev had to shake up a system that had become desiccated. Deng wanted to effect change in a country where 80 percent of the people were still peasants after forty years of communism and where state-owned industries were not responsible for an overwhelming percentage of the gross national product. Gorbachev had to cope with work habits formed by seventy years of communism. Although the Soviets had successfully transformed their people from illiterate peasants to educated com-

In the vast rural regions of the former Soviet Union there is a tradition of little experience with private farming. For centuries *mirs,* which were collective operations much like self-contained villages but ruled from above by a landed aristocracy, prevailed. The end of Russian serfdom in the 1860s did not result in land reform, and efforts to place land in the hands of the peasants from 1905 to 1911 also ended in failure. Ironically, it was Lenin who created a brief period of privatization in 1921 with his New Economic Policy (NEP), which helped create private ownership and a new prosperous middle class in rural Russia. But the Kulaks, who worked the land and became rich farmers, were destroyed by Stalin in 1928 when he sent party cadres into the countryside to turn landless peasants against their Kulak neighbors with the promise of all land to the people. Private farms were turned into collectives or large state farms. In the 1990s, with little experience and in the face of a disastrous financial situation, Russian and Ukrainian peasants are not anxious to try private farming.

rades, a large percentage of the people worked for the party, for the state, or in state-owned industries that barely functioned. After Stalin's brutal collectivization of agriculture, Soviet agricultural workers on state farms and collectives had adopted the same attitudes and work habits as their industrial comrades. Deng could begin simply by allowing China's peasants to sell some of the crops they produced on their plots of land. Gorbachev had no such simple option to initiate economic change.

## Similarities Between China and the Soviet Union

Some argue that too much is made of the differences, that actually many similarities exist between China and the Soviet Union. For example, Marshall Goldman, an expert on the Soviet economy, argues that Chinese agriculture suffers from the same capital deficiencies as did Soviet agriculture; yet the Chinese increased their output and shipments to urban areas with only a modest increase in storage facilities and without building new storage facilities. They did this through allowing the peasants to operate on their own,[29] something Gorbachev now regrets not doing. In January 1993 Gorbachev said, "I consider it my biggest miscalculation that we did not take agriculture as the starting point of the reform process and that we stopped halfway."[30] Goldman extends his critique of Gorbachev's methods of economic reform:

> Several important lessons arise out of China's experiences. Build institutions such as private businesses—banking and manufacturing first, or at least simultaneously. Agricultural reform, and the creation of private agriculture in particular, is crucial. Peasants, service personnel, and workers should also be encouraged to dabble in handicraft work and manufacturing. Economic incentives should be designed to tempt large numbers of people into becoming entrepreneurs.[31]

Closer analysis of the purported differences also reveals many similarities in terms of politics. Gorbachev's attempts to reform the Communist Party structure through opening it to criticism mortally wounded the party instead of revitalizing it. New and vigorous appointments could not reinvigorate a system that only a few old believers still had faith in. In China, the Communist Party apparatus survives, but it, too, is mortally wounded. Instead of the party imploding as it did in the Soviet Union, the Chinese Communist Party is becoming increasingly irrelevant. It is already despised by the Chinese people for its corruption. The new generation of entrepreneurs either ignore the party or bribe its cadres, and the best and the brightest join the party only if forced into it. Few believe that the Chinese Communist Party will maintain its vanguard role long after the death of Deng Xiaoping and the other veterans of the civil war. Instead, many believe that the Chinese Communist Party will either transform itself into a totalitarian ruler backed by the military or wither away as did the Communist Party of the Soviet Union. Thus, Deng's victory may be a pyrrhic one. The Chinese Communist Party still rules but with little support from the masses and few prospects for the future.

## How to Preserve Communism in China?

Despite the reluctance of many Chinese leaders to admit it, China was even more open to Western economic penetration than was the Soviet Union. The demonstrations at Tiananmen Square illustrated that values borrowed from the West, especially the value of democracy, were already affecting China's student population. Two groups argued over the approach the Chinese Communist Party would have to take to ensure that it, too, did not end up in the dustbin of history. Party conservatives argued that the collapse of the Communist Party of the Soviet Union showed that China should mount a class struggle and a vigorous campaign against bourgeois ideology. Deng Xiaoping, however, argued that the Soviet Communist Party's problems were caused by a lack of the sort of change he spearheaded in China. Poverty, Deng asserted, would lead to demands for change. Only continued reform and opening could save China.[32] Deng triumphed, and economic reform and growth became the guiding principle of the Chinese Communist Party in the post–Cold War era. The question that Deng's successors will have to face is whether economic reform and growth are enough to sustain a ruling Communist Party. It was not enough to sustain the Soviet Communist Party, the most powerful one in the world. Will the fate of the CCP be any different?

### RUSSIA AND CHINA IN THE NEW ERA

China's relations with Russia in the post–Cold War era will be governed by the same dynamics that govern all interstate relations in the international system. Issues of state sovereignty, interdependence, and balance of power will dominate China's policymaking with respect to Russia, the other states of the former Soviet Union, and the rest of the world. China and Russia will continue to be dominant military powers in East Asia in the twenty-first century by virtue of their size and their possession of nuclear weapons. The United States and Japan will also play a role. Their interactions with each other and with the other nations of East Asia will determine the nature of security issues in the region. And there are many security issues that will have to be addressed.

The Chinese may be among those who rue the end of the Cold War and the certain sort of security that a bipolar world system offered. Now, many Chinese balance a fear of a unipolar world led by the United States with an equally great fear of a nationalist, obstreperous Russia that will seek to reassert control over the Soviet Empire. Equally as frightening to the Chinese is the possibility of Russian political instability, which could spill over into the other members of the Commonwealth of Independent States and thereby threaten Chinese security. Both of these scenarios—a newly aggressive Russia or a state that is dissolving into further political and economic chaos—would threaten Chinese security, so much so that it might consider once again "tilting" toward the United States despite fears of U.S. hegemony.

Alternatively, Russia may overcome its current political and economic instability and develop a centrist foreign policy such that Russia and China will work together to solve East Asian security issues. Elements of this type of foreign policy have already been put into place by the Yeltsin government. For example, Russia and China have agreed to meet with Kazakhstan, Kyrgyzstan, and Tajikistan to reduce tensions by negotiating a solution to border disputes between China and these Central Asian states. China and Russia have also been working together with the United States to resolve the impasse over inspection of North Korea's nuclear facilities.

## Economic Relations

There are now opportunities to improve economic relations between China and its neighbors in the Commonwealth of Independent States. China can provide cheap consumer goods of relatively high quality, which are in short supply and in great demand in former communist countries. These countries, in turn, have many resources, such as oil and timber, that are badly needed in China and that might be exploited through joint ventures. However, China has been approaching trade relations with the Commonwealth states gingerly, perhaps because of its unfamiliarity with the political and economic conditions in many of these states. Fear of competition from Taiwan, though, may actually have spurred Beijing's leaders to become more involved in trade relations than their natural inclinations would have dictated. A desire to serve as a successful model of economic reform in communist societies may also be a driving force to increase economic interactions; indeed, Russian economic reformers have already visited China's special economic zones. Although trade between China and the Commonwealth states will undoubtedly increase and diversify, trade relations with the United States, Western Europe, Japan, and the Four Little Tigers will continue to be more important. Only those countries can provide China and Russia with the capital and the technical know-how needed to develop their economies successfully.

## Military Relations

In November 1993, Russia and China signed a five-year military cooperation agreement that would provide China with military technology. The agreement followed a year in which Russia sold China $1.2 billion in military hardware, including about twenty-four advanced SU-27 fighters.[33] There are also reports that China and Russia will make arrangements for coproduction in China of Russia's modern Mig-31 fighter and that hundreds of Russian technicians and engineers will be sent to China to help it with its nuclear weapons and missile programs.[34] In addition, China is purchasing large amounts of high-quality military equipment from former communist countries that are willing either to barter arms for Chinese consumer goods or, in the case of highly desired equipment, to sell it for hard currencies. For all of these reasons, trade has increased substantially in the 1990s between China and its former communist neighbors.

Yet the balance is delicate for all parties engaged in the arms trade. The United States is unnerved by signs of Russo-Chinese military cooperation, and at Washington's urging, Russia reportedly agreed not to sell China aircraft and certain long-range bombers.[35] At the same time, the Russians have been exercising all their options. Two senior Russian military officials visited Taiwan in June 1992, presumably to investigate the possibility of Taiwanese military purchases. Both Taipei and Moscow have apparently expressed the desire to enter into a normal, cooperative relationship;[36] Beijing's reaction to such a relationship would presumably be explosive.

This complicated military interchange among the United States, Russia, China, and Taiwan illustrates well the complexities of the post–Cold War world. Will Russia and China continue to expand military ties, or will a nationalist revival in Russia force China to improve relations with the United States? How will China deal with its fears of a bloc of Muslim states in central Asia? And will Russian and U.S. relations with Taiwan alarm the Chinese sufficiently to provoke them into action?

## Foreign Policy Decisionmaking

Before Russia and China can develop a comprehensive, long-term approach to security issues in East Asia, both sides will have to decide how they wish to develop the policymaking framework. In Russia today, the foreign policy establishment is in the midst of a debate over what principles will guide it over the next few decades. Should Russia adopt a Sino-

---

**Li Peng on Sino-Russian Relations**

China and Russia "share long borders which should be peaceful and friendly ones. . . . The economies of the two countries are strongly complementary and their economic and trade relations have experienced rapid development in recent years. . . . Both China and Russia should proceed from reality to explore new ways for further bilateral cooperation."

[BBC Summary of World Broadcasts, February 25, 1994.]

centric policy favoring ties with China, a Nippocentric policy favoring ties with Japan, or a pragmatic and flexible balance-of-power approach[37] that would balance Japanese economic strength through economic ties to China and balance Chinese military strength through ties to Japan, the United Nations, etc.?

China's leaders are asking similar questions. What are their foreign policy and security goals? First, they would like to avoid any spillover of disorder in neighboring regions into China's periphery regions. Although contact cannot be cut off between people with similar cultural traits on both sides of the border, Beijing seeks correct relations with its neighbors based on the principle of noninterference in each other's affairs. Second, even though China's leaders are highly critical of the present leadership in former communist countries, they realize that open antagonisms in the current situation serve no purpose, and they have therefore sought to establish correct relations with the new nations of Eastern Europe and the members of the Commonwealth of Independent States. Third, both China and its former communist neighbors have reason to cooperate politically to solve continuing problems, such as border issues that have poisoned relations in the past, as well as ideological disagreements. To that end, despite some misgivings, China has generally been supportive of the Commonwealth of Independent States as a source of stability and a protection against further spread of disintegrative nationalism, particularly in Central Asia.[38] It serves no purpose to create political and ideological tensions or to support particular groups in neighboring states during the 1990s' rapid and uncertain transition both inside China and in the former communist world.

In the 1990s, as China's leaders look to the north and northwest, the former republics of the Soviet Union pose both opportunities and dangers. Conservatives and reformers alike are still trying to recover from the shock of seeing the Soviet Union come apart, and they will do whatever is necessary to try to prevent similar happenings in China by avoiding the mistakes they think were made in Moscow. The collapse of the Soviet Union has changed the geopolitical power structure, ended the Cold War, and for the foreseeable future reduced any major security threat to China from its neighbors to the north and northwest. In fact, China, with its successful market developments since 1978, provides a model that now may have many lessons for its former communist neighbors on how to develop and modernize a society that has practiced communism for many years but wishes to adopt market capitalism.

## POLICY OPTIONS

China's leaders observed the collapse of communism with some disquiet, but Beijing's relations with the former communist world are as good or better than during the height of the Cold War. China's policy options in its relations with the former communist world and with the few remaining communist states are far more varied than at any time since the founding of the People's Republic.

## Option 1: Pursuing Nonalignment

China and Russia seek to maintain good relations based on the five principles of peaceful coexistence, while at the same time taking advantage of opportunities to cooperate on specific issues. Both Beijing and Moscow share a common interest in creating stable security conditions in Asia, especially in Northeast Asia, because this would reduce Japan's temptation to rearm. Beijing and Moscow also have an interest in increasing trade and good relations among countries in Southeast Asia because regional arms races could lead to a resurgence of U.S. military activity in Asia as well as a rapid militarization of Japan.

## Option 2: Sino-Russian Military Cooperation

Although it is not in Beijing's or Moscow's interest to seek formal military alignments in the post–Cold War era, both nations are already benefiting by sharing military technology and trading weapons for hard cash or consumer goods. The two nations also have a common interest in maintaining stability and preventing conflict in Northeast Asia. Continued military cooperation must, however, be carried out in ways that do not alarm Japan, the United States, and other nations in Asia. Moreover, China and Russia will have to overcome over two centuries of distrust and tension that in the past have led to military engagements.

- Current Russian sales of Mig-31 and SU-27 aircraft to China benefit both sides. Moscow gets hard currency for sales of advanced military aircraft and cheap Chinese consumer goods for sales of other weapons. The military complexes of both countries benefit from joint ventures to produce arms. These transactions are a major source of trade, involving billions of dollars of arms, consumer goods, and hard cash. China's arms purchases from the Russians are essential to the modernization of its military forces, especially because the United States, Japan, and other nations restrict sales of military technology to China.
- Both Beijing and Moscow share a common interest in creating stable security conditions in Asia, especially in North Asia. For example, both nations desire a resolution to difficulties on the Korean peninsula out of fear that increasing Korean tensions will prompt Japanese rearmament. To prevent regional arms races, which might

eventually involve the United States and Japan, both nations also have an interest in helping create a stable Southeast Asia.

## Option 3: Promoting Trade and Investment

In the economic realm, Moscow and Beijing have growing opportunities to increase both trade and investment. Beijing would like to diversify its trade, which is still heavily oriented toward the United States, Japan, Hong Kong, and Taiwan. The Russian market seems one obvious choice for expansion of Chinese trade. China may also serve as a model of reform to Russia as Moscow seeks to marketize its economy.

- Beijing increasingly views Russian Siberia as a treasure chest of raw materials just waiting to be developed through joint ventures involving China, Russia, and other Asian countries.
- China could provide skilled and disciplined labor for joint ventures while South Korea, Hong Kong, and Taiwan could provide the capital. Siberian raw materials, such as timber and minerals, could then be exported to all these countries in exchange for consumer goods.

## Option 4: Promoting Multipolarity

At the multilateral, global level, geopolitical realities dictate that in some instances Moscow and Beijing will have complementary interests while at other times they will be in conflict. Both nations, however, will have a vested interest in promoting multipolarity. Now that the Soviet Union is no longer one of the two global superpowers, fear of U.S. hegemony in the international system will drive both China and the Soviet Union to promote shifting alliances as a tactic to encourage a balance of power.

- Both nations are likely to work together to preserve current veto privileges and special rights of the five permanent members of the UN Security Council. Chinese and Russian leaders believe that other arrangements are likely to strengthen western or Third World domination of the global security system at their expense. China and Russia increasingly wish to limit UN intervention inside states to promote basic human rights. They agree that such intervention is a violation of the sovereign rights of states and the five basic principles of peaceful coexistence.
- Cold War–era rivalries continue on the Sino-Russian border and throughout the world. For example, China continues to back Pakistan, whereas Russia continues to back India. In addition, both nations are competing for trade, economic assistance, and technol-

ogy transfer from global economic regimes such as the World Bank and the International Monetary Fund, as well as from the United States, the European Community, and Japan.

- Should radical changes take place inside Russia leading to nationalist irredentism, China is likely, for geopolitical reasons, to join with the West and other regions in using global security structures to restrain Russian expansionism into the former Soviet Union.

## DISCUSSION QUESTIONS

1.  What were the reasons for cooperation between China and the Soviet Union in the 1950s?
2.  From the Chinese perspective, what were the sources of conflict between China and the Soviet Union during the Cold War years?
3.  From the Russian perspective, what were the sources of conflict between the Soviet Union and China during the Cold War years?
4.  From the perspective of China's leaders in Beijing, what were the reasons for the collapse of communism in Eastern Europe and the Soviet Union?
5.  With the end of the Cold War, why are relations between China and the former communist countries better than during the Cold War years?
6.  How has the collapse of the Soviet Union affected the balance of power in Asia?
7.  How do Chinese leaders view Gorbachev and Yeltsin?
8.  How relevant are current Chinese political and economic domestic developments as a model to be followed by the former parts of the Soviet Union?
9.  In what ways are the Chinese and Russian governments working together to create peace and stability in Northeast Asia during the post–Cold War era?
10. Although there is no Sino-Russian military alliance in the 1990s, why is military cooperation between the two countries increasing?
11. How does Beijing seek to deal with current developments taking place inside Russia and other former communist countries? Explain the reasons for China's current position on developments inside former communist countries.
12. How does Beijing view Russia's role in the United Nations in the post–Cold War era?

## SUGGESTED READINGS

Cohen, Warren I., and Akira Iriye, eds. *The Great Powers in East Asia, 1953–1960.* New York: Columbia University Press, 1990.

Diller, Daniel C. *Russia and the Independent States.* Washington, D.C.: Congressional Quarterly, 1992.

Dittmer, Lowell. *Sino-Soviet Normalization and Its International Implications, 1945–1990.* Seattle: University of Washington Press, 1992.

———. "China and Russia: New Beginnings," in Samuel S. Kim, ed. *China and the World: New Directions in Chinese Foreign Policy.* Boulder, Colorado: Westview Press, 1993, pp. 113–127.

Fletcher, Joseph. "Sino-Russian Relations, 1800–1862," in John Fairbank, ed. *The Cambridge History of China, Vol. 10, Late Ch'ing, 1800–1911, Part I,* Cambridge: Cambridge University Press, pp. 318–350.

Floyd, David. *Mao Against Khrushchev: A Short History of the Sino-Soviet Conflict.* New York: Frederick A. Praeger, 1963.

Ginsburg, George. "The End of Sino-Russian Territorial Disputes?" *The Journal of East Asian Affairs* 7, no. 1 (Winter/Spring 1993): pp. 261–320.

Kim, Ilpyong, ed. *Beyond the Strategic Triangle.* New York: Paragon House, 1992.

Klintworth, Gary. *Sino-Russian Detente and the Regional Implications.* Canberra, Australia: Strategic and Defense Studies Centre, Australian National University, 1992.

Levin, Norman D. "Evolving Chinese and Soviet Politics Toward the Korean Peninsula," in June Teufel Dreyer and Ilpyong J. Kim, eds. *Chinese Defense and Foreign Policy.* New York: Paragon House, 1988, pp. 187–213.

Levine, Steven I. "Chinese Foreign Policy in the Strategic Triangle," in June Teufel Dreyer and Ilpyong J. Kim, eds. *Chinese Defense and Foreign Policy.* New York: Paragon House, 1988, pp. 187–213.

Moskoff, William, *Hard Times: Impoverishment and Protest in the Perestroika Years.* Armonk, New York: M.E. Sharpe, 1993.

Nelsen, Harvey W., *Power and Insecurity: Beijing, Moscow, and Washington: 1949–1988.* Boulder, Colorado: Lynne Rienner Publishers, 1989.

Pi, Ying-hsein, "China's Boundary Issues With the Former Soviet Union." *Issues and Studies* 28 (July 1992): pp. 63–75.

Ross, Robert S., ed. *China, the United States and the Soviet Union: Tripolarity and Policy Making in the Cold War.* Armonk, New York: M.E. Sharpe, 1993.

Solomon, Richard H., ed. *Asian Security in the 1980s: Problems and Policies for a Time of Transition.* Cambridge, Massachusetts: Oelgeschlager, Gunn & Hain, 1979.

Stuart, Douglas T., and William H. Tow. *China, the Soviet Union, and the West: Strategic and Political Dimensions in the 1980s.* Boulder, Colorado: Westview Press, 1982.

Su Chi, "Sino-Soviet Relations of the 1980s: From Confrontation to Conciliation," in Samuel S. Kim, ed. *China and the World.* Boulder, Colorado: Westview Press, 1989.

Tow, William T. "Strategy, Technology and Military Development in Sino-Soviet Strategic Relationships," in June Teufel Dreyer and Ilpyong J. Kim, eds. *Chinese Defense and Foreign Policy.* New York: Paragon House, 1988, pp. 269–295.

White, Stephen. *Gorbachev and After.* 3d Edition. New York: Cambridge University Press, 1992.

Yahuda, Michael B. "Chinese Foreign Policy and the Collapse of Communism." *SAIS Review* 12 (Winter–Spring 1992): pp. 125–137.

## NOTES

1. Joseph Fletcher, "Sino-Russian Relations, 1800–1862," in John Fairbank, ed. *The Cambridge History of China, Vol. 10, Late Ch'ing, 1800–1911, Part I* (Cambridge: Cambridge University Press), p. 335.

2. Joseph Fletcher, "Sino-Russian Relations," p. 347.

3. Adam Ulam, *The Rivals: America and Russia Since World War II* (New York: Penguin Books, 1980), p. 138.

4. Ross Terrill, *Mao: A Biography* (New York: Harper & Row, 1980), p. 201.

5. Ross Terrill, *Mao,* pp. 201–202.

6. Allen S. Whiting, *China Crosses the Yalu* (Stanford, California: Stanford University Press, 1968).

7. Steven I. Levine, "Soviet Asian Policy in the 1950s," in *The Great Powers in East Asia, 1953–1960.* Warren I. Cohen and Akira Iriye, eds. (New York: Columbia University Press, 1990), p. 308.

8. Stuart Schram, *Mao Tse-tung* (Baltimore, Maryland: Penguin, 1975), p. 291.

9. Harold C. Hinton, "Sino-Soviet Relations: Background and Overview," in *China, the Soviet Union, and the West: Strategic and Political Dimensions in the 1980s.* Douglas T. Stuart and William H. Tow, eds. (Boulder, Colorado: Westview Press, 1982), p. 9.

10. Ross Terrill, *Mao,* p. 202.

11. Gordon H. Chang, "JFK, China, and the Bomb," *Journal of American History* 74, no. 4 (March 1988): pp. 1287–1310.

12. Steven Levine, "Soviet Asian Policy in the 1950s," p. 311.

13. Joseph L. Nogee and Robert H. Donaldson, *Soviet Foreign Policy Since World War II,* 3d edition (New York: Pergamon Press, 1988), p. 250.

14. Henry Kissinger, *White House Years* (Boston: Little Brown and Company, 1979).

15. William G. Hyland, "The Sino-Soviet Conflict: A Search for New Security Strategies," in *Asian Security in the 1980s: Problems and Policies for a Time of Transition,* Richard H. Solomon, ed. (Cambridge, Massachusetts: Oelgeschlager, Gunn & Hain, 1979), p. 40.

16. Chi Su, "China and the Soviet Union: Principled, Salutary and Tempered Management of Conflict," in *China and the World: New Directions in Chinese Foreign Policy,* Samuel S. Kim, ed. (Boulder, Colorado: Westview Press, 1989), p. 136.

17. Michael Yahuda, "Deng Xiaoping: The Statesman," *China Quarterly* (September 1993): p. 562.

18. Robert S. Ross, "Foreign Policy in 1987: Independent Rhetoric, Pragmatic Policy," in Anthony J. Kane, ed., *China Briefing, 1988* (Boulder, Colorado: Westview Press 1988), pp. 45–46.

19. Robert A. Scalapino, "The China Policy of Russia and Asian Security in the 1990s," in *East Asian Security in the Post–Cold War Era,* Simon W. Sheldon, ed. (Armonk, New York: M.E. Sharpe, 1993), p. 161.

20. Allen S. Whiting, "China's Foreign Relations After 40 Years," in *China Briefing, 1990,* Anthony J. Kane, ed. (Boulder, Colorado: Westview Press, 1990), p. 71.

21. David Shambaugh, "China's Security Policy in the Post–Cold War Era," in *At Issue: Politics in the World Arena,* 7th edition, Steven L. Spiegel and David J. Pervin, eds. (New York: St. Martin's Press, 1994), pp. 142–143.

22. John W. Garver, "The Chinese Communist Party and the Collapse of Soviet Communism," *China Quarterly* (March 1993): p. 1.

23. George Ginsburg, "The End of the Sino-Russian Territorial Disputes?" *The Journal of East Asian Affairs* 7, no. 1 (Winter/Spring 1993): p. 265.

24. John Garver, "The Chinese Communist Party and the Collapse of Soviet Communism," p. 11.

25. John Garver, "The Chinese Communist Party and the Collapse of Soviet Communism," p. 13.

26. Chai Chengweng, cited in David Armstrong, "Chinese Perspectives on the New World Order," *The Journal of East Asian Affairs* 8, no. 2 (Summer/Fall 1994): pp. 457–458.

27. Marshall Shulman, "Reform and Soviet Collapse Spur Discussions Between American and Chinese Specialists," *United States-China Relations: Notes from the National Committee* (Spring/Summer 1992): p. 6.

28. Paul H.B. Godwin, "China's Asian Policy in the 1990s: Adjusting to the Post–Cold War Environment," in *East Asian Security in the Post–Cold War Era,* Sheldon W. Simon, ed. (Armonk, New York: M.E. Sharpe, 1993), p. 127.

29. Marshall L. Goldman, "The Chinese Model: The Solution to Russia's Economic Ills?" *Current History* (October 1993): p. 321.

30. Marshall L. Goldman, "The Chinese Model: The Solution to Russia's Economic Ills?" p. 321.

31. Marshall L. Goldman, "The Chinese Model: The Solution to Russia's Economic Ills?" p. 324.

32. John Garver, "The Chinese Communist Party and the Collapse of Soviet Communism," p. 25.

33. Patrick E. Tyler, "Russia and China Sign a Military Agreement," *New York Times,* November 10, 1993.

34. See Andrew K. Hamani, "Japan and the Military Balance of Power in Northeast Asia," *The Journal of East Asian Affairs* 8, no. 2 (Summer/Fall 1994): pp. 374–375.

35. Patrick Tyler, "Russia and China Sign a Military Agreement."

36. Mette Skak, "Post-Soviet Foreign Policy: The Emerging Relationship Between Russia and Northeast Asia," *The Journal of East Asian Affairs* 7, no. 1 (Winter/Spring 1993): p. 165.

37. Mette Skak, "Post-Soviet Foreign Policy," p. 152.

38. Marshall Shulman, "Reform and Soviet Collapse Spur Discussions Between American and Chinese Specialists," pp. 12–13.

# China and the United States

Fifteen years ago our entire relationship with China was geo-strategic. They were a card to play against the Soviets. Now it is geo-economic. They know we need them as a market for exports, not a card to play. That gives them a lot more leverage when we make demands on them about human rights. Clinton will be meeting with a much more self-confident Chinese leadership than any President in the past.
—*Robert D. Hormats, former U.S. assistant
secretary of state for economic affairs, 1993*

## HISTORICAL BACKGROUND

### Sentimental Imperialists

It was Chinese tea that was dumped into Boston harbor in December 1773 to protest British rule over the thirteen colonies. U.S. trade with China in tea, china, spices, silks, and furniture predated even the American Revolution. The history of official Sino-U.S. contacts is nearly as long. In 1844, the United States signed a treaty with China that promised "peace, amity and commerce."[1] The treaty also guaranteed that the United States would be granted the same trading rights as the British, and the Chinese promised to grant automatically to Washington all future privileges given to other Western nations. Thus was born the most-favored-nation status, which the Chinese called "jackal diplomacy" and which continues to cause friction in Sino-U.S. relations to this day.

From the earliest Western contacts with China, the myth of the China market prevailed. The idea that the huge Chinese population would want to buy foreign products, creating a huge import market and huge profits for exporters, drove Western powers to demand spheres of influence in China. Those in the United States also believed in the myth, even though U.S. trade with China was only 1 to 2 percent of the total volume of U.S. exports for most of the nineteenth and early twentieth centuries. Still, the hope of expanding markets continued, and Washington viewed the ever-growing number of foreign enclaves with alarm. Successive U.S. administrations were not concerned enough with China to take the trouble to establish a U.S. sphere of influence; however, Washington very much wanted access to the markets in areas controlled by the Western powers. To effect this, in 1899 the McKinley administration sent letters to the Great Powers, including Britain, Germany, Russia, and Japan, asking that they promise to preserve commercial equality for all nations in any spheres that they controlled. Despite evasive responses, the administration declared the powers had agreed to Open Door status, and secret U.S. contingency plans to establish a U.S. sphere of influence in China never had to be put to the test.[2]

Besides trade, the United States' other great interest in China was promoting Christianity. Along with France, England, and Germany, the United States sent missionaries to China to convert the Chinese and run charitable institutions. Although never successful—only approximately 1 percent of the Chinese population converted—by 1930, half of the 3,000 missionaries in China were U.S. citizens.[3] The Chinese were generally uninterested in adopting a foreign religion, and most were especially resistant to accepting a religion that came to symbolize foreign imperialism in China. Few U.S. citizens at home, however, realized how unsuccessful the missionaries were; rather, most believed that their missionaries were being honored in China for their role in bringing Christianity to the country and for introducing the concept of public charity.

Trade and Christianity became the two factors determining Sino-U.S. interactions well into China's revolutionary era. Because it did not actually control any Chinese territory, the United States believed that it was behaving in a more benevolent manner than the other Western nations. This notion was particularly reinforced by the U.S. allocation of monies paid by the Chinese government to Western powers for damages incurred during the Boxer Uprising toward educating Chinese students in the United States. The people of the United States were *sentimental imperialists*—they believed they were unlike their more rapacious brethren in Europe and therefore had a special relationship with the Chinese.

Most Chinese, however, failed to notice the difference between the United States and the European powers. After all, the United States demanded the special rights and privileges of the other foreign powers in China, contributed troops to the forces fighting the Boxers in Beijing, and sought to demonstrate the superiority of Christianity to heathens. To many Chinese, the United States was little different from all the other powers that were eroding China's sovereignty and its pride. Their attitude was perhaps best stated by the Chinese minister to the United States in 1899 (the year of the Open Door) when he protested against "the utter disregard of the American government for the friendly relations that should exist between two governments."[4]

## Nationalism and Revolution

To many Chinese, the United States' less than honorable attitude toward China was demonstrated yet again at the Versailles Conference in 1919. Despite President Wilson's previous high-minded statements regarding U.S. respect for Chinese sovereignty, he acquiesced in the transfer of Shandong province from German to Japanese control. The Chinese students and intellectuals who protested did not prevent the transfer, but they did forge a new sense of Chinese nationalism that precluded foreign intervention. U.S. intervention in China was as little appreciated as that of other foreign powers. The fact that the United States refused to give up extraterritorial rights (immunity from Chinese law) for its citizens in China until after World War II had started did not increase respect for the United States in Chinese patriotic circles.

## World War II

During the late 1920s and the 1930s, Washington paid only intermittent attention to China. The rise of fascism in Europe was of paramount concern to most of the U.S. people, and China, divided into satrapies controlled by sparring warlords, was only of marginal interest. Even the myth of the China market had been proven false—as late as 1940, $78 million in U.S. exports went to China while $227 million went to Japan.[5]

Only as Japanese expansionism in the Far East continued, with images of the Japanese "rape" of Nanjing indelibly etched in U.S. minds through pictures in *Life* magazine and newsreels, did China come into focus as a component of U.S. security policy. After Japan joined the Axis (fascist Germany and Italy) in 1940, official and public opinion in the United States began to favor China. The United States then adopted a dual policy toward Japan: an oil embargo and a simultaneous attempt to find a diplomatic solution to the East Asian crisis. For the United States, one condition of any talks was a Japanese pledge to respect Chinese territory and sovereignty, but the Japanese refused to withdraw their troops from Manchuria. On December 7, 1941, the tide turned. Once the United States was at war with Japan, preservation of a free and independent China became a vital component of the U.S. international security agenda.

During World War II, the U.S. policy toward China was complicated by the growing strength of the Chinese Communists in their base areas and the virtual civil war between the Communists and the Nationalists. The primary U.S. goal was to defeat the Japanese invaders in China. To some, Chiang Kai-shek's goal seemed to be to defeat the Communists instead. President Franklin Roosevelt adopted a number of approaches. He sent a U.S. general, Joseph Stilwell, to train the Chinese Nationalist troops to fight the Japanese. But he also sent a group of U.S. diplomats to meet with the

Communists to determine if a united front against the Japanese could be arranged. He tried to massage Chiang's and China's pride by treating China as one of the four "global policemen," along with the United States, the Soviet Union, and the United Kingdom (who, with France, are now the permanent members of the United Nations Security Council).

Nothing seemed to work. Chiang forced Stilwell out, and the morale of the Nationalist troops remained low. The Nationalists and the Communists never effectively cooperated in the anti-Japanese war. The Communists always perceived the United States as pro-Chiang. And the United States could not create Chinese national pride. Ultimately, neither the Nationalists nor the Communists defeated the Japanese in China. The U.S. troops defeated Japan on its own territory and then faced the monumental task of disarming Japanese troops in China, which they did with the assistance of Chiang's troops, who benefited from the Japanese disarmament.

After 1945, Chiang's forces were free to fight Mao's troops for control of China. Communist and Nationalist troops fought each other with weapons confiscated from the Japanese and with weapons supplied to Chiang's forces by the United States but often appropriated by Mao's troops. U.S. efforts to mediate between the two parties in hopes of creating a coalition government came to naught. Both the Nationalists and the Communists were loathe to compromise, and the Communists believed that the United States was partial to Chiang Kai-shek. In January 1947, General George C. Marshall, the U.S. negotiator, left China in disgust after in effect pronouncing "a plague on both your houses."

## THE COLD WAR YEARS

### When the Dust Settles

The United States soon came to the decision that the Communists would be victorious, and it tried to limit the anticipated domestic political damage through education. The *China White Paper,* published in August 1949, was a report authored by the State Department to justify the administration's policy of disengagement to the U.S. public. In the foreword, Secretary of State Dean Acheson attempts to placate supporters of the Nationalists while also making the case that a Communist victory was inevitable no matter what the United States did:

> A realistic appraisal of conditions in China, past and present, leads to the conclusion that the only alternative open to the United States was full-scale intervention in behalf of a Government which had lost the confidence of its own troops and its own people. . . . The unfortunate but inescapable fact is that the ominous result of the civil war in China was beyond the control of the government of the United States. Nothing

that this country did or could have done within the reasonable limits of its capabilities could have changed that result; nothing that was left undone by this country has contributed to it. It was the product of internal China forces, forces which this country tried to influence but could not.[6]

The white paper was not enough to silence critics. In 1949, President Truman had to persuade Congress to lower its allocations for China aid, and he was forced continually to defend his administration from charges (particularly by Republicans) of abandoning the Nationalists to the Communists. The "Who Lost China" debate continued in Washington into the 1960s.[7]

As predicted, the Chinese Communists did soon prevail, largely because of better military leadership, a reputation for incorruptibility, and an appeal to Chinese nationalism. The People's Republic of China was established on October 1, 1949. Defeated, Chiang and his supporters were forced to flee to the southern island of Taiwan, where they established a rump Nationalist regime. Most U.S. policymakers expected that after the Chinese Communists had consolidated control of the mainland, they would then mount an amphibious invasion of Taiwan, thereby finally finishing the bloody civil war. Even the Truman administration reached the controversial decision, which was by no means unanimously accepted, particularly in the military, not to intervene when Chinese forces crossed the Taiwan Straits.

U.S. policymakers in 1949 and early 1950 were initially unsure of how to react to the establishment of the People's Republic. Two options were considered: to recognize the regime or to ignore it because of its communist government. Policymakers opposed to recognition cited the threat to the stability of Southeast Asia posed by a communist China, the degree to which the People's Republic marched in lockstep with the Soviet Union, the danger to the functioning of the United Nations if the Security Council were to have another communist permanent member, and the U.S. obligation to the Nationalist Chinese on Taiwan. Policymakers who favored recognition argued for it in the distant future, and then only because the prerogatives of international law would demand U.S. recognition of a stable communist regime.

This debate between absolutes had not been resolved by mid-1950. After the outbreak of the Korean War on June 25, 1950, recognition of the People's Republic was no longer considered a viable policy option. The invasion of South Korea by Communist troops from North Korea was perceived in Washington to be another example of militant communism driving toward world domination. Prior Soviet and Chinese knowledge of the attack was considered a given.

As a result, the United States reversed its East Asia policy. Washington sent troops to defend South Korea, which had only a few weeks earlier been considered outside the U.S. defense perimeter. The Truman administration also quickly reversed its laissez-faire position by sending the Seventh Fleet

into the Taiwan Straits. No longer would the United States allow the anticipated Communist invasion. Chiang's island regime became a U.S. protec-
torate.

Chinese entry into the Korean War in October 1950 after U.S. troops
marched toward the Korean-Chinese border fulfilled Washington's worst
fears of the Chinese Communists. U.S. and Chinese troops fought face-
to-face for nearly three years until an armistice was finally signed in July
1953. The legacy of distrust had been transformed into a legacy of hatred
engendered by open warfare.

## The Eisenhower Administration

Sino-U.S. relations during the Eisenhower administration were punctuated
by two episodes of near war, the Taiwan Straits Crises of 1954 and 1958. In
addition to the Sino-U.S. dispute over Taiwan's status, which threatened
world peace, a number of major issues of contention repeatedly arose
between the United States and the People's Republic during the Eisenhower
administration. These issues, which included recognition, United Nations
membership, trade, China's imprisonment of U.S. citizens,[8] and U.S. retention of Chinese citizens, formed a theme of Sino-U.S. relations from 1953
through 1960. A less important issue, but one that received tremendous press
coverage, was how Washington should respond to the Chinese invitation to
U.S. news reporters.[9] Not one of these issues was resolved during the
Eisenhower administration or, it might be added, the next two administrations.

## Taiwan

The Eisenhower administration mounted a complex effort to support the
Nationalist regime while at the same time subtly restraining its reckless
behavior toward the People's Republic. One of President Eisenhower's first
acts after taking the oath of office was to "unleash" Chiang Kai-shek, stat-
ing that the U.S. Seventh Fleet would not stand in the way of Nationalist
attempts to invade the mainland. The Mutual Defense Treaty of 1954 officially bound the United States to the defense of Taiwan should it be attacked,
and Congress endorsed the use of U.S. troops for the defense of Taiwan the
next year. At the same time, to curb any tendencies towards recklessness, the
administration elicited promises from Chiang's foreign minister that the use
of force would be "a matter of joint agreement." In addition, limitations were
placed on the use of some of the military equipment supplied to Chiang to
prevent employment for offensive purposes.

The first offshore island crisis was by far the more perilous. On
September 3, 1954, the People's Republic shelled the island of Quemoy, one
of the offshore islands that was held by the Nationalist Chinese despite the

fact that it lay no more than a few kilometers from the Chinese mainland and by international law belonged to the People's Republic. Nevertheless, the Nationalists responded by staging raids on the mainland, to which the Communist Chinese responded by bombarding the offshore islands more heavily. The United States supported Chiang's retention of the offshore islands because their loss might have affected the morale of not only the Nationalist government on Taiwan but also of the noncommunist governments of Southeast Asia. The U.S. position also lessened pressure from the right wing of the Republican party.

By January 1955, the situation flared up again when the Communists invaded the Tachen Islands, located 200 miles north of Taiwan. Although the Eisenhower administration had initially counseled the Nationalist Chinese to strengthen their position on these islands, when the situation became dangerous the administration changed its position and urged evacuation because it now regarded the Tachen Islands as indefensible. Subsequently, it supported only Chiang's claims to Quemoy, Matsu, and a small island group in the Taiwan Straits.

Despite pressure from his advisers to retaliate against the Chinese by bombing the Chinese mainland, the president counseled caution. The potential escalation of the violence had unnerved U.S. allies and even the administration. Later presidential hints that atomic weapons might be used in the dispute aroused the alarm of the U.S. allies, Congress, and public (not to mention the Chinese) and caused the president unsuccessfully to urge Chiang to withdraw some of his troops from Quemoy. This stalemate was then breached by the Chinese offer to negotiate with the United States, an offer the administration grudgingly accepted. With the advent of the talks, an informal cease-fire was established in the Taiwan Straits that lasted for three years.

In July 1958, the People's Republic announced its intention to "liberate" Quemoy and Matsu, and in August they once again began bombarding the islands. The hostilities sputtered through a number of phases, including debate in the United Nations, abusive letters from Khrushchev to Eisenhower, and abortive Communist cease-fires. Finally, the crisis ended in October with Communist pledges to shell only on alternate days and the development of a U.S. understanding with Chiang that the United States would not assist the Nationalists in any invasion of the mainland. After two major crises in Sino-U.S. relations, crises that many feared could lead to World War III, the situation in the Taiwan Straits remained virtually unchanged.

## Sino-U.S. Communication

Sino-U.S. relations during the Eisenhower administration were also characterized by several episodes of reluctant communication, such as the Geneva

Conference of 1954 and the Bandung Conference of 1955. These conferences were multilateral, and the Eisenhower administration worked hard to
ensure that the participants would not ratify a policy that was soft on communism.

More remarkably, after the Eisenhower administration reaffirmed that
it was not according the People's Republic de facto or de jure recognition,
the United States accepted the Chinese proposal to begin direct ambassado-
rial talks. Talks began in Geneva in August 1955. In September, the two
nations reached an agreement on repatriation of civilians that was never
fully effected; no other agreement was ever ratified during the entire course
of the talks, which sputtered on sporadically for another decade.

It was during this period, the mid-1950s, that the Chinese were the
most open to the outside world and to substantive negotiations with the
United States. Their reasons were pragmatic: a desire for international
recognition, a need for trade and credit, and a determination to solve the
Taiwan problem in its favor. Domestic politics constrained the Eisenhower
administration from discussing the status of Taiwan, however, and it was
unwilling to discuss recognition or trade publicly. By 1958, when the administration may secretly have been contemplating a "two Chinas" policy, the
People's Republic was in the middle of the Great Leap Forward and was
unwilling to compromise with imperialists.

## The Kennedy Administration

Sino-U.S. contacts during the Kennedy administration exhibited both the
patterns of the past fourteen years and the beginnings of a new pattern that
was to last until the beginnings of rapprochement. Although the rhetoric
remained hostile, the threat of direct Sino-U.S. hostilities diminished even
as the battle by proxy in Southeast Asia became more intense. The Chinese
avoided provocation in the Taiwan Straits, and the United States once again
"leashed" Chiang Kai-shek.

Direct contacts continued through the Warsaw talks, which continued
to be described by U.S. policymakers as "sterile." Nevertheless, both sides
made some effort at introducing an element of freshness in 1961. The
Chinese told U.S. representatives that they were waiting with "a great sense
of anticipation" for a new U.S. policy at the talks. In response, the United
States tried to develop new initiatives on exchanging news reporters, trade,
and aid. Nothing came of this, however, and the talks thereafter continued in
their familiar unprofitable mode.[10] At the same time, members of the foreign
policy decisionmaking apparatus in Washington openly began to voice their
desire for more meaningful contacts, which they hoped might occur in the
second Kennedy administration. Not even humanitarian aid—food for the
Chinese suffering through a famine—could escape the limits of Cold War
sensibilities, Chinese pride, and U.S. domestic politics. No U.S. food aid

was sent to China despite general approval of the concept by the administration and the U.S. public.

Washington's recognition of the fact that the Soviets and the Chinese were openly expressing different interests, even if they did not grasp the magnitude of the split, also increased fears. Kennedy and his advisers believed that a split might result in the two communist nations vying for power in Asia and the Third World, further destabilizing the international situation. Rather than fighting a monolith, the United States would now have to face two hostile regimes, neither of which had any influence over the other and both of which claimed they would "bury the West."

## The Johnson Administration

The Johnson administration's China policy was a mélange of the hard-line (its Vietnam policy), the predictable (finally implementing limited initiatives that had been under discussion in Washington for over a decade), and the unpredictable (President Johnson's alleged desire for a summit meeting in Beijing). It was a time of changing paradigms, and nobody in the bureaucracy was entirely sure of how to deal with the change, especially the Chinese leaders, who rejected most of the limited approaches fielded by Washington.

Several initiatives were also fielded through the Warsaw talks.[11] The U.S. representatives asked the Chinese if China would be willing to share meteorological information, exchange scientific data, and exchange seed and plant samples.[12] In addition, the State Department encouraged U.S. colleges to invite Chinese scholars to their campuses, and the United States Information Agency invited Chinese journalists to the United States to cover the 1968 election. According to the State Department, these initiatives were rejected.[13]

By 1966, revised passport regulations were issued.[14] Professional journalists, public health doctors, scientists, scholars, and U.S. Red Cross workers were to be allowed to travel to China, as was any individual who could prove a valid reason to visit the People's Republic other than tourism. The Chinese, however, issued only a few visas. In April 1967, a license was granted for the sale of drugs and medical supplies. Originally suggested by the State Department, the proposal was approved by the secretaries of state, the treasury, and commerce and by the president in less than two weeks. The Chinese denounced the attempted sale, however, and though other trade initiatives were discussed repeatedly during the Johnson administration, none were implemented.

The rhetoric changed as well during the latter part of the Johnson administration. Official pronouncements on the possibilities of better future relations with the People's Republic grew increasingly explicit during the administration's final years. According to the departments of state and defense, the administration wanted "to induce present and future communist leaders to reappraise US intentions" and to "arouse Peking's interest in developing a more constructive relationship with us."[15]

These administration initiatives were "too little, too late" (or too early), for the Cultural Revolution had erupted in China in June 1966. Any accommodation with the United States was extremely unlikely while millions of teenage Red Guards were causing chaos in China and while the government of the People's Republic nearly ceased to exist. The administration was dimly aware of this dilemma. Nevertheless, it fielded its cultural and trade initiatives for three reasons: the bomb, Vietnam, and the Cultural Revolution.

China's entry into the nuclear club in 1964 altered the balance of power in Asia to the apparent detriment of U.S. allies on the continent. Encouraging China's entry into the community of nations as a means of preventing potentially aggressive actions became critically important.[16] It became even more important after the United States began bombing North Vietnam, when the world began to worry about a direct Sino-U.S. conflagration. Policymakers in Washington believed that while the United States was acting tough in Vietnam, it could afford to introduce some flexibility into its China policy without appearing weak.

The Cultural Revolution posed a more complex policy problem. President Johnson's advisers well understood that the United States could not determine events on the mainland, and they had no desire to try. They did, however, believe that a new generation of leaders would emerge from the chaos and that the United States should try to impress these men and women with the United States' good intentions. Without any basis in reality, the U.S. policymakers wishfully believed that the limited changes in policy they had introduced would influence a new generation of Chinese to overcome two decades of nationalist and socialist propaganda. President Johnson could not wait for a new generation, however, and when rapprochement finally came, it was the older generation, both in Washington and Beijing, that spearheaded it.

## Nixon and Kissinger in China

On July 15, 1971, "without warning to friend or foe,"[17] President Nixon announced that his national security adviser, Henry Kissinger, had recently returned from a visit to the People's Republic and that he himself planned to visit the communist capital. The world was astounded and pleased, particularly because President Nixon's political career was based on vigilant anticommunism. With his television announcement, the People's Republic of China was transformed overnight in the minds of the U.S. public from a "red peril"—if Richard Nixon was willing to visit the capital of the People's Republic of China, it really must be all right—to a fascinating, exotic travel destination. Nixon and Mao, the two former archenemies, were drawn together by a desire to play two sides of the strategic triangle against the third. By opening a dialogue with Beijing, Washington expected it could enhance its security by playing off Beijing against Moscow. But before the United States could play its China card, it had to address the many issues that had prevented a meaningful Sino-U.S. dialogue for so many years. Official recognition was most imperative to the Chinese over the short term, and a resolution of the Taiwan question in favor of reunification was a long-term goal. U.S. goals, in addition to changing the dimensions of Soviet policy, were to lessen tensions in East and Southeast Asia. At a time when the United States was actively engaged in a war in Vietnam, this was no easy task.

In February 1972, President Nixon met Mao Zedong in Beijing, "which conveyed to the world that the period of Sino-American hostility was over—indeed, that the two great nations were moving toward cooperation on fundamentals of foreign policy."[18] During President Nixon's trip, the two nations replaced twenty-three years of hostility with an uneasy compromise—the Shanghai Communiqué—in which the United States and the People's Republic agreed to disagree about Indochina, Korea, the Indo-Pakistani conflict, and the status of Japan. To achieve "progress toward the normalization of relations between China and the United States," the United States ceased fighting for Taiwan:

> The United States acknowledges that all Chinese on either side of the Taiwan Strait maintain there is but one China and that Taiwan is a part of China. The United States Government does not challenge that position. It reaffirms its interest in a peaceful settlement of the Taiwan question by the Chinese themselves.[19]

Containment of communism had been replaced as the central tenet governing U.S. policy toward China; Nixon and Kissinger instead adopted the notion of the *strategic triangle,* with all the complex diplomacy that would entail to ensure a balance of power. It worked—the Soviets were soon courting the United States.

Despite President Nixon's promises to withdraw U.S. troops from Taiwan, de jure recognition would take another seven years, primarily because of congressional distaste for the complete abandonment of a long-time ally and because of leadership crises in both countries. Nevertheless, with China's entry into the United Nations in September and with U.S. acceptance of the permanence of the Communist Chinese regime, 1971 marked the end of the international isolation of the People's Republic.

## Recognition at Last

The United States and the People's Republic exchanged official delegations after the Nixon trip, and trade increased drastically between the two countries, but official recognition did not come about until the Carter administration. In 1979, because of fears that the Chinese would not tolerate an unofficial status of quasi-relations for much longer, the United States formally recognized the People's Republic of China, thirty years after its creation. Although late, the results were dramatic. Sino-U.S. trade increased 200 percent between 1978 and 1979, and U.S. tourism in China increased 300 percent.[20] Equally important, U.S. perceptions of China were evolving. Deng Xiaoping's trip to the United States in early 1979, when he visited Washington and Disney World, humanized China to millions of U.S. citizens who watched his visit on the nightly news. For a nation that only recently had been portrayed as armed and dangerous to U.S. security, normalization of perceptions was as important as normalization of diplomatic relations.

With full diplomatic relations between Washington and Beijing, the United States no longer recognized the Nationalist government on Taiwan as the government of China. To circumvent this derecognition, the U.S. embassy in Taipei became a nongovernmental agency that hired furloughed State Department employees (who miraculously became State Department employees again after their stint in Taiwan was up). The defense commitment to Taiwan was more difficult to abrogate, even though U.S. troops were withdrawn from Taiwan. Congress, however, refused to accept Chinese demands for immediate abrogation of the Mutual Defense Treaty of 1954. Rather, it passed the Taiwan Relations Act, which declared, "It is the policy of the United States to provide Taiwan with arms of a defensive character; and to maintain the capacity of the United States to resist any resort to force or other forms of coercion that would jeopardize the security or the social or economic system, of the people on Taiwan."[21]

The Chinese objected, but not too strenuously, because of their desire for leverage against the Soviet Union and, perhaps more important, because of their desire for increased access to U.S. capital and technology. Sino-U.S. relations continued to be difficult, however, particularly in the area of arms sales. The fact that $200 million in U.S. arms were delivered to Taiwan in 1979 and $625 million in 1980[22] confirmed Beijing's worst suspicions—that Washington was in reality trying to implement a two-Chinas policy. With the Soviet invasion of Afghanistan, however, the Chinese began cooperating with the U.S. military and purchasing U.S. arms. Following the visit of the U.S. secretary of defense to Beijing in January 1980, the Chinese even agreed to permit establishment of a joint intelligence listening post in Xinjiang to monitor Soviet military activities.[23] Fearful of Soviet expansionism and worried by their own recent military failure in Vietnam, China's leaders acceded to a de facto two-Chinas policy out of expediency.

## The Reagan Years

In his 1980 presidential campaign, Ronald Reagan adopted the conservative position, lambasting the Carter administration for its abandonment of the

United States' longtime ally, Taiwan. If elected, he promised he would review Sino-U.S. relations, with the goal of reestablishing relations with Taiwan. Supporters of continued U.S. relations with Beijing greeted Reagan's inaugural as president with great trepidation. China, too, was nervous.

Much to everyone's surprise, particularly many conservative Republicans, President Reagan eventually adopted a China policy that neither Henry Kissinger nor Jimmy Carter could object to. In August 1982, both countries issued the Communiqué on United States Arms Sales to Taiwan. In the communiqué, the Reagan administration agreed to continue the Shanghai Communiqué position that Taiwan is a part of China and that unification would be an internal matter. In addition, the United States agreed to not increase its arms sales to Taiwan and to "reduce gradually its sales of arms to Taiwan, leading over a period of time to a final resolution."[24] President Reagan explained his views on China as follows:

> Building a strong and lasting relationship with China has been an important foreign policy goal of four consecutive American administrations. Such a relationship is vital to our long-term national security interests and contributes to stability in East Asia. It is in the national interests of the United States that this important strategic relationship be advanced.[25]

To prove his point, President Reagan visited China in April 1984, his first visit to a communist country.

Though differences over international security issues, human rights, trade, and limitations on U.S. sales of dual-use technology remained, the Reagan administration sought to resolve these differences through diplomatic discussions. Many felt that Sino-U.S. relations had advanced to the point that, according to then undersecretary of state Michael Armacost, "we have been able to discuss the most difficult issues without major adverse consequences, while continuing to cooperate and advance our relationship as a whole."[26] Even Chinese suppression of Tibetan activists and its missile sales to Iran and Saudi Arabia, both in 1987, did not derail Sino-U.S. relations or prevent dramatic increases in U.S. military sales to China (see Table 5.1). Official and public perceptions of China continued to be positive.[27]

Why did Ronald Reagan change his China policy so dramatically once he became president? The most cogent explanation is the old adage "where you stand is where you sit." It was easy for a conservative candidate for president to argue for abrogation of diplomatic relations with the People's Republic of China in favor of relations with Taiwan, but for a president to do so was far more difficult. A complete rupture of relations with Beijing would have heightened tensions in the Taiwan Straits, and the Chinese might even have responded by putting increased military pressure on Taiwan. The rest of East Asia, too, feared a China not allied to either superpower more

**Table 5.1    U.S. Military Sales to China**

| Year | Total Deliveries |
|------|------------------|
| 1981 | $0 |
| 1982 | $1,000,000 |
| 1983 | $209,000 |
| 1984 | $8,043,000 |
| 1985 | $46,671,000 |
| 1986 | $55,790,000 |
| 1987 | $37,814,000 |
| 1988 | $88,013,000 |
| 1989 | $106,215,000 |
| 1990 | $3,615,000 |

*Source:* Harry Harding, *A Fragile Relationship: The United States and China Since 1972,* Washington, D.C.: Brookings, 1992. p. 371. Reprinted with permission.

than a China with ties to the United States. President Reagan realized that China was strategically, militarily, and politically more important than Taiwan. In view of Reagan's initial belligerent attitude towards the Soviet Union, Sino-U.S. ties were important to ensure that the strategic triangle would be organized in a way detrimental to Moscow.

## THE POST–COLD WAR ERA

### Bush, Beijing, and Baghdad

When George Bush was inaugurated as president in January 1989, Sino-U.S. relations were perhaps better than they had ever been. Even with the continual problems over Taiwan and controversies over trade issues, which increased as trade increased, it seemed that relations between Washington and Beijing had stabilized into a normal pattern characterized by diplomatic interchanges to resolve difficulties. Moreover, George Bush had real China experience; he had headed the United States Liaison Office in Beijing for a few years in the 1970s. The future of Sino-U.S. relations looked, if not bright, at least stable.

But any illusions of normalcy in Sino-U.S. relations collapsed on June 4, 1989, as Chinese tanks crushed demonstrations in the environs of Tiananmen Square. The world was outraged, and the U.S. people and Congress called for sanctions. On June 5, 1989, President Bush announced that the following steps would be taken in response to the Chinese military actions against the demonstrators in Beijing:

- suspension of all government-to-government military sales and commercial exports of military materials

- suspension of exchange visits by U.S. and Chinese military personnel
- extension of assistance to the Red Cross for its work in China
- sympathetic review of requests by Chinese students studying in the United States to extend their stay
- a review of other U.S.-China programs and activities[28]

President Bush was reluctant, however, to cut China off completely. Anxious to maintain contact and believing that direct talks would have more influence on China than studious avoidance, Bush sent his national security adviser and deputy secretary of state on a secret mission to Beijing in July 1989 and on another mission in December that was announced to the public after the fact. Pictures in the press of two aides toasting the very leaders that had ordered the military to fire on unarmed protestors led to severe criticism of the Bush administration. Why, many critics asked, was it necessary to send secret envoys to China? Why drink toasts to the "Butchers of Beijing"? Would it not have been better to condemn the Tiananmen massacre while at the same time allowing cool but correct contacts through official diplomatic channels, rather than engaging in secret shuttle diplomacy?

Subsequent public and congressional criticisms of President Bush's China policy led to two congressional attempts to legislate conditions on renewal of MFN trading privileges. Both were thwarted only by presidential vetoes. President Bush's philosophy of Sino-U.S. relations, articulated in a 1991 address at Yale University, was that "if we withdraw MFN or imposed conditions that would make trade impossible, we would punish South China . . . that very region where free-market reforms and the challenge to central authority are the strongest."[29]

Perhaps equally as persuasive to President Bush was the fact that he

---

### Most-Favored-Nation Status

China was accorded most-favored-nation (preferential tariff) status, which the United States accords to virtually every nation in the world, in 1980. The Jackson-Vanik amendment of 1974, however, prohibits the U.S. government from establishing MFN status with communist countries that do not allow free emigration. To circumvent the amendment, the president can issue a waiver if he has received "assurances" that the country's practices would "henceforth lead substantially to freedom of emigration."

[Tan Qingshan, *The Making of U.S. China Policy: From Normalization to the Post–Cold War Era* (Boulder, Colorado: Lynne Rienner Publishers, 1992), p. 60.]

needed China in 1990 and 1991. China could veto any United Nations Security Council resolution condemning Saddam Hussein's invasion of Kuwait, and twelve resolutions were voted on in the four months following the Iraqi invasion of Kuwait in August 1990. Official U.S. censure of Beijing's handling of the Tiananmen demonstrations was therefore toned down. For this, the People's Republic showed its thanks by abstaining on the vote to use force against Iraq (Resolution 678). China thus had it both ways—it had not approved of the use of force, but it had not disapproved either. It had not angered its African and Asian allies by condoning U.S. intervention, yet it had not incurred U.S. wrath by vetoing the operation. Some call this approach a policy of "maximizing China's rights and interests and minimizing China's responsibility and normative costs."[30]

After defeating Iraq, the Bush administration had perhaps the highest public opinion ratings ever. It seemed that arguments over China policy would be won without difficulty by a president who had demonstrated his foreign policy expertise. And President Bush was still intent on maintaining good relations with China. To that end, Secretary of State Baker visited Beijing in November 1991, officially ending the suspension of high-level contacts.

During the remaining year of the Bush administration, China and the United States had some good times, some bad. Several agreements were signed that seemed to create a framework for resolving the trade and human rights problems that continued to plague Sino-U.S. relations. On August 7, 1992, the United States and China formally signed a memorandum of understanding to ensure that products made by forced labor in China are not exported to the United States, and both nations signed a memorandum of understanding in which China agreed to reduce controls on imports by December 31, 1993. China also acceded to the Missile Technology Control Regime (MTCR) in early 1992,[31] after having agreed to join the Nuclear Non-Proliferation Treaty in 1991. These signs of progress were counteracted, however, on September 2, 1992, when the Bush administration approved the sale of F-16 fighter jets to Taiwan. In a desperate election campaign, President Bush abandoned his many years of promoting U.S. relations with Beijing in favor of courting conservative votes at home. The Chinese, needless to say, were not pleased, and Bush's China policy ended on a sour note. Once defeated, President Bush changed course again. He ended his presidency by revising his China policy to allow official interchanges and resume trade and arms sales, allegedly to allow the Clinton administration to begin with a clean slate.[32]

## Bill Clinton's Engaging of China

Candidate Bill Clinton severely criticized China's human rights record, and in his first year of office the situation did not improve. The State Department's annual review found that China's "overall human rights record in 1993 fell far short of internationally accepted norms as it continued to repress domestic critics and failed to control abuses by its own security forces."[33] Yet the Clinton administration moderated its campaign position by seeking to step up engagement with China in order to give Beijing an incentive to meet human rights demands before Congress voted to limit renewal of most-favored-nation status. In May 1993, President Clinton determined "that a one-year extension of his waiver authority for China would substantially promote the objectives of the Jackson-Vanik amendment." At the same time, he issued Executive Order 12850 naming the conditions that China would have to meet to continue to receive renewals. China's will to meet these demands, some of which it believes infringe on its sovereignty, was put into doubt during Secretary of State

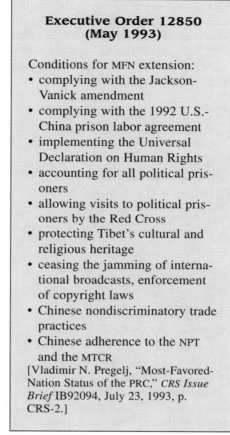

**Executive Order 12850 (May 1993)**

Conditions for MFN extension:
- complying with the Jackson-Vanick amendment
- complying with the 1992 U.S.-China prison labor agreement
- implementing the Universal Declaration on Human Rights
- accounting for all political prisoners
- allowing visits to political prisoners by the Red Cross
- protecting Tibet's cultural and religious heritage
- ceasing the jamming of international broadcasts, enforcement of copyright laws
- Chinese nondiscriminatory trade practices
- Chinese adherence to the NPT and the MTCR

[Vladimir N. Pregelj, "Most-Favored-Nation Status of the PRC," *CRS Issue Brief* IB92094, July 23, 1993, p. CRS-2.]

**Table 5.2    Illustrative MFN and Full Duty Rates Applicable to Imports from China**

| Import | MFN Rate | Full Rate |
|---|---|---|
| Shellfish | free | free |
| Men's trousers (synthetic fiber) | 29.7% | 90% |
| Knit women's sweaters, vegetable fiber (excluding cotton) | 5% | 45% |
| Women's silk apparel | 6.9% | 65% |
| Artificial flowers (synthetic fiber) | 9% | 71.5% |
| Crude petroleum | 0.62% | 1.24% |
| Audio tape players | 3.7% | 35% |
| Hair dressing appliances | 3.9% | 35% |
| Luggage and handbags (textile fiber) | 20% | 65% |
| Plastic handbags | 20% | 45% |
| Stuffed toys | free | 70% |
| Various other toys | 6.8% | 70% |

*Source:* Vladimir N. Pregelj, "Most-Favored Nation Status of the PRC," *CRS Issue Brief* IB92094, July 23, 1993, p. CRS-4.

Warren Christopher's visit to Beijing in March 1994, during which time a number of Chinese dissidents were imprisoned. Pushing most-favored-nation renewal through Congress becomes more and more a political liability for each successive U.S. administration. Table 5.2 shows the difference in MFN and full duty rates on imports from China, highlighting the incentive China has to maintain MFN status.

Trade issues also continue to plague Sino-U.S. relations in the Clinton era. Again, instances of cooperation are followed by acrimonious disputes over the United States' negative balance of trade and China's limited markets. China's trade surplus with the United States is approaching $25 billion per year, second only to Japan's.[34] Many believe this is due to unfair Chinese trade practices. To discuss trade issues, President Clinton convened the Joint Economic Committee, which had not met since the Tiananmen massacre.[35] Among the agreements reached with China was a textile accord that limited growth in Chinese textile imports to the United States and promised greater enforcement to prevent cheating on quotas.[36]

However, in August 1993, the administration imposed sanctions on an estimated $1 billion in high-technology trade after intelligence indicated that China was shipping missiles to Pakistan in violation of the Missile Technology Control Regime. After announcing the sanctions, the administration also quickly sought to negotiate their end, and by November 1993 it had agreed to allow a U.S. company to sell a supercomputer to China's State Meteorological Administration. Despite Pentagon and congressional misgivings that the supercomputer might be put to mili-

---

**Standing Up to China**

"When dealing with China, it sometimes helps to see matters through Chinese eyes. As Beijing views it, a great power must always insist on being treated with due respect. To behave otherwise is to acknowledge inferiority and therefore to forfeit influence. During Secretary of State Christopher's weekend visit to Beijing, Chinese leaders aggressively asserted what they see as the prerogatives of China. . . . For the sake of a healthy U.S.-China relationship, Washington is now obliged to respond with equal firmness. . . . The Clinton Administration needs instead to be forthright about its continued determination to insist on human rights progress. It especially needs to dispel China's impression that it can exploit differences between various policy makers in the Administration, Congress, and the business community.
[Excerpts from a *New York Times* editorial, March 16, 1994, p. A20.]

tary use, the Clinton administration was more concerned with promoting trade and alleviating the United States' trade deficit with China.[37]

In 1993 the United States and China also agreed to resume contacts between the Pentagon and the Chinese Army.[38] In November 1993 high-level Chinese and U.S. military officials met for the first time since Tiananmen. Weapons sales were not discussed, but the two sides agreed to "future dialogue" on topics like international peacekeeping operations and the problems of converting defense industries to civilian use. The U.S. delegate to the talks praised China's peacekeeping record in Cambodia and its diversification of its military industries into civilian areas, but stated that the Tiananmen Square massacre "has taken its toll in terms of mutual understanding."[39]

The two intertwined issues of human rights and trade will continue to determine the course of Sino-U.S. relations over the next few years. So long as Beijing's leaders perceive Washington's linking of trade with human rights as an infringement on China's security, they will react strongly to any admonishments from the United States. Their attitude was never more clearly illustrated than when Secretary of State Warren Christopher visited Beijing in March 1994. Arriving, unfortunately for him, when the National People's Congress was in session, Communist Party leaders perceived the need to take a strong stance against U.S. admonitions on human rights issues because of their need to appear strong to an increasingly disaffected governmental and party bureaucra-

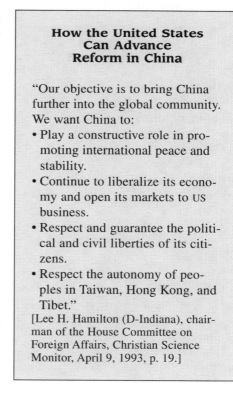

**How the United States Can Advance Reform in China**

"Our objective is to bring China further into the global community. We want China to:
• Play a constructive role in promoting international peace and stability.
• Continue to liberalize its economy and open its markets to US business.
• Respect and guarantee the political and civil liberties of its citizens.
• Respect the autonomy of peoples in Taiwan, Hong Kong, and Tibet."
[Lee H. Hamilton (D-Indiana), chairman of the House Committee on Foreign Affairs, *Christian Science Monitor*, April 9, 1993, p. 19.]

cy. Secretary Christopher was greeted almost rudely by his Chinese hosts and was left with nothing to show for his trip except criticism from home for allowing himself to be humiliated. The official Chinese position is that "dialogue is beneficial, while pressure is futile."[40]

Bill Clinton came to appreciate the Chinese resistance to pressure by May 26, 1994, when he announced, "I have decided that the United States should renew Most Favored Nation trading status toward China. This decision, I believe, offers us the best opportunity to lay the basis for long-term sustainable progress in human rights and for the advancement of our other interests with China. . . . I am moving, therefore, to delink human rights from the annual extension of Most Favored Nation trading status for China."[41] His only qualification was to ban the import of munitions, principally guns and ammunition, from China.

Why did President Clinton's China policy develop to the point where it was indistinguishable from President Bush's China policy? At the same time that China and the United States were heatedly discussing the relationship of human rights issues to trade, China was expected to spend about $560 billion in infrastructure projects between 1994 and the end of the century. U.S. companies hope to contract for some of these projects, and the Chinese leadership is encouraging them. Now that the anti-Soviet rationale for Sino-U.S. relations no longer exists, China's rulers counted on U.S. capitalists to blunt the efforts of human rights advocates to abrogate MFN status, and they were correct in their assessment. The U.S.-China Business Council and other representatives of the U.S. business community mounted a large lobbying effort in favor of MFN renewal. They were joined, paradoxically, by Chinese intellectuals and Chinese entrepreneurs, who feared that termination of MFN status would strengthen hard-liners in Beijing and that increasing foreign trade would be a better lever to liberalize the regime than would economic pressure. Ironically, party moderates worked with U.S. capitalists and industrialists, who feared loss of investment in China if MFN status was not renewed, to promote economic development in the People's Republic. Both nations would have suf-

---

**U.S. Interests in Sino-U.S. Relations**

Global Interests
• United Nations Security Council
• Military Modernization
• Environmental Protection
• Migration
• Arms Sales
Regional Interests
• North Korean nuclear program
• Cambodia
• Sino-Indian rapprochement/Sino-Pakistani relations
• Taiwan
• Hong Kong
• U.S. relations with Japan and with China/security balance in East Asia
Bilateral Interests
• trade/jobs
• human rights
• arms sales
[Atlantic Council of the United States & National Committee on United States-China Relations. *United States and China: Relations at a Crossroads,* February 1993.]

fered: China would have lost an export market for its textiles, toys, etc., while the United States would have lost a market for its agricultural and high-technology products. Although dollar estimates of the potential disruption in trade differed, the damage to Sino-U.S. amity would have been immense, and political relations would have been disrupted to an even greater degree than economic relations.

## POLICY OPTIONS

Ultimately, the disposition of each of the issues affecting Sino-U.S. relations will be greatly affected by the results of the coming succession struggle in China. How the next generation of leaders redefines Chinese security and sovereignty will do much to define China's place in the post–Cold War era. How China's next generation of leaders chooses to respond to Washington will affect not only Sino-U.S. relations but also China's future role in regional and international fora. The state of Sino-U.S. relations, too, will be predicated on who succeeds Deng Xiaoping.

### Option 1: Security in Asia

China's Communist leaders and even its intellectuals view the United States with a mixture of dread and desire. Many acknowledge that the Chinese goal of a socialist market economy will be difficult if Sino-U.S. trade relations are disrupted, but some also fear U.S. hegemony in the post–Cold War era. One classified Chinese analysis states, "The United States may be running out of energy, but it has never abandoned its ambition to rule the world, and its military interventionism is becoming more open."[42] Some even believe that Washington is not averse to disrupting Sino-U.S. trade relations in the hope that the resulting economic dislocation would bring political and social dislocation similar to that seen in Eastern Europe and the former Soviet Union. Continued indiscriminate U.S. pressure and even threats on human rights issues, which the Chinese leadership regard as an infringement on their sovereignty, only fuel Chinese fears of the U.S. drive to control and dominate.

　　Other Chinese security analysts fear that China will replace the Soviet Union as the justification for a continued U.S. military presence in Asia.[43] The increases in Chinese defense spending since 1989, as well as Chinese arms sales, fuel U.S. fears of a Chinese drive for military domination of the area. Concerns over the security of Japan, South Korea, and Southeast Asia—particularly in light of possible conflict over control over the Spratly and Paracel islands—are likely to dictate a continued U.S. presence. If Sino-U.S. relations break down over other contentious issues, such as Chinese reluctance to adhere to the Missile Technology Control Regime, China may

> ### U.S. Tasks in Asia
> ### for the Next Decade
>
> • "Involve itself more extensively in
> Asia's economic expansion and con-
> tribute to making that expansion
> durable and equitable. The growing
> Chinese economy will be a major part
> of Asia's overall expansion.
> • Assist the region in developing eco-
> nomic and security relationships that
> will encourage cooperation, discour-
> age destructive economic competition
> and regional arms races and conflict,
> and contribute to the peaceful resolu-
> tion of conflicts that do arise. Since
> the global nature of U.S. interests
> would unavoidably involve the U.S. in
> any large-scale conflict in Asia, it is
> best to help prevent the emergence of
> conflict through multilateral coopera-
> tion that encompasses the region and
> spans both sides of the Pacific.
> • Encourage further development of
> free-market economies and pluralistic
> forms of governance."
> [Atlantic Council of the United States and
> National Committee on United States–China
> Relations. *United States and China:*
> *Relations at a Crossroads,* February 1993,
> pp. 3–4.]

well be used to provide the rationale by which U.S. officials convince the U.S. public to remain engaged in East Asia.

In the post–Cold War era, the balance of power in East Asia may shift in several directions. The United States will be forced to develop a coherent response to each of the possible scenarios. Winston Lord, former U.S. ambassador to China, told Congress, "We must develop new mechanisms to manage or prevent emerging concerns. We have enormous stakes in the Pacific. We need to integrate out economic, political and security policies. We need fresh approaches and structures of cooperation."[44] One scenario was enunciated by former Secretary of State Alexander M. Haig, Jr., who argued in October 1993 that Tiananmen should not guide U.S. policy and that the United States cannot impose its human rights standards. Rather, he advocated a balance-of-power approach to U.S. relations with East Asia, whereby the United States pursues good relations with both China and Japan, thereby keeping these two potential superpowers balanced.[45] Many Asian leaders also want the United States to act as a balance between China and Japan, but not at the price of Washington domination of the area.

China, concerned over perceived U.S. attempts to interfere in its domestic affairs (e.g., promoting human rights and political openness), may also ally itself with other nations that are concerned that the United States as the sole superpower may attempt to become the global police force. One U.S. analyst suggests, "Should the relations between Washington and

Beijing continue to unravel, China would then become a viable partner for Russia or Japan if either finds itself at odds with U.S. policy in the region. A Sino-Russian or Sino-Japanese alliance thus is possible if the balance-of-power game is steadfastly played in a twenty-first century multipolar world."[46] For now, however, China seeks informal security arrangements in Asia that preclude any one nation from being too influential. From the Chinese perspective, it is better to solve security problems by bilateral diplomacy or through the United Nations than through formally structured security pacts. China's goal is to keep the United States, Japan, Russia, etc., from dominating the decision-making process on East Asian security issues.

> ## To Talk About Modernization Without Mentioning Human Rights Is Like Climbing a Tree to Catch a Fish
>
> "Lately there have been many incidents in which people have been arrested or detained in Beijing and Shanghai for interrogation because of their ideas and their exercise of free speech. World public opinion has reacted strongly. People of insight who are dedicated to the cause of our country's modernization are shocked, upset and worried. . . . We appeal to the authorities to bravely end our country's history of punishing people for their ideas, speeches and writings, and release all those imprisoned because of their ideas and speeches. We believe that only after human rights are respected and all rights of citizens are secured will society achieve true stability. Other contradictions will intensify, causing unmanageable turmoil."
>
> [Statement issued by seven Chinese intellectuals during Secretary of State Warren Christopher's March 1994 visit to Beijing, *New York Times,* March 11, 1994, p. A10.]

The United States, for its part, will have to decide whether to continue its military presence in East and Southeast Asia. Despite a resurgent U.S. isolationism, many still argue that "continued U.S. presence will not stop or even significantly slow the growth of indigenous forces, but it will provide a framework for orderly growth and conservative use of these forces. The sudden decompression resulting from the disappearance of both Soviet and U.S. power from Southeast Asia is not desirable."[47] Yet the United States will also have to recognize the fears of Asian leaders that a formal security structure dominated by the United States would lead to another era of U.S. preponderance in the region. The Chinese leadership, in particular, demands that the United States treat the People's Republic with a respect and dignity befitting the largest regional power in East Asia. If the United States remains militarily engaged in Asia in the post–Cold War era, even as the sole remaining superpower, it will have to play by the new rules, which place greater value on local dignity and sovereignty.

## Option 2: Economic Relations

The increasing U.S. trade deficit with China, second only to Japan in 1992, combined with the continuing controversy over MFN renewal, use of prison labor, evasion of quotas through transshipment to Hong Kong, etc., may lead to increased Sino-U.S. tensions and potential future trade disruptions. These might include congressional approval of only conditional MFN status, U.S. sanctions on Chinese products, U.S. opposition to Chinese entry into GATT, etc. Although China is still accorded MFN privileges, controversies over trade issues will continue. Obvious problems over the next decade—including Chinese efforts to circumvent textile quotas, U.S. efforts to limit sale of advanced technology to China, etc.—will continue to make economic relations difficult. If Sino-U.S. diplomacy is successful, trade issues will be addressed through bilateral diplomacy, with each side compromising somewhat to prevent a breakdown in relations; if diplomatic discussions break down, a trade war may well ensue.

## Option 3: Greater China

China has never ruled out the use of force to reunite Taiwan with mainland China. Although Chinese leaders in Beijing have always been unwilling to send their military across the Taiwan Straits, primarily because of fears of international sanctions, a resurgent China may chose the military options, particularly if the Taiwanese independence movement becomes stronger and more outspoken. In addition, if the Beijing succession struggle becomes too disorderly, one or another faction might well seek support by mounting an expedition to unify China. Successful integration of Hong Kong would allow China's leaders to present the "one country, two systems" approach as a model for Taiwanese integration into the mainland. In that case, China's leaders could remind Washington of its commitment to a Chinese solution to the Taiwan issue and to a cessation of arms sales to Taiwan.

 The implications for both the People's Republic and the United States are obvious. If the People's Republic mounts a military expedition against Taiwan, congressional and public opinion will be aroused. Though commitment of U.S. troops to the actual defense of Taiwan is uncertain, given Washington's reluctance to become involved in ground wars in Asia, U.S. air and naval support activities might be provided to the Taiwanese military. Thus would end any U.S. rapprochement with China.

 What the United States must hope for is the gradual integration of Hong Kong into China, followed by the economic integration of Taiwan into greater China. The economies of China, Hong Kong, and Taiwan are becoming increasingly interwoven. As the three economies become one large inter-connected entity, the impetus to maintain good trade relations with Europe and the Americas will increase. At the same time, as China's economy becomes more marketized, its political system will be forced to become more open, which will reduce friction with those nations concerned about human rights violations. The development of the Greater Chinese economy is important to the United States for at least four reasons:

- With the increasing ties between southern China and Hong Kong and Taiwan, the Chinese people in Guangdong and Fujian provinces are increasingly influenced more by their capitalist neighbors than by Beijing.
- With the southern Chinese, Hong Kong, and Taiwan economies becoming interdependent, the security of the latter two nations is enhanced.
- The greater Chinese economy provides a platform from which the United States can develop its economic and cultural ties throughout the East Asian region.
- Greater economic growth will lead to the growth of a middle class that will begin to demand change, especially because this middle class will be in contact with the slowly liberalizing societies of Hong Kong and Taiwan.[48]

Greater economic integration would lead to more political cooperation. Closer political ties between the People's Republic and Taiwan would be the next obvious step, perhaps eventually leading to peaceful political unification or at least a Chinese economic and political community.

## Option 4: Quiet Diplomacy

Scholars of Sino-U.S. relations now advocate "quiet diplomacy." Instead of threatening China each year, they advocate a carrot-and-stick approach. This approach might include trying to pressure China to improve its human rights record through international organizations instead of revocation of most-favored-nation status. According to Barber Conable, former president of the World Bank,

> We need to develop other instruments to promote our human rights objectives, not only in China, but elsewhere as well. . . . I am inclined to move conflict over human rights into multilateral fora where the accumulated weight of world opinion can have its effect. . . . A package of moves needs to be put together in the next couple of months in which both the PRC and the US seek to meet concerns of the other. A set of confidence inducing, reciprocal, and parallel moves that are clear and understood to both sides should be sufficient. . . . Among the compo-

nents of such a package might be: further significant moves forward by Beijing in areas mentioned above and in the President's May 28th executive order; staunch American support for China's accession to GATT as appropriate; Washington's removal of most of the sanctions imposed on Beijing since 1989; high-level visits in both directions, including a visit to China by the President or Vice President at an appropriate time in the not-too-distant future; and, increased Chinese vigor in faithfully implementing the various trade and intellectual property agreements arrived at in 1992 and this year. Further, progress might be made in controlling the flow of conventional and unconventional weaponry and technology in the region and increasing Chinese support for firmness in the current nuclear problem with North Korea. And finally there are areas of potential cooperation between China and the United States that we have not previously exploited . . . for example, allow China to participate in USAID's US-Asia Environmental Partnership Program.[49]

Isolating China is no longer an option, according to this school of thought; rather, the best way to change a nation is by engaging it.

## DISCUSSION QUESTIONS

1. In the 1990s, to what extent is it in China's interest to comply with U.S. demands for changes in its domestic policies?
2. What is the current status of Sino-U.S. relations? Are the two nations partners, opponents, or a combination of both? Explain.
3. As an emerging world power, is China entitled to greater respect for its sovereignty and more equal treatment from the United States?
4. If Taiwan seeks to abandon the "one China" policy, establish a democratic political system, and seek membership in the United Nations, how should China and the United States react?
5. Is China justified in demanding that its MFN status with the United States not be made conditional on Beijing's human rights or arms sales policies?
6. In what ways can China utilize the assistance of other states to influence Washington to respect its sovereignty and treat it more equally in the international community?
7. To what extent do other Asian states agree with China in opposing Washington's demands for more formal structures in the Asia Pacific rimland to deal with political-security and economic problems?
8. How do different interests inside China affect its relations with the United States? How do different interests inside the United States affect U.S. policy toward China?
9. How can Beijing take advantage of different interests inside the United States to foil U.S. attempts to link China's human rights policy to the extension of China's MFN status?
10. To what extent do Beijing and Washington disagree on the role that China should play in different regions of the world?
11. To what extent do Beijing and Washington disagree on the role that the two states should play in the United Nations?
12. What are the possibilities for overcoming Sino-U.S. disagreements on issues such as nuclear testing and eliminating nuclear weapons and other weapons of mass destruction, as well as delivery systems for such weapons?
13. Now that the Cold War is over and China is undergoing major changes as it seeks to improve its relationships with the outside world, to what extent should the United States cooperate with China in modernizing its military forces? Explain.
14. In the twenty-first century, to what extent are China and the United States likely to be rivals or partners in the emerging global system? Explain.
15. In the 1990s, why is the United States likely to have a greater effect on China than any other country? With the passage of time, is the U.S. impact on China likely to increase, decrease, or remain stable? Why?

## SUGGESTED READINGS

Alexander, Bevin. *The Strange Connection.* New York: Greenwood Press, 1992.

Bernstein, Robert L., and Richard Dicker."Human Rights First." *Foreign Policy,* no. 94 (Spring 1994): pp. 43–47.

Bert, Wayne. "Chinese Policies and U.S. Interests in Southeast Asia." *Asian Survey* 33, no. 3 (March 1993): pp. 317–332.

Bush, Richard. "Clinton and China: Scenarios for the Future." *China Business Review* 20 (January–February 1993): pp. 16–20.

Cohen, Warren. *America's Response to China: A History of Sino-American Relations.* 3d edition. New York: Columbia University Press, 1990.

Copper, John Franklin. *China Diplomacy: The Washington-Taipei-Beijing Triangle.* Boulder, Colorado: Westview Press, 1992.

Drinan, Robert F., and Teresa Kuo."The 1991 Battle for Human Rights in China." *Human Rights Quarterly* 14 (February 1992): pp. 21–42.

Harding, Harry. *A Fragile Relationship: The United States and China Since 1972.* Washington, D.C: Brookings, 1992.

Kim, Hong N., and Jack L. Hammersmith. "U.S.-China Relations in the Post-Normalization Era, 1979–1985." *Pacific Affairs* 59, no. 1 (Spring 1986): pp. 69–91.

Kim, Ilpyong J., ed. *Beyond the Strategic Triangle.* New York: Paragon House, 1992.

Kristof, Nicholas D. "The Rise of China." Foreign Affairs 72, no. 5 (November/December 1993): pp. 59-73.

Levine, Steven I. "China and America: The Resilient Relationship." *Current History* 5, no. 91 (September 1992): pp. 241–246.

Lilley, James R. "Freedom through Trade." *Foreign Policy* no. 94 (Spring 1994): pp. 37–42.

———, and Wendell L. Willkie, II, eds. *Beyond MFN: Trade with China and American Interests.* Washington, D.C.: The AEI Press, 1994.

Munro, Ross H. "Awakening Dragon: The Real Danger in Asia Is from China." *Policy Review* no. 62 (Fall 1992): pp. 10–16.

Oxnam, Robert B. "Asia/Pacific Challenges." *Foreign Affairs* 72, no. 1 (1993): pp. 57–73.

Ross, Robert S., ed. *China, the United States and the Soviet Union: Tripolarity and Policy Making in the Cold War.* Armonk, New York: M.E. Sharpe, 1993.

Ross, Robert S. "U.S. Policy Toward China," in Robert J. Art and Seyom Brown, eds., *U.S. Foreign Policy: The Search for a New Role,* New York: Macmillan, 1993, pp. 338-357.

Schaller, Michael. *The United States and China in the Twentieth Century.* New York: Oxford University Press, 1979.

Tan Qingshan. *The Making of U.S. China Policy: From Normalization to the Post–Cold War Era.* Boulder, Colorado: Lynne Rienner Publishers, 1992.

United States Congress, House Committee on Ways and Means, Subcommittee on Trade, *United States–People's Republic of China Trade Status for China,* 102nd Congress, 1st Session, June 12, 1991. Washington, D.C: U.S. Government Printing Office.

United States Congress, Senate Committee on Finance, *China Most-Favored-Nation Status,* Hearings Before the Committee on Finance, 102nd Congress, 1st Session, June 19–20, 1992. Washington, D.C: U.S. Government Printing Office.

———, *Extending China's MFN Status,* Hearing, 102nd Congress, 2nd Session on S. 2808 and H.R. 5318, July 30, 1992, Washington, D.C: U.S. Government Printing Office, 1993.

Zweig, David. "Clinton and China: Creating a Policy Agenda That Works." *Current History* (September 1993): pp. 245–252.

## NOTES

1. Warren I. Cohen, *America's Response to China,* 3d edition (New York: Columbia University Press, 1990), p. 2.
2. Michael Schaller, *The U.S. and China in the Twentieth Century* (New York: Oxford University Press, 1979), p. 30.
3. Michael Schaller, *The U.S. and China in the Twentieth Century,* p. 16.
4. Warren I. Cohen, *America's Response to China,* p. 42.
5. Thomas G. Paterson, J. Garry Clifford, Kenneth J. Hagan, *American Foreign Policy: A History Since 1900,* Lexington, Massachusetts: D.C. Heath & Co., 1988, p. 383.
6. U.S. Department of State, *The China White Paper: United States Relations with China with Special Reference to the Period 1944–1949* (Stanford, California: Stanford University Press, 1967), XV–XVI.
7. Many U.S. citizens believed that the Communist victory was not inevitable but rather was a result of a "stab in the back" by members of the State Department who supported the Communists. In 1945, Ambassador Hurley's bitter resignation letter charged that the "China Hands" had sabotaged his efforts in China because they favored a Communist victory. Several Foreign Service officers were singled out for being "soft on communism. "John Service was arrested as part of the Amerasia case in 1945 and was subject to loyalty and security hearings in 1946, 1947, and 1949 (as well as 1950 and 1951) that were all resolved in his favor. John Carter Vincent was accused of sabotaging the U.S. China policy in 1947, and only after a spirited defense by Secretary Acheson did the Senate confirm his appointment as career minister. John Paton Davies was also investigated in 1949 and was cleared. Thus began the McCarthy era in the State Department and in the United States.
8. As a result of the Korean War approximately fifty U.S. citizens were incarcerated in the People's Republic, including eleven members of the U.S. Air Force who were sentenced as spies. Dag Hammarskjold, the U.N. Secretary-General, traveled to China to lobby for their release in January 1955, but renewed fighting in the Taiwan Straits delayed any further discussions until the issue of direct Sino-U.S. negotiations was raised by the Chinese. To show their goodwill, they released four of the U.S. airmen at the end of May and the eleven accused of spying at the end of July. Nine more were released in September after the ambassadorial-level talks had begun in Geneva. At the same time, the United States agreed to allow any Chinese citizen still in the United States to return to China if he or she so desired. By 1957, only eight U.S. citizens were still being held by the Chinese. After this initial success, however, the prisoner issue stalemated until President Nixon's visit to China in 1972, and so long as even one U.S citizen was in a Chinese jail, the issue remained a potent rallying factor for the China lobby.
9. The debate between the United States and the People's Republic over the admission of U.S. news reporters to China was the subject of a furious controversy in the late 1950s. Three U.S. newsmen visited China in early 1957, one as a representative of the *Baltimore Afro-American* and two as representatives of *Look* magazine, and many other representatives of the U.S. press criticized the State Department ban on China travel for reporters. Secretary of State Dulles initially defended the ban, citing the U.S. prisoners, and he stated that "the issuance of passports to a regime which is not recognized is something which is never done." By mid-year, to

defend himself against charges that the United States was deliberately trying to prevent information on the People's Republic from reaching the U.S. public, Dulles was forced to modify his position. He proposed that a limited number of U.S. reporters be allowed seven-month trial periods in China, but he refused reciprocal privileges to Chinese reporters. There, notwithstanding considerable legal nitpicking by both sides but particularly by the U.S. government, the matter died.

10. Jacob Beam, *Multiple Exposure: An American Ambassador's Unique Perspective on East-West Issues* (New York: W.W. Norton & Company, Inc., 1978), pp. 139–143.

11. Amazingly, even after the Cultural Revolution, some meetings were held in Warsaw. Altogether, twenty-one meetings were held during the Johnson administration, with three in 1966, two in 1967, and one in 1968. Communications between representatives of the United States and the PRC were also facilitated: "As the interval between the talks grew longer, the channel between the Embassies in Warsaw was used increasingly to pass messages of interest between the two governments." In addition, from September 1966, U.S. officials stationed abroad were allowed to have social contacts with Chinese officials if appropriate.

12. The U.S. Department of Agriculture was particularly interested in a crop exchange because China was "historically a principal source of some major US crops." [*Administrative History of the Department of State, 1945–1973*, (Lyndon B. Johnson Library), 42.]

13. *Administrative History,* pp. 42–43.

14. James Thomson describes the efforts to ease travel regulations, once again blaming the secretary of state for delaying initiatives. [James Thomson, Jr., "On the Making of U.S. China Policy, 1961–69: A Case Study in Bureaucratic Politics" *China Quarterly* 50 (April–June 1972): pp. 220–243.

15. Special State-Defense Long-Range Study on Communist China, S/P 66-71-2a, June 1966, *Administrative History,* p. 26.

16. There was some talk in Washington of pushing a "two Chinas" policy in the UN more blatantly after the annual General Assembly vote on PRC admission tied. That talk faltered, apparently because of both bureaucratic reluctance in Washington and the onset of the Cultural Revolution. James Thomson once again blames Dean Rusk. [Thomson, "On the Making of U.S. China Policy," p. 240.]

17. Warren L. Cohen, *America's Response to China,* 3rd ed. (New York: Columbia University Press, 1990), p. 198.

18. Henry A. Kissinger, *Years of Upheaval* (Boston: Little Brown and Company, 1982), p. 1124.

19. "The Shanghai Communique," in *The China Factor: Sino-American Relations and the Global Scene,* Richard H. Solomon, ed. (Englewood Cliffs, New Jersey: Prentice-Hall, 1981), pp. 296–300.

20. Hong N. Kim and Jack L. Hammersmith, "U.S.-China Relations in the Post-Normalization Era, 1979–1985," *Pacific Affairs* 59, no. 1 (Spring 1986): p. 72.

21. The Taiwan Relations Act, Public Law 96-8, April 19, 1979, 93 Stat 14.

22. Kim and Hammersmith, "U.S.-China Relations in the Post-Normalization Era," pp. 77–78.

23. Kim and Hammersmith, "U.S.-China Relations in the Post-Normalization Era," p. 73.

24. United States-China Joint Communiqué on United States Arms Sales to Taiwan, August 17, 1982. [Harry Harding, *A Fragile Relationship: The United States and China Since 1972* (Washington, D.C.: Brookings Institute, 1992), pp. 383–385.]

25. Tan Qingshan, *The Making of U.S. China Policy from Normalization to*

*the Post–Cold War Era* (Boulder, Colorado: Lynne Rienner Publishers, 1992), p. 101.

26. Harry Harding, *A Fragile Relationship,* p. 209.

27. During the Reagan administration, favorable U.S. public opinion of China ranged from a low of 43 percent in 1983 to a high of 71 percent in 1985. By July 1989, only 31 percent of respondents reported a favorable opinion of China. [Harry Harding, *A Fragile Relationship,* p. 363.]

28. From 1984 to 1989, the United States delivered $79 million of military assistance to China. In addition, weapons valued at $195 million were delivered through commercial sales.

29. Donald M. Snow and Eugene Brown, *Puzzle Palaces and Foggy Bottom* (New York: St. Martin's Press, 1994), p. 134.

30. Samuel S. Kim, quoted in Michael Yahuda, "Deng Xiaoping: The Statesman," *China Quarterly,* no. 135 (September 1993): p. 557.

31. China's record is not worse than that of the NATO countries on sales to Iraq. [Robert Ross, "Foreign Policy in 1987," p. 343.]

32. Specific measures included the following: formally resuming high-level contacts with the Chinese government; resuming regular exchanges of commercial and scientific commissions; allowing the delivery of specific U.S. military equipment to China agreed on and paid for in the 1980s but held in storage in the United States after the Tiananmen incident; allowing some higher-level military interaction with China; actively considering high-technology sales to China; and reducing export controls on communications and telecommunications equipment. [Robert G. Sutter, *CRS Report for Congress: China Policy Decisions at the Start of the 103rd Congress,* January 19, 1993, p. CRS-3.

33. Steven Greenhouse, "State Department Castigates China on Rights Record," *New York Times,* February 2, 1994, p. A9.

34. Thomas L. Friedman, "U.S. Pares Imports of Chinese Fabrics," *New York Times,* January 7, 1994, p. D2.

35. Thomas L. Friedman, "Bank Rules Are Eased by China," *New York Times,* January 22, 1994, p. 37.

36. Patrick E. Tyler, "Textile Accord with China Averts Trade Clash," *New York Times,* January 18, 1994, p. D1.

37. Elaine Sciolino, "U.S. Will Allow Computer Sale to Court China," *New York Times,* November 19, 1993, pp. A1, A5.

38. Elaine Sciolino, "U.S. will Allow Computer Sale to Court China," p. 10.

39. Patrick E. Tyler, "U.S. and China Agree to Expand Defense Links," *New York Times,* November 3, 1993, p. A13.

40. John Kohut, "Arms Sellers Accused of Stirring Fears," *South China Morning Post,* March 24, 1993.

41. "Clinton's Call: Avoid Isolating China," *New York Times,* May 27, 1994, p. A8.

42. Nicholas D. Kristof, "The Rise of China," *Foreign Affairs* 72, no. 5 (November–December 1993): pp. 72–73.

43. Bonnie S. Glaser, "China's Security Perceptions: Interests and Ambitions," *Asian Survey* 33, no. 3 (March 1993): pp. 259–261.

44. John R. Faust, "East Asia's Emerging Security System," *The Journal of East Asian Affairs* 8, no. 1 (Winter/Spring 1994): p. 89.

45. Patrick E. Tyler, "Haig Scorns U.S. for Its Tough China Policy," *New York Times,* October 28, 1993, p. A14.

46. Charles W. Kegley, Jr., and Gregory Raymond, *A Multipolar Peace? Great-Power Politics in the Twenty-first Century* (New York: St. Martin's Press, 1994), p. 207.

47. Wayne Bert, "Chinese Policies and U.S. Interests in Southeast Asia,"

*Asian Survey* 33, no. 3 (March 1993): p. 332.

48. "Triangular Chinese Economy Quickly Emerging," *United States-China Relations: Notes from the National Committee* (Spring/Summer 1992): pp. 3, 11.

49. Testimony on U.S.-China Relations from Barber Conable, submitted to the Subcommittee on Trade, Committee on Ways and Means, February 24, 1994.

# China and Its Neighbors in the Post-Cold War Era

In contrast to a turbulent Europe, the Asia-Pacific region enjoys relative stability. The signing of the Paris Agreement has laid the foundation for a final settlement of the Cambodian conflict. Following their simultaneous admission to membership of the United Nations, the North and the South of Korea have signed a protocol on mutual non-aggression and a joint declaration on the denuclearization of the Korean peninsula. The situation on the peninsula is moving towards relaxation and stability. Quite a few countries in the Asia-Pacific region have enjoyed a rather high economic growth rate thanks to political stability at home. This region has now become a dynamic and promising region in world economic development.

*—Premier Li Peng, in a speech at the*
*UN Security Council* (January 31, 1992)

One of China's major challenges in the 1990s will be to develop a policy with respect to an East Asian security system. Forced by the exigencies of the Cold War to follow military policies independent of its neighbors, China now has the opportunity to work with these neighbors, as well as with major actors in the UN Security Council, to solve a number of dangerous security problems in Asia. These include the following:

- rivalry on the Korean peninsula, with the potent dangers of a nuclear arms race
- uncertainty over the future status of Taiwan spurred by Chinese recidivism
- continuing fears over a future military rivalry between China and Japan
- political instability in the Philippines
- rivalries among China, Vietnam, Taiwan, and the Philippines over control of economic resources in the South China Sea
- continued political instability in Cambodia, leading to the possibility of renewed civil war
- instabilities in the Central Asian republics newly independent from the former Soviet Union and bordering on China

159

Through spearheading efforts at multilateral cooperation, China could choose to be a key to East Asian stability. Or it could choose a route that leads to further bloodshed and the escalation of violence, particularly if it continues to export military equipment to selected neighbors. An important example is China's selling of over $1.2 billion of military equipment to Myanmar (formerly Burma), a Southeast Asian state that is largely isolated from the international community because of its human rights atrocities and its refusal to cooperate in stamping out the drug trade, some of which crosses through Chinese territory.

China's future security role in Asia is an increasing concern to its Asian neighbors, especially because of the large increase in Chinese military expenditures since 1989.[1] Although military expenditures are decreasing in the world as a whole in the 1990s, military expenditures are increasing in Asia as a region and especially in China. Samuel Huntington, a Harvard expert on military affairs, believes that China's current military buildup has important implications at both the regional and global levels:

> Centrally important to the development of counter-West military capabilities is the sustained expansion of China's military power and its means to create military power. Buoyed by spectacular economic development, China is rapidly increasing its military spending and vigorously moving forward with the modernization of its armed forces. It is purchasing weapons from the former Soviet states; it is developing long-range missiles; in 1992 it tested a one-megaton nuclear device. It is developing power-projection capabilities, acquiring aerial refueling technology, and trying to purchase an aircraft carrier. Its military buildup and assertion of sovereignty over the South China Sea are provoking a multilateral arms race in East Asia.[2]

Three of the world's greatest arms races are now going on in Asia: North and South Korea; China and Taiwan; and India and Pakistan. Moreover, between 1985 and 1991, military expenditures in constant U.S. dollars have increased by 60.14 percent in China, 15.83 percent in North Korea, 27.82 percent in South Korea, 15.61 percent in Japan, 24.59 percent in Taiwan, 12.05 percent in Thailand, 23.36 percent in Malaysia, 24.59 percent in the Philippines, and 30.95 percent in Singapore.[3] Currently, there is an even greater military buildup in Asia than in the Middle East, which along with Asia experienced the greatest amount of war and violence during the Cold War era.

Since the end of World War II, the government in Beijing has been involved in military skirmishes along most of its borders, as well as in a major war in Korea. In the 1990s, military tensions continue at high levels to the northeast (the two Koreas), to the east (an arms race between Beijing and Taipei), to the southeast (naval skirmishes between China and Vietnam in the South China Sea, as well as violence in Cambodia and Myanmar), and in South Asia (an arms race and military confrontation over Kashmir between Pakistan and India).

In contrast to continuing military tensions along its borders, China's economic relations with its neighbors have improved dramatically since the implementation of the Open Door policy. Unlike the United States and some of its European allies, China's noncommunist Asian neighbors seem little disturbed by the events of Tiananmen Square. As a result, there has been a rapid increase in Chinese trade and tourism with Japan, Taiwan, and Hong Kong especially, but also increasingly with South Korea and Russia. Political, economic, and social transactions continue to grow with nearly all of China's neighbors through bilateral relations.

Multilateral transactions, however, have largely taken place through China's growing but limited role in the United Nations system, not at the regional level. An East Asian security community similar to NATO or an economic community similar to the European Community is not likely in the near future. A traditional regional distrust of China, combined with Chinese nationalism and isolationism, is likely to prevent a security alliance. Similarly, the export-based economies of Japan, South Korea, Taiwan, and Hong Kong do not form a logical basis for a common economic community. To analyze China's post–Cold War role in Asia, it is therefore necessary to examine China's relations with Japan, the two Koreas, Southeast Asia, South Asia, and Central Asia on a bilateral basis.

## THE QUESTION OF TWO KOREAS

To date, the end of the Cold War has been felt most dramatically in the southern part of the Korean peninsula. Surprisingly, China, rather than the United States, has been the pivotal actor affecting the changing status of South Korea. First, China supported the admission of the two Koreas into the United Nations in 1991. Second, China extended diplomatic recognition to South Korea in 1992, two years after the Soviet Union had done so.

Both China and South Korea clearly had a tremendous amount to gain by normalizing relations. In playing its China card, South Korea further isolated North Korea, its long-time rival, while reducing its dependency on the United States and Japan. By playing the South Korea card, China created a major new trading partner—over $5 billion in 1992. South Korea is now the sixth largest investor in China. These economic ties with South Korea have reduced Chinese dependence on trade and investment from other major partners, especially the United States and Japan, giving China greater leverage and bargaining power.

By playing the South Korea card, China also furthered one of its most important foreign policy goals. During the Cold War years, South Korea and

Taiwan were united by passionate anticommunism into a strong alliance. Now, as traditional security and economic goals have replaced ideology as a guide to developing foreign policy, South Korea has abandoned Taiwan in favor of rapprochement with China. With Korean-Taiwanese relations reduced to nongovernmental economic arrangements similar to those between Taiwan and its major trading partners, Taiwan has lost one of its very few remaining diplomatic ties.

The Korean War began on June 25, 1950, when North Korean troops moved south of the thirty-eighth parallel. Although some military skirmishes had occurred at the parallel since Korea was divided at the end of World War II, the events in June were perceived as an invasion of the South. President Harry Truman masterminded a United Nations military operation that was initially successful in driving back the North Koreans. Indeed, U.S. and United Nations troops were so successful that China felt its security was threatened, and it sent one million volunteers to Korea to fight. After three years of bloody fighting that ended with troops arrayed along the thirty-eight parallel as they had been before the war, an armistice was finally signed in July 1953.

South Korea has clearly benefitted from the end of the Cold War. North Korea is the clear loser. Now that ideological score cards are not being kept, Soviet/Russian and Chinese aid to the isolated, neo-Stalinist regime has decreased dramatically with devastating results. North Koreans are being asked by their leaders to eat only two meals per day as a patriotic duty. Patriotism only extends so far, however, and the North Korean leadership has resorted to rattling its sabers. In March 1993, North Korea announced it would withdraw from the Nuclear Non-Proliferation Treaty and bar international inspections on its soil, presumably to be free to develop nuclear weapons without on-site inspections by United Nations officials. A North Korea armed with nuclear weapons is enough to scare every nation in East Asia into working together to develop means to counter this potential security threat. Alternatively, though, a nuclear North Korea could be the catalyst for a nuclear South Korea, Japan, and Taiwan.

## Arms Race or Peaceful Coexistence?

Regardless of whether the Cold War has come to an end elsewhere or not, the two Koreas have continued to confront each other with the largest concentration of military forces in Asia. North Korea maintains an active military force of nearly one million (5 percent of its population), and South

Korea's active force numbers over 700,000. In addition, nearly 40,000 U.S. military personnel are still stationed in South Korea.

North Korea's superior numbers are balanced by South Korea's more modern equipment and technology. No longer supported by Russia and increasingly unsure of Chinese support, North Korea's military might is its own. South Korea has double the population and a far more vibrant economy, so time and international circumstances seem to be working against North Korea. That leaves North Korea's leadership with only the nuclear option to ensure its grip on power.

*The world's response.*   The world is trying to convince the North Koreans not to even consider using the nuclear option as a bargaining chip. Japan has firmly informed North Korea that any investment and help from Japan depends on the cessation of North Korea's nuclear arms program. The United States removed its nuclear weapons from the peninsula and offered to guarantee that South Korea will not embark on a nuclear weapons development program, contingent on similar guarantees from the North. As a friend of North Korea, one of the world's few remaining communist regimes, China has been unwilling to pressure the North Koreans openly, but symbolic gestures may be conveying the message to the north. The South Korean president visited Beijing in August 1992, a first. At the same time, the Chinese stopped allowing barter trade and began demanding cash for its exports to North Korea. North Korea now has two unpalatable choices: impoverished isolation while working on a nuclear weapons development program or peaceful coexistence probably leading to eventual reunification with the South.

*Reunification—Who wants it?*   The Koreans on either side of the thirty-eighth parallel have always stated publicly that reunification is both desirable and inevitable. The question is how. The always suspicious North Korean leaders are unlikely to trust their southern compatriots. Quick reunification is therefore unlikely, especially after the example of Germany, where precipitate reunification led to social and economic distress. Most South Koreans believe that reunification will be a slow process of building mutual trust, expanding trade ties, and defusing the military threat. How long the process will be and how difficult is open to debate.

## Future Chinese Relations with the Two Koreas

There are a number of reasons improved relations between China and South Korea promote China's national interests. First, increased South Korean investment in China reduces China's economic dependence on other outside sources such as Japan. Second, close relations with both Koreas increase Chinese political bargaining with respect to both Japan and Russia because

Kim Dae Jung, a South Korean opposition leader who ran for president of South Korea, believes that accommodation with North Korea will have to come about very gradually. Kim advocates that South Korea first establish a full democracy that will be flexible enough to accommodate the stresses of reunification. To heal the deep wounds brought about by forty years of suffering and separation, Kim suggests that trade and communication barriers be lifted first. At the same time, measures to ensure peaceful coexistence should be promoted. The next generation of Koreans will then have to solve the problems of how to unify their governments and their peoples.

China and South Korea have a mutual interest in constraining both Japanese and Russian influence in Northeast Asia. Third, because China, Japan, the United States, and Russia all have a common interest in bringing the arms race on the Korean peninsula to an end, close Chinese relations with both Koreas gives Beijing the key role in working with both Koreas and others to bring the two sides together.

There are also a number of reasons China wishes to retain good relations with North Korea. To be trustworthy as a mediator, Beijing must retain the respect of the leadership in Pyongyang. Therefore, China's leaders cannot allow North Korea to become isolated and abandoned by threatening to lessen China's traditional security commitments to North Korea. Good relations with North Korea will also enable China to encourage Pyongyang's participation in regional economic projects, including special economic zones in the border areas between Russia, China, and North Korea, which will benefit all three countries. Helping North Korea modernize and develop through using the Chinese model will help stabilize Northeast Asia, reducing the danger of outside intervention in the future. Finally, China's support for North Korea's vital interests enables Beijing to work behind the scenes to head off a dangerous nuclear arms race on the peninsula. China will be a key player in negotiating alternative security arrangements that may enable North Korea to give up its nuclear card, which is one of its only bargaining chips in getting more favorable terms in settling its differences with Seoul.

In the 1990s, China's leaders officially continue to support North Korea's view on the unification question—including the call for wide-ranging concessions from South Korea, such as political sharing of power on an equal basis, even though the South's population is double that of the North and its productivity is many times higher. With the passage of time, however, Beijing may gain more advantage from a unified Korea—one that comes gradually, rather than through a "shotgun marriage," as was the case with the two Germanies. In the twenty-first century, a unified Korea, because of its own interests and traditional experiences with the Japanese, is likely to align with China on balance-of-power issues in Northeast Asia, both on the questions of Japanese influence in the region and on any resurgence of Russian chauvinism. Should a separate Siberian republic emerge in Northeast Asia, China and a unified Korea would have a common interest in working together with their new neighbors to the north to create stability in the region. Japan, on the other hand, may wish to promote the emergence of a non-nuclear and stable North Korea in order to maintain a balance of power on the peninsula. Tokyo has always looked upon the Korean peninsula as its sphere of influence, and it is aware that with further economic development throughout the region, a united Korea might have more in common with the Chinese than the Japanese in the twenty-first century.

President Kim Il Sung, referred to by the people of North Korea as the Great Leader, established the Communist government after the end of World War II. Kim had been part of the armed Communist opposition to Japanese domination of Korea, and when the Soviets moved into North Korea, they handed the reins of government over to Kim. His regime was one of the most reclusive on earth, with few diplomatic or economic contacts with the outside world. Kim's philosophy of self-reliance, however, was severely tested by the collapse of communism—the nation is currently virtually bankrupt. Kim's son Kim Jong Il, the Dear Leader, is set to inherit the throne—a first in communist countries—despite a reputation for dissoluteness that may be accurate or may be promoted by the South Korean intelligence agencies.

## GETTING ALONG WITH SOUTHEAST ASIA

The end of the Cold War has altered the balance of power not only in Europe but throughout many other areas of the world as well. The withdrawals of the Soviets from Vietnam and the United States from its Philippine bases have dramatically altered the map in Southeast Asia. In the 1980s, the issue most concerning the members of the Association of Southeast Asian Nations (or ASEAN, which is composed of Thailand, Indonesia, Malaysia, Singapore, the Philippines, and Brunei) was the growing Soviet presence in the region and the expansion of Vietnamese influence into Cambodia and Laos. Now, ASEAN's major concerns are the growing economic domination of Japan in Southeast Asia; intraregional disputes; and the political fragility of the coalition regime in

Cambodia, the military regime in Myanmar, and the potential for political unrest in the Philippines.

China's range of political and economic options in Southeast Asia is wider now than at any time during the Cold War era. However, China's southeastern Asian neighbors have always been wary of their gigantic northern neighbor. If China seeks to broaden its influence in Southeast Asia, it will have to tread carefully. Thus far, China has focused its efforts on cutting its ties to the remaining communist revolutionaries in the Philippines and on improving relations with Indonesia, formerly one of its most ardent foes.

China's ties to the Southeast Asian nations are varied and complex. Each ASEAN country has a large Chinese minority, which is often the backbone of the nation's commercial and business community. Resentments and prejudices have festered. Even now Chinese in Malaysia are officially discriminated against, and Thai Chinese were forced to adopt Thai surnames. Large numbers of Chinese were killed in Indonesia in 1965 during the overthrow of President Sukarno's pro-Beijing government because of lingering fears that the Chinese living in Southeast Asia would have primary loyalty to China rather than the country they lived in. Many overseas Chinese were not even citizens of the countries they and their forebears lived in. Though many Southeast Asians resent Chinese clannishness, they both fear and admire Chinese business successes. The Chinese in Southeast Asia, in turn, believe that their economic success is due to hard work, and they resent the limitations many Southeast Asian nations attempt to place on expressions of Chinese culture.

Though Beijing has now normalized relations with all nations in Southeast Asia, trade between these countries and China has remained at relatively low levels compared with growth of their trade with Japan. In fact, most Southeast Asian nations are rivals with China for international investors seeking cheap labor residing in relatively stable political environments. Over time, however, Chinese economic ties with ASEAN nations will undoubtedly increase. With South Korean and Taiwanese trade with Southeast Asia also increasing, Japan's coprosperity sphere may become a reality in the twenty-first century.

China's moves in the political-security spheres will be more difficult. Within the region, there has been little success in creating multilateral structures to compensate for the withdrawal of the Soviet and U.S. military presence. Even ASEAN has failed to move beyond economic cooperation to some type of regional collective security system. This is probably due in part to U.S. opposition (until very recently) to multilateral Asian security ties rather than bilateral security ties with Washington. Similarly, China ignored Mikhail Gorbachev's calls for an Asian collective security system in the late 1980s, and it refused to participate in an Asia Pacific security conference sponsored by Australia, Canada, and Japan. Beijing, too, has favored bilateral security arrangements. China's leaders fear that they would have little influence over multilateral Southeast Asian security arrangements. Chinese interests, they believe, are best promoted through security ties with each Southeast Asian nation separately.

## China's Role in Cambodia

One of the major tests of China's future relations with Southeast Asia depends on the outcome of the United Nations peacekeeping efforts in Cambodia. Since the Khmer Rouge took over the country and marched the residents of Phnom Penh into the killing fields, over one million people, one-fifth of the population, have been butchered. Now, after most members of society with any education, business experience, or ties with the "bourgeois" classes have been eliminated, the nation's political and economic problems are beyond imagining. Continued Khmer Rouge resistance in the countryside may well doom the United Nation's best efforts to create a coalition government.

Throughout the worst years of Khmer Rouge excesses, China supported Pol Pot and his revolutionary murderers, at least partially through revolutionary affinity. Probably more important, however, was the historic antagonism between China and the Vietnamese. The Soviet-supported Vietnamese government invaded Cambodia in 1978, ostensibly to end the killings but also in no small part because Vietnam has traditionally coveted Cambodia's rich agricultural areas. The Vietnamese established a puppet regime in Phnom Penh led by Hun Sen, but the Khmer Rouge continued to fight in the countryside.

Thailand, another traditional rival of the Vietnamese, entered into an informal alliance with the Chinese to back the Khmer Rouge, who used Thai territory and Khmer Rouge–controlled refugee camps inside Thailand as bases to conduct warfare against Hun Sen's Vietnamese-backed regime in Phnom Penh. Chinese economic and military assistance flowed through Thailand to the Khmer Rouge, and Beijing also ordered a military incursion across China's southwestern border into northern Vietnam in late 1978 and 1979 to try to force Hanoi to stop its military intervention in Cambodia. Vietnamese military forces were successful enough to embarrass the Chinese military. Despite the failure of China's military effort, China remained a major participant in the internal struggles in Indochina. By 1980, Vietnam controlled most of Laos and Cambodia, and the Khmer Rouge occupied sizable rural areas of western and northwestern Cambodia on the Thai border.

Vietnam's increasing power, as well as the Soviet support for Vietnam's expansionism, alarmed many other Asian nations. To check Vietnam, ASEAN joined with the United States to promote a tripartite coalition government involving two non-Communist Cambodian resistance movements and the Khmer Rouge. This so-called coalition government even received the imprimatur of the United Nations, which allowed the coalition to assume Cambodia's seat in the General Assembly. The supporters of this anomalous coalition were more concerned with the expansion of Soviet and Vietnamese influence in Southeast Asia than they were with the moral and ethical implications of allying themselves with the Khmer Rouge.

The end of the Cold War ended Asian fears of Vietnamese expansionism. Vietnam withdrew most of its forces from Cambodia in 1989, and Russia, which is no longer interested in or able to provide aid to its former ally, withdrew its forces from Vietnam. Now Vietnam is seeking normalization of relations with the West—even with China and the United States—and investment funds. Taiwan, with $600 million in investments, and Japan have been leading the way. In 1992, Japan provided $400 million to help rebuild Vietnam's infrastructure. Japanese and other business people are interested in Vietnam's large, educated, and cheap work force.

The end of the Cold War has also allowed more concerted efforts to find a solution to the problems in Cambodia, led by the permanent members of the Security Council, along with the ASEAN countries, Australia, and New Zealand. In October 1991, the Security Council passed the Comprehensive Political Settlement of the Cambodian Conflict. Twenty-two thousand UN forces were sent to Cambodia to supervise the demobilization of all factions and the steps necessary for writing a new constitution that would lead to elections of a new government. To date, however, the Khmer Rouge is still defying UN attempts at disarmament.

China therefore has a problem in Cambodia. As a member of the Security Council, it is obligated to support UN efforts in Cambodia. Yet China may still be providing its former ally with some aid. Beijing is also afraid of Japanese influence in the region. The United Nations appointed a Japanese representative to lead the UN effort. This, in turn, led Japan to pledge to send troops to Cambodia to perform nonmilitary duties. The idea of Japanese troops being mobilized anywhere on the Asian mainland is an issue of the greatest sensitivity to China's leaders—so much so that during his visit to Japan in 1992, Party Secretary Jiang Zemin called on the Japanese government to cancel plans for nonmilitary troop deployment in Cambodia.

All the UN's best laid plans may well come to naught, however, because the Khmer Rouge is slowly moving from reliance on Chinese political and economic support to finding its own means of support. By 1992, it had built up a reserve of over $100 million through clear-cutting timber operations and through the mining of rubies, which were then sold on the world market through illicit conduits in the Thai military. The Khmer Rouge now has funds to replenish any weapons stores lost to UN disarmament efforts. When the UN-supervised elections were held in May 1993, the Khmer Rouge refused to participate, and they continue to control territory in western and northwestern Cambodia. Peace in Cambodia will continue to be elusive.

## Territorial Disputes

China's territorial claims in Southeast Asia extend beyond the island of Taiwan to the South China and East China seas. In February 1992, China passed a territorial waters law claiming control of the Spratly Islands, which are also claimed by every other nation in the area; the Paracel Islands; and the Senkaku Islands, which are currently administered by Japan. Potential oil reserves were the incentive for China's claiming of the Spratly Islands. First, China stunned the world in 1988 when it engaged Vietnam in a military clash over the islands. Then, in 1992, Beijing entered into an agreement with a Denver-based oil company to begin joint exploration for oil near one of the Spratlys. Dangerously, Vietnam and other Southeast Asian nations still stake their claims to the Spratlys, which are far closer to their borders than to China's borders; some of the nations have a military presence on one or more of the thirty-three islands.

## Future Chinese Relations with Southeast Asia

The decline of Soviet and U.S. military influence in Southeast Asia, continuing instability in Cambodia, regional territorial disputes, and growing Chinese military capability are causing concern to all nations with an interest in Southeast Asian security. Over the next decades, Beijing will have to choose among a number of difficult options. Its decisions will have an enormous effect on the future course of Southeast Asian security.

If China opts to provide continued behind-the-scenes support to the Khmer Rouge, Pol Pot's followers could continue their dominance of part of Cambodia's countryside even though they boycotted the UN-sponsored elections. Continued backing of the Khmer Rouge would serve to announce to the world that China remains steadfast in its efforts to preserve client regimes while also preventing foreign interference within its sphere of influence. Conservative military leaders in Beijing would very much like to demonstrate to the other major powers, including the Japanese, that multilateral United Nations operations cannot be used to prevent Chinese-supported military forces from exercising power in Southeast Asia.

Beijing could adopt a hard-line policy of threatening to use force, as well as bilateral deals, to assert Chinese control over the island chains in the South China and East China seas. Such threats would undermine efforts to create regional security arrangements and would work to the detriment of China's good relations with its neighbors. By playing one territorial claimant against another, while offering economic deals to investors from outside the region, Beijing might be able to take advantage of existing disagreements between Southeast Asian states and their inability to create effective regional collective security arrangements.

If Beijing is controlled by conciliators rather than those who favor the use of the military over the next decades, China might signal to its neighbors and the global community that it wishes to avoid bilateral power plays. China might reaffirm the policy it always has adhered to in theory, if not in fact: noninterference in the internal affairs of other states. It could demand similar pledges from its neighbors. In addition, as the sole Asian member of the Security Council, China could become an active partner in guaranteeing the peace and stability of Southeast Asia.

If the influence of those in Beijing who seek peaceful relations with China's neighbors grows, they might seek to reach an accommodation on territorial disputes. In the fall of 1993 China began negotiations with Vietnam in an effort to bring about a peaceful settlement of disputes over islands in the South China Sea. It is hoped that this will lead to a sharing of oil resources. A new policy of seeking joint solutions to regional problems could be the missing link in gradually building an East Asian security community to match the growing economic cooperation in the region. Whereas military confrontation in the South China Sea could lead to regional arms races (especially between China and Japan), as well as to China's isolation from its neighbors, partnership in solving regional disputes could strengthen Asia's role in the emerging global system. See Table 6.1 for a comparison of China's combat forces with those of other countries in the region.

## THE BALANCE OF POWER IN SOUTH ASIA

Throughout the Cold War, South Asia has been an important crossroads of confrontation, involving not only the two principal actors in the region, India and Pakistan, but also the two superpowers, the United States and the Soviet Union. The People's Republic of China has also become involved in South Asia through its accession of Tibet in 1950 and a number of border skirmishes with India, particularly in the 1960s. India's sheltering of the Dalai Lama after he finally fled Tibet in 1959 led to increasing Chinese mistrust of Prime Minister Nehru's government. Increasing Soviet support for India only heightened Chinese security sensitivities, and Nehru's aspirations to Third World leadership directly conflicted with China's own bid for that title.

Pakistan, adopting the philosophy "The enemy of my enemy is my friend," became China's ally and hence anti-Soviet. The more military equipment the Indians received from the Soviet Union and Eastern Europe, the more U.S. and Chinese military assistance went to Pakistan. By the time of the 1971 war between West and East Pakistan, in which India intervened to ensure the independence of East Pakistan (Bangladesh), the Indo-Pakistani conflict had become a proxy war for the superpowers. The Soviet Union assisted India,

**Table 6.1  Comparative Combat Forces of China and Some of Its Neighbors**

| | China | Japan | North Korea | South Korea | India | Pakistan |
|---|---|---|---|---|---|---|
| Army Forces | People's Liberation Army: 2 million troops | Army: 150,000 troops | Active army of 930,000; 26 reserve infantry divisions | Active army of 550,000; 23 reserve infantry divisions | 1.1 million army (3 armored divisions, remainder light infantry); 30 reserve infantry divisions | 480,000 army (4 armored divisions, remainder light infantry) |
| Tanks | 7,500 | 800 (light type) | 3,200 (main battle type) | 1,600 (main battle type) | 3,000 (main battle type) | 1,700 (main battle type) |
| Combat Aircraft | 5,000 | 400 | 650 | 450 | 800 | 450 |
| Sub-marines | 88 (1 nuclear) | 14 | 23 | 3 | 17 | 6 |
| Missile Craft | — | — | 29 | 11 | — | — |
| Destroyers | 56 | 60 | — | — | 25 | 17 |
| Amphibious Ships | — | 6 | — | — | 10 | — |

*Source:* Rand National Defense Institute, *Understanding the Evolving U.S. Role in Pacific Rim Security* (Santa Monica, California: Rand, 1992), pp. 26, 33.

whereas the United States "tilted" toward Pakistan as a reward for Pakistani assistance with the Nixon administration's overtures to Beijing.

The Sino-U.S.-Pakistani anti-Soviet alliance found its true cause in Afghanistan in 1979. Not since the end of World War II had the Soviets so blatantly expanded their sphere of influence, although the Russians and the British had been vying for control of the area for nearly two centuries. China and the United States intervened on the side of the anticommunist Afghanis. Predictably, India sided with the Soviet Union and voted against United Nations condemnations of the invasion. Because many of the anticommunist fighters operated out of camps on the Afghani-Pakistani border, Pakistan became the major supply line for the anticommunist resistance movement in Afghanistan. The civil war heightened tensions in South Asia, and until Mikhail Gorbachev withdrew his troops in 1989, the war became the Soviet Union's Vietnam. Withdrawal may have gotten the Soviet Union out of its quagmire, but it did not fully resolve the situation in Afghanistan. Now the various groups of "freedom fighters" continue to fight among themselves.

With the end of the Cold War, tensions in South Asia have actually heightened, and the security alignment has become more complex than ever. India and Pakistan allegedly nearly went to war again in the late 1980s, and there were rumors that both nations were considering the possibility of using nuclear weapons. India exploded a nuclear device in 1974, and Pakistan began its nuclear development program in the 1980s with Chinese aid. So long as the Soviet intervention in Afghanistan continued, the United States turned a blind eye to Pakistan's efforts to join the nuclear club. In the late 1980s, however, the Bush administration implemented congressional resolutions that denied foreign aid to any country seeking nuclear capability. The United States also pressured China, presumably unsuccessfully, to cease assisting Pakistan with its nuclear and missile programs. Commercial sales of U.S. military equipment to Pakistan continued, however, just as Russian president Yeltsin has continued to sell arms to India. Just to complicate the situation, the United States has at the same time been successfully pursuing better relations with India. In 1992, India conducted joint naval maneuvers with the United States in the Indian Ocean, and the United States has become India's largest trading partner.

## Post–Cold War Alignments

Post–Cold War alignments in South Asia have an Alice in Wonderland character—they become curiouser and curiouser. Unfortunately, they also become more and more dangerous as the two superpowers (the global police forces) are less concerned with restraining their allies and client states. Despite the reduced roles of Washington and Moscow, all of the same rivalries and conflicts remain, and new dangers are arising. Nuclear proliferation alarms all, as the possibility of yet another war between India and Pakistan becomes more and more real. Pakistan may feel the need to respond to the increasing violence directed at India's Islamic minority by intervening, border tensions may increase, and tensions over Indian control of Kashmir may flare up yet again. Although Pakistan's military capabilities are far inferior to India's, it could resort to the use of nuclear and chemical weapons to make up for its inferior conventional forces, and India could respond in kind. All in all, the arms buildup on the subcontinent is exceeded only by the arms buildup in the Middle East. Any warfare between India and Pakistan would involve two of the world's largest military forces.

## Arms Control on the Subcontinent

Pakistan, disingenuously hedging its bets, has announced that it will sign the Nuclear Non-Proliferation Treaty if India also signs it. Pakistan has also joined the United States in calling for a five-power negotiating team (the United States, Russia, China, Pakistan, and India) to bring about a permanent solution to the nuclear proliferation problem in South Asia. India is unwilling to become involved in a multilateral discussion of its nuclear options, however, until China removes its own missiles from Tibet, where they are currently targeted at South Asia, and agrees to discuss eliminating its nuclear forces. But China is unwilling to discuss its own nuclear weapons until all other nuclear states agree to discuss a total global ban on nuclear weapons and nuclear development programs. In fact, any Asian security system that relies on China as the only regional nuclear power is totally unacceptable to India. Thus, the arms race continues in India, Pakistan, and China.

## Future Sino-Pakistani Relations

Beijing has a long-term interest in seeing that Pakistan remains a viable counterforce to Indian domination of the subcontinent and the surrounding regions. So long as domination through force is the order of the day in South Asia, China has a vital interest in supporting a balance of power based on mutual deterrence in the region. Until India itself agrees to pursue a nuclear-free zone in the region, which the United States, Russia, and Pakistan allegedly support, China will not have to face the difficult decision of whether or not to support multilateral discussions to end the nuclear arms race in South Asia.

In the future, it may be in China's interest to continue providing conventional arms to Pakistan but to cease aiding its nuclear program. China's arms sales provide foreign currency to its military industrial complex, and China and Pakistan have a common interest in creating a military balance on the subcontinent to prevent Indian domination of the region.

China may avoid taking any official stand on the conflict between India and Pakistan while in reality supporting the Pakistanis. Working behind the scenes, Beijing may wish to use Pakistan as a balance against extremist groups in Afghanistan and Central Asia, which in the future may cause trouble for Beijing in China's far-western province of Xinjiang.

It may be in China's interest to discourage the creation of an internationally sponsored nuclear-free zone in South Asia. The conventional as well as nuclear arms race on the subcontinent reduces India's ability to challenge China for leadership of the Third World as well as in Southeast Asia. In addition, instability in South Asia makes this region less attractive as a competitor to China in seeking international investment.

Beijing's relations with Pakistan are complicated by its desire to keep a low profile in Afghanistan. As noted above, China has an interest in Pakistan as a counterweight to Afghanistan and Central Asia, but strong Chinese backing for pro-Pakistani factions in Afghanistan might alienate Beijing's relations with Iran at a time when China wants to increase arms sales to Tehran.

As an alternative to taking a pro-Pakistani stand in South Asia, Beijing could emphasize peaceful economic trade ties with all South Asian countries and avoid supporting any country in the region militarily. A policy of non-interference, including cessation of military sales to Pakistan and Myanmar, as well as giving up the option of building a naval base in Myanmar on the Bay of Bengal, could strengthen China's reputation as a supporter of peace in the post–Cold War era. From the perspective of the reformist and non-militarist interests inside China, it could also be a means of encouraging trade and investment in consumer goods rather than the arms trade coming from military-controlled factories inside China.

## China and India as Role Models

China and India are often compared as models of the successes and failure of capitalism versus communism in raising the popular living standard. India has pursued modernization through state capitalism and improvements in agrarian technology. A large, well-educated middle class has developed since World War II, and crop yields have increased markedly. Yet, because of the caste system, both the urban and rural social structures remain unaltered, ensuring that the distribution of wealth remains inequitable. Thus, many rural poor migrate to Calcutta and other large cities to join the low-caste urban population in eking out a miserable existence at odd jobs. To create more efficient and productive industries that will lead to job creation, the Indian government began taking steps in 1992 to privatize its large state industrial sector, create laws more favorable to foreign investment, and even set up special economic zones.

China's model of development has been dramatically different. The Communist Party's first priority was to create a classless society through political controls at all levels of society. Then, it utilized a Stalinist model for industrialization that involved collectivization of the peasantry to create a surplus for use in developing heavy industry. The Communist Party claimed that it provided each citizen with a decent diet, but many starved during the politically induced famines during the Great Leap Forward and the Cultural Revolution. Not until agriculture was freed from party control did crop yields rise substantially, and China's state industries have had their own inefficiency problems. After Deng Xiaoping's reforms, China's economy began to grow rapidly but unevenly and inequitably, not unlike India's economy. As both India and China reform their economies, discussion of each as a discrete model of development becomes less persuasive.

Few clear winners emerge in any comparison of Chinese and Indian development statistics. Per annual capita income in China is $370, compared with $300 in India.[4] Human rights are generally considered to be more honored in India, the democracy, than in China. Yet many minorities in India, including the large Muslim minority—and especially women—are often treated ruthlessly by government authorities.[5] China definitively bests India in the areas of primary education and preventive health care. The current literacy rate in China is reported to be 73 percent, whereas in India it is only 43 percent. In China, the average life span for men is 68 years and for women is 72 years. In India, it is 57 years for men and 59 years for women. But the discrepancy in life span may decrease as China abandons its basic health care system, one of the most prized outcomes of the Communist revolution. In the post–Cold War world, doctrinaire models of development are giving way to messy experimentation with elements of socialism and capitalism. Neither China nor India can present any clear model to the other developing countries of the world.

In the early twenty-first century, China and India may be partners in promoting Third World issues in the emerging global regime and preventing Western dominance of the international system. For example, both India and China have abstained on Security Council censure votes aimed at Third World nations such as Iraq and Libya. In addition, Chinese premier Li Peng recently called for a negotiated settlement of the Sino-Indian border controversy so that the world's two largest developing nations would not only "enhance understanding and strengthen cooperation" but "would also produce a positive impact on the situation in Asia and the world."[6]

More likely, China and India will continue their traditional rivalry, which is not unusual for two regional powers with contiguous borders. China is unlikely to abandon its support for Pakistan, both because Pakistan is a counterweight to India on the subcontinent and because a friendly Pakistan might be able to influence moderates in the new Central Asian

Islamic republics on China's borders. Further, in the post–Cold War era, Sino-Indian economic rivalry will become an issue. Despite recent increases in Sino-Indian trade,[7] the two nations will compete with each other for foreign investment and development aid from the World Bank. China and India will also compete for export markets in Southeast Asia, and India's recent attempts to improve relations with Vietnam must concern China.

Either as a competitor or as a potential partner, relations between China and India will have a tremendous effect on the stability of southern Asia as well as on the leadership alignments within the Third World in the emerging global system. If the past is a key to the future, China may pursue both approaches simultaneously. Beijing wishes to improve both political and economic relations with India on a bilateral basis. Yet multilateral arms control negotiations seeking to end the nuclear and conventional arms race in South Asia would undoubtedly at some point raise India's demand for China to dismantle its nuclear capability as a condition for New Delhi's agreement to abandon the nuclear military option. Up to now, China's political and military leaders have refused to consider such an option other than as part of a total world package to eliminate all nuclear arms.

## HOW TO DEAL WITH CENTRAL ASIA?

Five central Asian republics have emerged from the wreckage of the Soviet Union: Kazakhstan, Turkmenistan, Uzbekistan, Kyrgyzstan, and Tajikistan. Together these republics have a population of 50 million indigenous peoples who adhere to Islam. But there is also a large Russian minority. Three have a common border with the province of Xinjiang in northwestern China. The non-Han residents of Xinjiang have far more in common with their brethren in the new Islamic republics (sometimes even close relatives) than they do with the Chinese leaders in Beijing. Always a source of tension, the Xinjiang border area is becoming more fluid and at the same time more potentially volatile. Formerly, Xinjiang abutted the Soviet Union, and no other outside influences were allowed. Now Turkey, Saudi Arabia, Iran, and Pakistan are all competing to win friends in the Islamic areas of the former Soviet Union.[8]

What are China's policy choices in dealing with the newly independent Central Asian republics? Although the newly independent status of these republics might seem to be a stimulus to demands for independence in Xinjiang, long an extremely sensitive issue in Beijing, China's leaders are unlikely to allow any such eventuality. Since the era of the Sino-Soviet split, China has exerted strong control over Xinjiang, and it has been careful to settle the province with Han Chinese loyal to Beijing. Rather, the greatest danger to regional security is probably the danger of civil war within the republics. Recent fighting in Tajikistan illustrates the fragility of the new nations. That Kazakhstan still has nuclear weapons on its territory can only exacerbate Chinese fears, despite President Nazarbayev's agreement to return the weapons to Russia for dismantling.

Beijing's leaders are probably united in their desire to keep a low profile in Central Asia while trying to establish regular lines of communication. China's interests in the area are defensive, trying to avoid any instability in the region from reaching its borders. Though agreeing to the normalization of relations with the five new republics, China's leaders will have to deal with some difficult issues in the future. How should China respond to feelers from Kazakhstan, Kyrgyzstan, and some of the other new republics for creation of an Asian political association similar to the Conference on Security and Cooperation in Europe? In the past, China has preferred bilateral relations, pursuing a balance-of-power system rather than any regional collective arrangements. Beijing's conservatives, following their traditional state-centric point of view, will probably eschew such involvements. Others in Beijing, however, may realize that Russia, Turkey, Iran, Pakistan, and perhaps even the United States may work to create some type of security guarantees for Central Asia. China cannot afford to be left on the sidelines if this occurs. However, the initiative for such a pact is unlikely to come from China.

> The Sino-Soviet Friendship Treaty signed by Mao and Stalin in 1950 created a joint stock company that was to exploit Xinjiang's natural resources, ostensibly for the benefit of both nations. The company was very much resented by the Chinese, and Khrushchev renounced any Soviet interest in it. Even this could not prevent the downward spiral of Sino-Soviet relations in Xinjiang. By the late 1960s, the two nations fought several times in the area of their border.

Beijing, in order to earn hard currency, has been increasing its arms exports. Pakistan, a longtime ally of China because of both nations' hostility toward India, is reportedly receiving Chinese assistance for its nuclear program. Iran, a nation that aspires to regional dominance, is another large purchaser of Chinese weapons. Because both Pakistan and Iran are competing for friends in the Central Asian republics, Sino-Pakistani and Sino-Irani relations could become strained.

## POLICY OPTIONS

In dealing with its neighbors during a time when its leaders are involved in a struggle for succession at home, China's easier choices would be to continue most of its current policies with Japan, the two Koreas, Southeast Asia, South Asia, and Central Asia. Based on past behavior, this means reliance on bilateral rather than multilateral transactions with all its neighbors. From Beijing's perspective, the advantages are clear. Because multilateral fora may create alignments more favorable to other regional actors than to China, in terms of both political-security and economic issues, it is to the advantage of Beijing to deal with each neighbor separately. China's leaders seem to feel this approach may pay even greater dividends in the future as China's development increases its bargaining power on both security and economic issues.

## Option 1: Emphasis on Bilateral Relations

Beijing will have to work diligently to try to convince its neighbors that bilateral rather than multilateral arrangements are in everyone's best interest. This may become increasingly difficult if other Asian countries see China's rising military expenditures as a growing threat to their security. In the economic sphere, however, many of China's neighbors may agree with Beijing that rather than belonging to regional economic groupings dominated by Japan, the dominant Asian economic actor in the 1990s, it is better to work out individual arrangements to protect each Asian country's interests. By the turn of the century, if China's economy continues to grow at its present rate and if Japan has internal economic troubles, perhaps Beijing may feel more confident of its ability to protect its interests in any regional economic groupings.

## Option 2: Support for Regionalism as a Last Resort

If regional organizations emerge regardless of Beijing's wishes, then China will no doubt join them, if only for the purpose of protecting its interests (i.e., to limit damage should others support policies that seem unfavorable to Beijing).

## Option 3: Settlement of Regional Disputes in Northeast Asia

It is logical for China to work with its neighbors to settle Asiatic disputes that might upset the current balance of power in Asia, which currently seems favorable to Beijing. Especially in Northeast Asia, a settlement of differences would benefit China because it would minimize the danger of a remilitarized Japan or of disturbing developments in Russian Siberia. It is in China's interest to defuse the nuclear arms race on the Korean peninsula. Beijing is currently attempting to do this by working quietly behind the scenes as a mediator between the two Koreas, while at the same time publicly reaffirming its security commitments to North Korea and Pyongyang's policy positions in its negotiations with Seoul.

From the point of view of all the actors in the region, with perhaps the exception of the current leaders in North Korea, the ideal security arrangement would be the emergence of a low-key, informal security community similar to the one that exists between Canada and the United States. For 150 years, these two countries, without any formal regional security structures, have been able to settle all their political and economic conflicts through peaceful negotiations without the threat of force. Logically, it is in China's interest to encourage the emergence of such an informal regional security system, which is most likely to come about through functional economic integration. An informal zone of peace would reduce the danger of future coercive actions by two of China's greatest protagonists in modern history: the Russians and the Japanese.

## Option 4: Exercising Influence in Southeast Asia

The situation in Southeast Asia, from the Chinese perspective, seems to be very different from that in Northeast Asia. Now that Russia and the United States have either left or reduced their presence, China may emerge as the dominant military force in the region, especially in the South China Sea. China's current buildup of air and naval power gives Beijing the ability to defeat any other regional actors that might wish to contest its control of the Paracel and Spratly island chains. But in building up their military, China's leaders must be careful not to stimulate a buildup of arms or a renewal of alliances with countries outside the region. This could be difficult to avoid, however, because the vast majority of China's people take pride in the fact that the post–Cold War era is the first time in modern history that China has the possibility of restoring some former parts of the Middle Kingdom to Chinese control—mostly in Southeast Asia.

## Option 5: Creating Peace in Southeast Asia

If it wishes to avoid remilitarization of Southeast Asia, which in turn may stimulate a Japanese military buildup, Beijing may find it necessary to pursue an approach that it has so far been reluctant to undertake: promoting a settlement of regional disputes, especially in the South China Sea, so that no one power or alliance could dominate the area. But achieving an informal security community similar to the one that exists in North America could be very difficult. To achieve this, China may have to put pressure on the Khmer Rouge to accept a Cambodian coalition government in which it would participate but not control, an offer proposed by President Sihanouk in November 1993. China would also clearly have to change its policy of viewing the South China Sea as its exclusive zone. In the past, Beijing has not shown any willingness to share oil and fishing rights in the South China Sea with others, including Vietnam, Malaysia, Singapore, Brunei, the Philippines, and Taiwan. Beijing would also have to give up the possibility of building a Chinese naval base in Myanmar because this could become a destabilizing factor both in Southeast Asia and South Asia.

## Option 6: Promoting a Peaceful Balance-of-Power System in South Asia

China's future options may be quite different in South Asia because the current leaders in Beijing seem unwilling to take any active steps to defuse the growing arms race between Pakistan and India. Since the Communists came to power in China in 1949, Chinese security along its borders with South Asian countries has seemingly been enhanced by instabilities within the region. If India and Pakistan concentrate their military efforts against each other, the balance of power in the region helps China protect its interests in Tibet against any outside influence. Because a balance of power in South Asia seems to enable China to exercise more influence in South Asia than would a zone that has been demilitarized—in both nuclear and conventional terms—it is unlikely that China will change its current policy of discouraging any multilateral approaches to peacemaking in the region. Nor is China likely to place bilateral pressure on either Pakistan or India to settle their differences.

## Option 7: Promoting a Peaceful Balance-of-Power System in Central Asia

Beijing is likely to continue its current policy in Central Asia of supporting a balance of power among the Central Asian states and their neighbors. This seems preferable to the future unification of the five Islamic states in the region. At the same time, Beijing may work to lessen tensions in the area because the most destabilizing and threatening scenario to China would be the rise of fundamentalist Islamic forces; such a scenario might promote instability among the indigenous Islamic groups inside Xinjiang, China's northwestern province. By working closely with both Iran and Pakistan, Beijing hopes to maintain some type of balance within the region, lessening the danger that overt hostilities will spill over into China's western border areas.

## DISCUSSION QUESTIONS

1.  In pursuit of nationalist pride and a leadership role in Asia, will China's modernization and buildup of its military capabilities strengthen or undermine China's role in Asia in the 1990s?
2.  Can future Chinese security in Asia be enhanced more by unilateral and bilateral relations with its neighbors or by cooperation in the creation of multilateral security arrangements in East Asia, Southeast Asia, South Asia, and Central Asia?
3.  Would China be more secure in the future with the continued existence of North Korea and South Korea as separate states or with a reunified Korea?
4.  What can China do to become an equal to Japan as an economic power in the early twenty-first century?
5.  Would it be to China's advantage to support a common economic market in Asia similar to the European Community or the North American Free Trade Agreement?
6.  Should China continue its policy of occupying parts of the Spratly and Paracel island chains in light of conflicting claims by its neighbors? Would it be more to China's advantage to enter into arrangements with its neighbors to jointly exploit the economic resources located in these island chains than seek to exploit them through unilateral solutions?
7.  To what extent should Beijing continue to support the interests of the Khmer Rouge in challenging efforts to bring about peace and stability in Cambodia?
8.  Should China seek a partnership with Japan in determining Asia's future development, or should it try to join with other Asian states to contain Japan's dominant economic and potential political role in Asia?
9.  Is it in China's interest to seek an end to the conventional and nuclear arms race between India and Pakistan?
10. What policy toward the newly emerging, former communist states in Central Asia would best promote Chinese national interests?
11. What policies should Beijing's leaders pursue with Iran and Pakistan in order to promote Chinese interests in Central Asia?

## SUGGESTED READINGS

Baldinger, Pamela. "The Birth of Greater China." *China Business Review* 19 (May–June 1992): pp. 13–15, 17–20, and 22.

Bennett, Michael. "The People's Republic of China and the Use of International Law in the Spratly Islands Dispute." *Stanford Journal of International Law* 28 (Spring 1992): pp. 425–450.

Brown, Frederick, ed. *Rebuilding Cambodia.* Washington, D.C.: The John Hopkins Foreign Policy Institute, 1992.

Clark, Cal, and Steve Chan, eds. *The Evolving Pacific Basin in the Global Political Economy: Domestic and International Linkages.* Boulder, Colorado: Lynne Rienner Publishers, 1992.

Deng Yong. "Sino-Thai Relations: From Strategic Cooperation to Economic Diplomacy." *Contemporary Southeast Asia* 13 (March 1992): pp. 360–374.

Faust, John R. "The Emerging Security System in East Asia." *Journal of East Asian Affairs* 8, no. 1 (Winter/Spring 1994): pp. 173–204.

Funabashi, Yoichi. "Japan and America: Global Partners." *Foreign Policy* (Spring 1992): pp. 24–39.

Goodman, David S. G., and Gerald Segal, eds. *China in the Nineties: Crisis Management and Beyond.* New York: Oxford University Press, 1991.

Gregor, James. "China's Shadow over Southeast Asian Waters." *Global Affairs* 7 (Summer 1992): pp. 1–13.

Iriye, Akira. *China and Japan in the Global Setting.* Cambridge, Massachusetts: Harvard University Press, 1992.

Ji Guoxing, and Hadi Soeastro, eds. *Sino-Indonesian Relations in the Post–Cold War Era.* Jakarta: Centre for Strategic and International Studies, 1992.

Kim Dae Jung. "The Once and Future Korea." *Foreign Policy* (Spring 1992): pp. 40–55.

Kim, Samuel S. "China as a Regional Power." *Current History* (September 1992): pp. 247–252.

———. "New Directions and Old Puzzles in Chinese Foreign Policy," in *China and the World: New Directions in Chinese Relations,* Samuel S. Kim, ed., Boulder, Colorado: Westview Press, 1989, pp. 3–30.

Klare, Michael. "The Next Great Arms Race." *Foreign Affairs* 72, no. 3 (Summer 1993): pp. 136–152.

Klein, Donald W. "China and ASEAN," in June Teufel Dreyer, ed., *Chinese Defense and Foreign Policy.* New York: Paragon House, 1988, pp. 135–165.

Lee Keun. *New East Asian Economic Development: The Interaction of Capitalism and Socialism.* Armonk, New York: M.E. Sharpe, 1993.

Lin Yu-fang. "The German Unification Model: Applicable to China and Korea?" *Issues and Studies* 28 (May 1992): pp. 88–109.

Mack, Andrew. "North Korea and the Bomb." *Foreign Policy* (Summer 1991): pp. 87–104.

Mirsky, George I. "Central Asia's Emergence." *Current History* (October 1992): pp. 334–338.

Munro, Ross H. "Awakening Dragon: The Real Danger in Asia Is from China." *Policy Review,* no. 62 (Fall 1992): pp. 10–16.

Ono, Shuichi. *Sino-Japanese Economic Relations: Direct Investment and Future Strategy.* Washington, D.C.: World Bank, 1992.

Scalapino, Robert. *The Last Leninists: the Uncertain Future of Asia's Communist States.* Washington, D.C: Center for Strategic and International Studies, 1992.

Schrader, John Y., and James A. Winnefield. *Understanding the Evolving U.S. Role in Pacific Rim Security: A Scenario Based Analysis.* Santa Monica, California: Rand, 1992.

Senguptaa, Prasum. "China Expands Air Forces: Implications for Asia-Pacific Balance of Military Power." *Military Technology* 16 (August 1992): pp. 49–56.

Shambaugh, David. "China's Security Policy in the Post–Cold War Era." *Survival* 34 (Summer 1992): pp. 88–106.

Simon, Sheldon W., ed. *East-Asian Security in the Post–Cold War Era.* Armonk, New York: M.E. Sharpe, 1993.

Sutter, Robert. "Implications of China's Modernization for East and Southeast Asian Security: The Year 2000," in *China's Global Presence,* David M. Lampton and Catherine H. Keyser, eds., Washington, D.C.: American Enterprise Institute, 1988, pp . 201–227.

Whiting, Allen S. "The Politics of Sino-Japanese Relations," in *Chinese Defense and Foreign Policy,* June Teufel Dreyer, ed., New York: Paragon House, 1988, pp. 135–165.

## NOTES

1. Samuel S. Kim, "China As a Regional Power," *Current History* (September 1992), p. 248.

2. Samuel P. Huntington, "The Clash of Civilizations?" *Foreign Affairs* 72, no. 3 (Summer 1993): p. 47.

3. Michael T. Klare, "The Next Great Arms Race," *Foreign Affairs* 72, no. 3 (Summer 1993): p. 139. His data comes from *SIPRI Yearbook, 1992,* and *IISS Military Balance, 1992–1993.*

4. Wen Wei Po, Japan Economic Newswire, November 19, 1992.

5. M. Ali, "Kashmir Keeps South Asia Hostage While Visitors to U.S. Seek Solution," *Washington Report on Middle East Affairs* (October 1992): pp. 43–44.

6. "Li Reiterates Principles of Peaceful Coexistence," *Xinhua,* December 9, 1991, p. 4.

7. "India Enters Chinese Steel Market," *India News,* October 1–15, 1992, p. 3.

8. In a summit conference held in Turkey in 1992, all of the Central Asian Republics except Tajikistan met with Turkey and Azerbaijan to consider a proposal by Turkey's president, Turgut Ozal, for a free trade zone and eventual economic union. President Ozal also called for a regional investment bank and pipelines to carry Central Asian oil and natural gas to Europe via Turkey. ["Turkey Seeks an Economic Muslim Union," *New Arabia,* November 12–25, 1992, p. 24.]

# China and Japan:
# Partners or Rivals in
# the Twenty-first Century?

As the twentieth century draws to a close, the geopolitical structure in Asia and the world looks very different from that of a decade earlier. China and Japan loom ever larger as Asia's dominant powers. How they perceive and interact with each other, as partners or rivals, may well determine whether the next 100 years will be an Asian century of prosperity and global leadership or one of tragedy and suffering. Chinese and Japanese experience during the past century, in which both have suffered in world wars and regional conflicts, should be incentive enough for them to avoid such tragedies in the future.

But if this is to happen, Beijing and Tokyo will have to make difficult decisions at home and in their relations with each other. The economic miracles in both China and Japan, as well as their potential military capability, mean that their future relations will vitally affect not only their very existence, but the well-being of the rest of Asia and the world as a whole. Even before the collapse of the Soviet Union, Japan had become the world's second largest economy, with three-fifths of U.S. production but only half its population. The World Bank estimates that if China continues its 1992–1993 rate of 11–12 percent increases in annual production, mainland China alone will exceed Japanese production in the year 2010 and rival that of the United States or the European Union. If Greater China (made up of the Chinese mainland, Hong Kong, and Taiwan) is included, the World Bank estimates that these goals can be reached in the year 2002.[1]

But many critics are questioning the ability of both China and Japan to continue their economic miracle because of problems both at home and in their market relations abroad. In Japan, major political parties have been discredited by charges of corruption involving high-level politicians. Liberal Democratic Party (LDP) leaders, as well as those of other Japanese parties, have been exposed by the mass media for taking bribes from corporate interests for favors. In addition to political scandals, Japan's economy has fallen into recession, with GNP increasingly at the rate of only 1–2 percent. Japan also continues to have a huge foreign trade surplus, exceeding over $100 billion a year; over half of the surplus is with the United States. This has been a major factor in the rise of the Japanese yen, which in 1994 brings less than 100 yen to the dollar (the lowest rate in post–World War II history), making it difficult for Japan to compete on world markets. In the first half of 1994, the weak coalitions replacing the former ruling LDP have mostly been treading water, unable to make the necessary tough decisions in both domestic and foreign policy.

Decisionmakers in Beijing and other capitals wonder when and if Japan's decisionmakers will take steps to play a regional and global political-security role commensurate with Japan's powerful economic role, both as Asia's dominant economic power and as a world trader and investor, second only to the United States. Beijing likes the fact that Japan has maintained only a self-defense force since World War II. Since the Deng reforms, China has also been a primary beneficiary of Japan's powerful economy. In the future, both China and Japan will, however, have to make difficult decisions about how far to open up their economies to foreign competition. How to avoid a Sino-Japanese arms race, which could undermine the economic and military security of both countries, will also be critical. Yet observers believe that Japan's identity crisis about its future role is only temporary. Japan, they believe, is destined to emerge as both a strong economic power, dedicated increasingly to the liberal open borders paradigm, and a world leader in dealing with political-security issues.[2]

## JAPAN: PARTNER OR RIVAL?

With the end of the Cold War, China and Japan are the two major powers in East Asia. The United States and Russia, the two other great powers that have exerted a dominant influence in Asia over the past century, are reducing their Asian commitments. Sino-Japanese relations will therefore become the key to stability and peace in the Far East over the next decade. The forces for a partnership are strong: Japan is China's most important trading partner and both nations are still wary of their Russian neighbor. But the forces for rivalry are equally strong: a historic animosity that was heightened during World War II. How these two nations manage these forces for rivalry and for partnership over the next decade will shape the future of international relations in East Asia and perhaps the entire globe.

### Military Rivalry

Any contest for military superiority between China and Japan would seemingly favor China, given its population, its location on the Asian land mass, the fact that it has the largest standing army in Asia, and its possession of nuclear weapons. Yet Japan, with only a self-defense force, has the third largest military budget in the world, ranking it after only the United States and contemporary Russia. Japan's technology and its budget allocations allow it to maintain a military force that revives fears of World War II imperialism among Japan's neighbors.

After Japanese efforts to create an Asian coprosperity sphere collapsed at the end of World War II, the nation's military position during the Cold War was solely defensive. The postwar Constitution, written by U.S. general Douglas MacArthur, states that Japan will never again have any offensive military capability. As a consequence, Japan's self-defense force has been limited to 250,000 soldiers. With memories of the U.S. firebombing of Tokyo and of the nuclear explosions in Hiroshima and Nagasaki still vivid, a majority of the Japanese people and all the major political parties have endorsed the antiwar provision in the Constitution.

During the Cold War, a time of great instability in East Asia, Japan accepted this provision at least in part because Japan was protected by U.S. ground troops and by the U.S. nuclear umbrella. There are currently about 50,000 U.S. military personnel in Japan, and the United States has the ability to support rapid mobilization of Japan's military potential, including the possibility of deploying nuclear and thermonuclear warheads and delivery systems. The next generation of Chinese leaders will all ask how China can avoid such a Japanese scenario while at the same time increasing the prestige and capability of its own military services, to which it feels rightfully entitled.

## Economic Interdependence

In the early part of the twentieth century, when Chinese intellectuals were seeking models of nation building that would allow China to drive out the European powers, they looked to the Japanese model. Sun Yat-sen, the "father" of modern China, studied in Japan, as did many other Chinese revolutionaries. All were searching for ways to lead China to "wealth and power," the motto of their movement.

Japanese military power inspired the respect of all Asians through its defeat of the Russian Empire in 1905. Japan's quick modernization and industrialization were also admired. A country that had its initial contacts with the Netherlands, Portugal, and then the United States (via Commodore Perry in 1853) inflicted a humiliating defeat on one of Europe's mightiest land powers within a few short decades. Quick modernization and industrialization were the basis of this military victory. With the Meiji Restoration in 1868, Japanese society was reorganized and opened to Western science, technology, and capitalist economic structures. The *zaibatsu,* the huge industrial conglomerates such as Mitsubishi, were established; government administration was modernized; and popular education was emphasized. All this was achieved with very little actual foreign penetration of Japanese society and the Japanese economy. After World War II, fearful of disrupting what was left of the Japanese economy, General MacArthur limited his economic initiatives to land reform in the countryside. The zaibatsu were allowed to survive and, as many U.S. car owners can attest, to prosper.

Japanese models of development were discounted by the Communist Chinese, who initially looked to the Soviet Union for guidelines to quick industrialization. Just as Stalin had brutally collectivized the Soviet farmers, so Mao collectivized Chinese peasants. Just as Stalin promoted heavy industry above all else, so did Mao. In his mercurial way, Mao experimented with models of economic development, but within the socialist mode of production. Japan's statist capitalism was considered neither by Mao nor by those within the ruling hierarchy who still looked to Moscow, despite the fact that Japan's gross national product came to exceed that of the Soviet Union in the 1980s.

Zhou Enlai's announcement that China would pursue the Four Modernizations changed the Chinese attitude toward the Japanese economic model. Zhou and Deng Xiaoping, Zhou's successor, observed that the Japanese model (as noted in Chapter 3) inspired the economic miracles in the Four Little Tigers (Taiwan, South Korea, Hong Kong, and Singapore). The combination of centralized, authoritarian power with land reform, emphasis on industrial investment leading to quick growth, and promotion of exports was attractive to the Chinese leadership. It calls for continued political control with economic growth.

To implement the Four Modernizations, China needed capital investment. Although concerned about becoming too dependent on a single country, China has nonetheless allowed a high level of Japanese investment; for example, capital loans totaled over $800 million in 1992 alone. Yet Japan's growing economic dominance in East Asia, with the growing dependence of not only China but also most of Southeast Asia on Japanese investment and trade, is a major worry for China's leaders. Japan is China's largest source of technology and capital goods, whereas China is a major source of raw materials for Japanese industry. Japan is the major market for Asian, Australian, and potentially Siberian raw materials. Japanese high-technology products already dominate most Asian markets, either through imports, joint ventures, or Japanese subsidiaries. Further agreements amongst Asian countries to lower trade barriers might further promote Japanese domination, in effect creating the Japanese coprosperity sphere through peace rather than war. Like many other Asian countries, China has an unfavorable balance of trade with Japan because it sells low-priced raw materials and labor-intensive industrial goods while purchasing expensive high-technology and finished products from Japan.

## Future Sino-Japanese Relations

In view of the continuing military buildup in Asia in the 1990s, the time when the Asian rimland has become the world's most rapidly developing economic region, Sino-Japanese relations perhaps provide the key to both Asian economic progress and regional security. Up to the present, all Sino-Japanese interactions have been in nonsecurity fields: trade, technology, investment, academic exchanges, tourism, and diplomacy. China is concerned about Japan's growing domination of trade and investment throughout Asia, but it nonetheless needs more investment, a higher level of technology, and more trade with Japan. Basically, Japan and China are natural trading partners, with China providing a wide range of natural resources, including coal, oil, timber, and agricultural products.

These economic relationships are extremely beneficial to both countries, but there are also problems. As China continues to develop economically, both countries see each other as rivals throughout the Asian rimland. Japan may play the Southeast and South Asian cards by seeking cheap raw materials, markets for its products, and labor-intensive investments in these Asian regions as an alternative to further dependence on China. In addition, Japan's more advanced technology is not exported to China because Japan seeks to maintain its technological advantages over its chief Asian rival in the twenty-first century. Japan is also concerned about China's modernization of its military forces, through both arms purchases and development of military technology inside China, which Japan avoids helping, a policy also followed by Japan's Western allies.

Currently, neither China nor Japan poses major security problems to the other. The problem is in the future. If military arms races continue to grow in Asia, it is highly unlikely that Japan will accept a situation in which China uses its growing economic strength to develop a dominant military capability in Asia. China is also concerned about Japan's growing political and security role in Asia, for example, through its leadership in UN peace-keeping in Cambodia, including the sending of Japanese troops to a Southeast Asian country for the first time since World War II.

## TRADE AND INVESTMENT

Growing complexity in Asian trade and investment patterns increasingly tie China to Japan and both to the rest of Asia. Japan, according to Chinese sources, is now China's largest trading partner, with $16 billion in Chinese exports to Japan in 1993 and $23 billion in imports from Japan. But the United States remains the largest market for both Chinese and Japanese exports. Asia's two emerging economic giants also have the world's largest trade surpluses with the United States. Japan's is the largest ($59.3 billion in 1993), but China's is second ($23 billion).[3]

The complexity and importance of economic interdependence among China, Japan, the United States, and the rest of Asia is also revealed by investment patterns in the 1990s. As noted in earlier chapters, mainland

China receives over 75 percent of its investment from Hong Kong, Taiwan, and overseas Chinese. But Japan and the United States are also key investors. Japan is especially important for infrastructure development, including power, transport, and communications, whereas the United States is now the major source of Chinese passenger airliners. Japan is the largest investor in Southeast Asia, and overseas Chinese in the ASEAN countries work very closely with the Japanese. At the same time, Southeast Asian overseas Chinese are a major source of investment in mainland China.

Growing economic interdependence in Asia is closely tied to interdependence with other regions, especially the United States. This suggests the need for China and Japan, as Asia's two economic dynamos, to adjust economic relations not only with each other, on the basis of mutual self-interests, but also with the rest of Asia as well as the United States and the West. In the 1990s, Asia has become the United States' largest trading partner, larger than either Western Europe or Latin America. But as Table 7.1 shows, both Japan and China will have to work out more equitable trade relations with the United States, as will most other U.S. trading partners in Asia, to prevent future trade wars.

**Table 7.1    U.S. Exports and Imports with Selected Asian Nations (in millions of dollars)**

|                              | 1990     | 1991     | 1992     |
|------------------------------|----------|----------|----------|
| Imports from ASEAN countries | 27,181.8 | 28,918.0 | 36,053.0 |
| Exports to ASEAN countries   | 18,953.6 | 20,775.3 | 23,985.6 |
| Imports from China           | 15,237.3 | 18,969.0 | 25,729.1 |
| Exports to China             | 4,806.4  | 6278.3   | 9,068.6  |
| Imports from Hong Kong       | 9,621.6  | 9,278.5  | 9,799.2  |
| Exports to Hong Kong         | 6,816.7  | 8,137.1  | 9,068.6  |
| Imports from Japan           | 89,684.1 | 91,510.6 | 97,181.4 |
| Exports to Japan             | 48,579.6 | 48,125.3 | 43,763.9 |
| Imports from South Korea     | 18,484.1 | 17,018.5 | 17,690.8 |
| Exports to South Korea       | 14,404.1 | 15,504.9 | 14,630.1 |
| Imports from Taiwan          | 22,685.9 | 23,023.0 | 24,601.3 |
| Exports to Taiwan            | 11,490.8 | 13,182.4 | 15,204.7 |

*Source:* John Bresnan, *From Dominoes to Dynamos: The Transformation of Southeast Asia* (New York: Council on Foreign Relations Press, 1994), data from Table 7 on p. 31 and Table 8 on p. 32. Bresnan's data come from United States Department of Commerce, Bureau of the Census, Compiled by Gary Brook, Office of the Pacific Basin.

## POSSIBILITIES FOR SINO-JAPANESE PARTNERSHIP

Indecision about Japan's political and security role at the regional and global levels has not prevented Tokyo from playing a key role in opening up

China to the outside world. Japan also helped China finesse the problem of how to normalize diplomatic relations with other nations while these nations continued their trade and nondiplomatic ties to Taiwan. In 1971, eight years before formal Sino-U.S. diplomatic relations were established, Tokyo simultaneously established diplomatic relations with Beijing, broke diplomatic relations with Taipei, and established a nongovernmental office on the island of Taiwan to conduct economic and other nondiplomatic functions. This ingenious arrangement not only benefitted China, Taiwan, and Japan, but it also served as a precedent for the United States and other countries when they switched their diplomatic relations from Taipei to Beijing.

Japan has also played a key role in opening up China to trade and investment. Tokyo successfully supported renewal of China's membership in the World Bank and the International Monetary Fund. While the United States convinced the World Bank to cut off further lending to China after the Tiananmen Square incident, Japan played a leading role in persuading the other G-7 nations to support renewal of World Bank lending to China. Today, while World Bank and IMF lending to Russia is limited because Moscow cannot meet the lending standards, China is the largest recipient of World Bank loans. Japan also supported China's participation as an observer at the 1987–1993 Uruguay Round negotiations, sponsored by GATT, to further reduce international trade barriers and upgrade GATT to a new World Trade Organization (WTO, the successor organization to GATT). Japanese support will be a key factor in China's admission to the newly created WTO despite U.S. efforts to get Beijing to take further steps to meet GATT/WTO trade standards prior to China's inclusion. Tokyo has taken the position that internal Chinese human rights policies should not be a criterion for integrating China into the global economic system and that conditionalities should not be placed on China's international trade relations.

What has Japan received in return? During the first six months of 1993, Japan increased its investments in China 58 percent over the first six months of the previous year. Opportunities beckon. For example, Japanese retail chains are hoping to expand retail sales in China following recent relaxation of restrictions.[4] One Japanese retail chain, Yaohan, says that it can employ twenty-eight Chinese workers for the same cost as one Japanese.[5] China is also a major source of raw materials, including oil, coal, and agricultural products, as well as a growing source of cheap consumer goods, which are popular in Japan.

China's ties to overseas Chinese are also important to Sino-Japanese relations. Overseas Chinese, as noted earlier, provide much of the business class in Southeast Asian countries. Through informal relationships that help Japan's multinationals, which are the major source of investment in Southeast Asia, they have worked very closely with Japanese investors and traders. The triangular partnership that has developed, based on informal business ties among overseas Chinese, mainland China, and Japan, further promotes economic integration and interdependence among Japan, Southeast Asia, and Greater China, as well as with the rest of the world.

A key advocate of growing Asian economic and political cooperation is Singapore's senior statesman and former prime minister Lee Kuan Yew. Lee speaks for most Asians when he says that they share a common heritage, take pride in Asia's growing modernization and development, and share common values such as Confucianism (family values and a desire for order) and a desire to work hard and improve themselves. Lee, who is himself Chinese, believes that Asians share many desirable traits, some of which he thinks are declining in the West, including the desire to strive hard to improve oneself through education and hard work. Most of all, Lee believes that the Chinese, Japanese, South Koreans, and Southeast Asians share a common desire to work together as partners to make the twenty-first century an Asian century.[6]

To achieve this, Lee rejected Malaysia's proposal for a closed Asian trading system in favor of one in which barriers not only between Asian countries but also with the rest of the world are gradually eliminated. China and Japan agree with Lee and with President Clinton on the need to avoid closed trading systems in Asia, in North America, or between Asia and North America; however, China and Japan oppose formal structures for eliminating trade barriers between Asia and North America because they fear U.S. domination of such structures.

Japan and China instead prefer to work through the global trading system through the Uruguay GATT agreement. Both countries resent U.S. bilateral economic threats aimed at changing Chinese and Japanese policies on access to internal markets. A greatly strengthened new World Trade Organization, which is scheduled to come into being in January 1995, will handle some complaints between trading partners that were previously handled through bilateral negotiations. In the future, disagreements between China and the United States over the relationship between trade and human rights (with threats to cut off China's MFN privileges) and between Japan and the United States (with threats to impose specific penalties on Japan as a means of opening up Japanese markets) will theoretically be resolved through the WTO. Thus, both China and Japan stand to gain from China's reentry into the world trade regime via GATT/WTO.

## Cooperation on Security Issues

Sino-Japanese security relations are more difficult. Both countries have reaped security benefits from the new Asian geopolitical structure emerging after the Cold War. To continue to reap these benefits, as East Asia's two major powers, China and Japan will have to work out ways to avoid rivalry between themselves. If they do not, arms races are likely to occur not only between China and Japan, but also in other Asian countries, to the detriment of all.

Economic well-being and the prevention of Asian instability and disorder are the prime reasons China and Japan should cooperate on security matters. But the history of Sino-Japanese relations during the first half of the twentieth century makes it difficult for Chinese and Japanese leaders to cooperate other than through informal talks, which, indeed, have occurred between Tokyo and Beijing in the 1990s. They can cooperate on security issues such as defusing the North Korean nuclear threat. Yet unless they can gain confidence in each other's security roles, Beijing and Tokyo could potentially become bitter rivals and even military enemies in a new type of cold (or hot) war based solely on geopolitical and nationalistic considerations rather than on disagreement over political ideologies. China and Japan, with their future military potential, hold the key to Asia's future security and well-being in the twenty-first century.

Since the end of the Cold War, with the reduced influence of outside powers in the region, Japan's greatest initiative to promote regional stability and security came in 1992–1993 when Japanese prime minister Miyazawa enunciated what became known as the Miyazawa Doctrine, a Japanese initiative to create a regional forum to discuss Asian security issues, modeled on the Conference on Security and Cooperation in Europe (CSCE). Throughout the Cold War era, Japan had followed the Yoshida Doctrine, named after Prime Minister Yoshida's policies of the 1950s, which mandated that Japan concentrate on economic development at home and increased trade and investment with Asia and the rest of the world. Japan pursued economic development while relying on the U.S. security umbrella to protect itself militarily, thus avoiding any Japanese military buildup other than the Self-Defense Force (SDF) of 250,000 personnel who were responsible only for the defense of the main islands. The Japanese people, as well as most political leaders, accepted Article 9 of the Japanese Constitution, which outlaws the right to make war except for strictly defensive purposes.

Under the new Miyazawa Doctrine, Japan seeks to continue its military alliance with the United States while at the same time undertaking initiatives of its own to play a more normal regional and global security role. Participating in United Nations peacekeeping operations, gaining a permanent seat on the United Nations Security Council, and promoting an Asian regional forum to discuss growing Asian security issues in the post–Cold War era are possible initiatives. Under the Bush administration, Washington at first hesitated to support a multilateral forum to discuss Asian security issues, even though Tokyo insisted on including the United States, Canada, and the European Community (now the European Union). But the Clinton administration has supported the Japanese initiative, which was presented to ASEAN at its June 1993 meeting and to ASEAN's dialogue partners (South

Korea, Australia, New Zealand, Canada, the United States, and the European Union) thereafter. ASEAN and the dialogue partners also agreed to include Russia, China, and Vietnam as observers to the Asian Regional Security Forum, which first met in September 1993.

Japan has always insisted that any regional security structure must include China. However, the inclusion of China, Russia, and Vietnam along with other Asian actors (except for Taiwan because of Chinese opposition and Myanmar because of its extreme domestic policies) is only a beginning. For an East Asian security organization to be successful, its members must be willing to work within its structures. NATO and the European community achieved this goal primarily because of the perception of an outside threat. That sort of threat does not currently exist to unite the leaders of all the East Asian nations; instead the smaller nations in the area are increasingly nervous over the growing economic and military might of both China and Japan. And, as previously noted, Beijing prefers either bilateral talks (but no formal structures) or limited actions through the United Nations Security Council rather than regional security arrangements.[7]

## Sino-Japanese Rivalry: Structural Realism and the Balance of Power

> China may get a lot more pushy, while Japan becomes somewhat less so. More-realistic is that an age is dawning for the smaller Asian countries, an age in which they face not one but two giant neighbors impinging heavily, each increasingly interested in politics inside and outside the region, and each increasingly capable of making a host of new demands.[8]

Just as a triangular relationship of economic interdependence has emerged among China, Japan, and the rest of Asia, a structural power system is emerging in Asia in which the little states of East and Southeast Asia find themselves fearful of Asia's two major powers. Japan and other Asian countries share a fear of China as an emerging military power that may try to exert pressure on its neighbors to the east and south. Their fear is fueled by the fact that China, already one of the world's greatest military powers, has doubled its military budget in the last four years. Estimates of China's military expenditures range from $22 billion to $36 billion, the latter taking off-budget income into account.[9] This is income from sources not listed in the official military budget.

China's continuing military buildup, especially its expansion and modernization of its air naval units and its deep-sea naval capability, is a matter of growing concern to Japan's political leaders. China has made specific territorial claims that pose difficult choices for Tokyo. How should it respond, either politically or through additional measures, to China's authorization of deals for oil exploration in the East China Sea? These waters are closer to the Senkaku Islands than to mainland China. The Senkaku Islands, which are halfway between Taiwan and Okinawa (the latter of which is part of Japan's home islands), were claimed by Japan in 1890. It was not until over 100 years later, in its February 1992 proclamation, that China claimed these islands, along with the Paracel and Spratly island chains in the South China Sea, as Chinese territory.

All of this is occurring while Russo-Japanese tensions continue over Japan's request for the return of the four Kurile islands seized by the Russians from the Japanese at the end of World War II. Tensions on the Korean peninsula over North Korea's presumed development of nuclear arms also continue to heighten. At a time when other states such as the United States, Russia, France, Germany, and Great Britain are cutting back their military budgets, China's military expansion and its territorial claims alarm its neighbors, including the Japanese.

In response to these developments, a great debate is raging in Japan over its future security policies. But a consensus seems to be emerging, supporting the Miyazawa Doctrine, as follows: (1) continue Japan's military ties with the United States, keeping a residual (even if reduced) U.S. military presence in Japan; (2) incrementally build up Japan's air and naval capability, including coproduction of the next-generation FSX fighter with the United States; (3) keep Japan's self-defense forces at their current level (250,000—less than one-tenth the size of China's PLA); and (4) reserve the decision whether to go nuclear for the future.[10]

There is also a consensus developing amongst Japan's policy elites over their country's role in the United Nations. If Japan sends military personnel outside the home islands, for now peacekeeping operations will be the instrument. In the summer of 1992, after great debate in the Japanese Diet (parliament), the government was authorized to send up to 2,000 military personal to serve as United Nations peacekeepers, but only in a nonmilitary capacity. Following the passage of the resolution, 600 Japanese noncombatants (engineers and service personnel) were sent to Cambodia to serve with the United Nations Transitional Authority (for details of this operation see Chapter 6), which was under the direction of Yasushi Akashi, a Japanese. Later, a token noncombatant unit of fifty Japanese SDF personnel was sent to Mozambique to serve with the United Nations peacekeeping operation, the first time that Japanese soldiers have ever been sent to the African continent.

Japanese citizens also serve in other capacities in the United Nations system, for example, as head of the UN's World Health Organization (WHO) and as the UN High Commissioner for Refugees (UNHCR). Because of his success in directing the United Nations operation in Cambodia, Akashi was later appointed by the United Nations to head its peacekeeping operation in Bosnia, an even more difficult task. The one United Nations leadership role that has eluded Japan, even though Japan has been a major financial contributor to United Nations security operations, is a permanent seat on the

Security Council. This would require a formal amendment of the United Nations Charter, which would require a supporting vote of both China and Russia—potential security threats to Japan in the post–Cold War era.

## CHINESE PERCEPTIONS OF JAPAN'S SECURITY ROLE

Beijing does not wish to see Japan emerge as a major regional or global military actor. According to Gerald Segal, "China will expect Japan to accept a subordinate role."[11] "When Japan's self-defense forces participated in the United Nations Transitional Authority in Cambodia, Beijing objected strongly because China hopes to keep Japan in "an abnormal state so it would not challenge China."[12]

Beijing would like to discourage Japan's military buildup and any increase in its regional and global security role for a number of reasons: memories of Japanese imperialism, China's own desire to be the major military power in Asia, and China's current inability to match Japan's dominant economic role in Asia.

Beijing is also going through a period of internal debate over its own role in the United Nations. It has been unwilling historically to make major contributions to United Nations peacekeeping operations, which from its perspective are mostly Western initiatives to dominate global security arrangements. Other than a token Chinese force serving as peacekeepers in the United Nations Transitional Authority in Cambodia, Beijing's other contribution has been 100 UN observers along the border between Iraq and Kuwait following the Gulf War.[13]

Japan's contribution was much greater, although it did not involve United Nations observers. Under pressure from the coalition fighting against Iraq (following a heated debate in the Japanese Diet), Japan contributed $13 billion to the costs of the operation. Then, after the fighting was over, Japan sent four mine sweepers to help clean up the shipping lanes in the Gulf. Should Japan decide to increase its support for peacekeeping operations, for example, by raising its current limit of 2,000 Japanese troops serving under United Nations command as peacekeepers, this would pose a problem for Beijing. Nevertheless, the other permanent members of the Security Council, given the current constraints on their military budgets, will push Japan to contribute more economically and perhaps militarily to any future peacekeeping operation.

## ASIA'S FUTURE BALANCE-OF-POWER SYSTEM

Asia's balance-of-power system in the twenty-first century may take many forms based on the different geopolitical and economic variables. In all likelihood, Japan will react to events beyond its four main islands rather than initiating new power structures. Japan benefits from the present system, in which relative stability exists with no immediate threats to Japan's security. At the same time, as Asia's economic dynamo, prime investor, and trader, Japan has been able to emphasize its regional and global economic primacy while remaining essentially a free-rider on security issues. As noted earlier, a continued U.S. presence in Japan, as well as in South Korea, even with only 100,000 personnel (approximately the same as in post–Cold War Europe), enables Japan to use its resources and scientific research to promote its economic primacy. Japan's 125 million people are overwhelmingly dedicated to maintaining a low military profile, including avoidance of the nuclear option if possible. Other than among the far right, there is little hankering for restoration of Japan's past military grandeur as Asia's hegemon during the first half of the twentieth century.

## China as Hegemon

The situation may be very different in mainland China. Tokyo's concern over China's continuing military buildup in the 1990s, even though China's neighbors pose no major threat to mainland China's security, has already been noted. Some possible reasons Beijing may wish to be the dominant Asian military power in the twenty-first century were given in earlier chapters. Before looking at Japan's probable reactions, it is important to review future Chinese policy choices:

- Should Beijing's central authority be threatened, including the power base of China's ruling Communist elite, the leaders in Beijing may appeal to nationalist revisionism and pride in China's ancient grandeur as the Middle Kingdom.
- Should the next generation of leaders seek to demonstrate China's new prowess as Asia's regional hegemon to head off further decentralization of power to China's regions, the continuing Chinese military buildup will be perceived as threatening by the surrounding nations.
- Should China continue to grow economically at its present rate, and should other states including Japan continue their current rates of investment in China, this may lead to further dependence on the Chinese market. Beijing may then believe that others will have no choice but to kowtow to China's views on how disputes should be settled with its neighbors.
- Should China gain both economic and military regional supremacy after the turn of the century, Beijing may wish to use its new strength to further expand its territorial claims (on both land and sea) based on ancient Chinese maps of the Middle Kingdom.

- Should Taiwan at some point declare itself an independent state, Beijing may seek to coerce it into submission by confiscating Taiwanese investments on the mainland. Or Beijing might seek to use its increasing military capability to coerce the independently minded Taiwanese into submission.
- Should instability develop inside Russian Siberia, Beijing may wish to use its growing economic and military strength to increase its influence inside the region, which at one time was either part of the ancient Middle Kingdom or under its sphere of influence.
- Should China gain military supremacy, it may be tempted to expand its claims to territorial waters and their resources in the East China and South China seas at the expense of its neighbors.

How would Japan react to any combination of the above scenarios? Such events surely would serve as a wake-up call to the Japanese.

## Nuclear Options

Because pacifist and antinuclear sentiments are likely to remain very strong in Japan, it is highly unlikely that Japan will enter into a conventional or nuclear arms race with China. More likely is a scenario in which Tokyo will seek to create a limited second-strike capability to deter nuclear and conventional attacks from abroad. To date, Tokyo has relied on the U.S. nuclear umbrella, as have the NATO countries and South Korea. In the face of a massive nuclear threat from abroad, however, Tokyo may fear that Washington, not wanting to risk its own destruction to save the Japanese, would renege on promises to come to its aid. A continually declining U.S. military presence in Asia after the turn of the century might further convince the Japanese that U.S. security guarantees will have to be supplemented with a second-strike nuclear capability.

Japan will not be able to match China tit for tat in conventional and/or nuclear forces for the foreseeable future. Rather than trying to match China in each weapon category, Japan's best option is to provide for a strong defense, but one that would not threaten the Chinese mainland through an equal or superior capability. The Japanese are well aware of their geopolitical situation, one in which four one-megaton thermonuclear bombs could obliterate Japan's four main islands. To counter the threat posed by an expanded Chinese nuclear military capability in the twenty-first century, Tokyo may seek a deep-ocean second-strike option. In this scenario, all of Japan's nuclear capability would be on submarines, and Japan would have the ability to cause grave damage to the Chinese mainland, thereby deterring attack. Japan would not, however, have the capability of destroying China's existence through a first strike—the ability to win by destroying the opponent's nuclear capabilities through a surprise attack.

## Balance of Power

Should China seek to be the Asian hegemon in the twenty-first century, Japan is likely to become its chief opponent. There is little likelihood that Japan will seek to match China's ground forces, or even contemplate a major use of ground forces, either in mainland China or other parts of Asia. Not only does Japan's past militarism continue to stir up fears in China and the rest of Asia, but the realities associated with the attempt to occupy and control other countries by force argue against such a response. Napoleon, Hitler, Mussolini, Stalin, and Tōjō come to mind, as do more recent U.S. efforts to control Vietnam and Russian efforts to control Afghanistan through military force. All ultimately ended in failure.

Instead, Japan would join together with other nations to oppose future Chinese hegemony in the region. Other powers, such as the United States and Russia, might play a backup role, but Japan would be the logical leader of future coalitions reacting to Chinese threats of coercion or actual initiation of military conflict. This would echo the classical balance-of-power era in Europe, when Great Britain used its naval power to play the role of balancer. Japan, too, may seek to use its extensive air power to take on the role of balancer.

## Conflict Inside China

Another scenario that could also stimulate Japan to play a greater political-security role in Asia would be the development of tensions inside China that might lead to the decentralization of power or even internal regional conflict. Such possibilities were noted in earlier chapters. Tokyo's reactions to such developments might include the following scenarios.

Because the PLA is increasingly a government within a government, with 80 percent of its economic facilities producing civilian goods that provide much of its income, in a future internal crisis between Beijing and different regions, the military could conceivably back regional rather than central forces. This could cause problems for Japan because China's nuclear forces, as well as its ground, air and naval units, might be divided into opposing factions, some backing the leadership in Beijing and others backing powerful regional provinces.

Should mainland China actually break apart into different regions, logically Japan would at least tacitly support those groups advocating liberal economic and political values. A divided China is a weak China, which (unless the devolution of power leads to chaos) the Japanese prefer. Japan's primary security interest is maintaining a stable order in Asia conducive to trade and investment. Should open conflict break out on the mainland—most likely through Beijing's efforts to reassert its central control in a manner similar to the role Moscow is now attempting to play within the

Commonwealth of Independent States—Japan is unlikely to become involved militarily. Japanese leaders are more likely to seek the role of mediator while avoiding direct intervention. Currently, this is the role which the Conference on Security and Cooperation in Europe is attempting to play in Eastern Europe and the former Soviet Union. But there is no similar regional structure in Asia—yet.

## CHINA AND JAPAN AT THE CROSSROADS

The above scenarios are only conjectures. More likely, China and Japan will be partners rather than rivals in the twenty-first century. Both are likely to see the increasing advantages of complex interdependence and of Chinese and Japanese partnership at the regional and global levels. China and Japan, as well as other Asian countries, also share feelings similar to those of Singapore senior statesman Lee Kuan Yew. They are likely to reject a future Asia with extreme forms of individualism in favor of an orderly civil society with strong community values. Similar societal values and strong economic ties may be the ties that bind.

It has already been noted how Japan is likely to act in its relations with China, as well as other Asian countries. As for China, its leaders during and after the transition following Deng Xiaoping's passing from the scene will have a wide variety of domestic and foreign policy choices. If they increasingly adopt the liberal paradigm and seek regional stability through negotiation and compromise with their neighbors, they are likely to find Tokyo a strong friend and partner rather than rival. Should China seek to play the role of hegemon, however, it will surely find Japan uniting with other Asians to try to persuade Beijing to abandon such a role.

Rivalries over economic and political ideologies are giving way to alternative scenarios as the Cold War recedes into the past. Renewed nationalistic conflict vies with the growing appeal of complex interdependence, in which all benefit from seeking solutions based on mutual self-interest, as the dominant force in the world. To prevent future conflict, Japan will have to take further steps to avoid using its economic power to gain benefits at the expense of its neighbors, and China will have to decide whether to impose a more liberal paradigm in economic as well as political-security concerns.

## POLICY OPTIONS

Beijing's decisionmakers face both opportunities and dangers that should lead them to consider seriously the following policies toward Japan:

## Option 1: Make Japanese Trade and Investment Conditional on Better Terms

- In return for further trade and investment concessions, Japan should agree to more coproduction agreements that would provide China more advanced technology, especially dual-use technology such as advanced computers.
- Further Chinese concessions should be contingent on Japan opening up its markets further to Chinese consumer goods and other products.

## Option 2: Balance Concessions to Japan and Other States

- As China's domestic market and production grows, Beijing should balance the influence of Japan or any other country by making similar concessions and demands with others, taking advantage of China's improved bargaining position.
- Bilateral negotiations with other states, including Japan, may be preferable to general concessions through GATT, WTO, or regional economic regimes.

## Option 3: Seek Further Japanese Aid Without Conditionalities

- Unlike the United States, Japan has provided China assistance without questioning domestic human rights policies after Tiananmen Square. Because decisionmakers in Tokyo have a greater understanding and willingness to avoid attaching conditionalities on trade, investment, and aid, Beijing can use Tokyo as a mediator in supporting Chinese interests in global regimes such as the IMF, the World Bank Group, and GATT/WTO. Japan strongly supports Chinese readmission to GATT.

## Option 4: Work Informally with Tokyo to Solve Asian Security Problems

- Both Beijing and Tokyo have problems with formal regional security structures. But as Asia's key powers, they share a common interest in defusing regional security threats, assuming that neither Beijing nor Tokyo wishes to use force or the threat of force to promote its own regional influence.

- If Beijing wishes Japan to limit its own military buildup, it must work informally with Tokyo's decisionmakers in deciding the legitimate military capabilities of each country, as well as the capabilities of other regional actors. Beijing cannot expect Tokyo to avoid indefinitely the nuclear military option if it continues to build up its own nuclear capability while others in East Asia have no nuclear forces.
- In the immediate future, Beijing needs to work closely with Tokyo to defuse the danger of nuclear and conventional conflict on the Korean peninsula, as well as in South Asia.
- Beijing and Tokyo can work quietly behind the scenes to avoid not only arms races and potential conflicts between themselves (for example, over the Senkaku Islands), but also potential conflicts throughout the region, thereby strengthening nonmilitary solutions to regional tensions.

## Option 5: Seek Understanding with Tokyo on Global Security

- Beijing can work with Tokyo to reform the United Nations Security Council structure to provide a better balance between the roles of the rich Western countries and developing countries. Seating Japan, from Beijing's perspective, would require not only greater agreement on the respective security roles of the two countries but also cooperation in increasing the security role of the non-Western world (with permanent seats for non-Western countries in addition to China).
- Both Tokyo and Beijing are undergoing major debates about their own future global security roles, including support for and participation in United Nations peacekeeping operations in Asia and other regions, so both states need to come to a better understanding of each other's UN security roles to ensure they will not be a source of tension in the twenty-first century.

## DISCUSSION QUESTIONS

1. In what ways has China patterned its economic development on the Japanese model?
2. How have Sino-Japanese economic relations benefitted each country?
3. In what ways do China and Japan share similar or different views on economic relations at the regional and global levels?
4. What is the relationship between mainland Chinese, overseas Chinese, and Japanese business interests?
5. What are the reasons China and Japan are likely to be economic partners in the twenty-first century? Economic rivals?
6. In what ways are political-security decisions in Beijing likely to affect Japanese political-security decisions in the future, including the question of Japan's nuclear option?
7. Regardless of what happens, why are the capabilities and purposes of Chinese and Japanese military forces likely to be different in important ways in the twenty-first century?
8. In what ways do Chinese and Japanese decisionmakers share similar or different views on regional and global security structures, including their perceptions of the United Nations Security Council and its activities?
9. What circumstances might lead to Sino-Japanese rivalry on security issues in the future?
10. In what ways does Asian preeminence and well-being in the twenty-first century depend on how China and Japan perceive and interact with each other and the rest of Asia?
11. In what ways do the decisionmakers in Beijing and Tokyo share similar or different views of their relationships with Washington?

## SUGGESTED READINGS

Anderson, Stephen J. "Japan As an Activist State in the Pacific Basin: Japan and Regional Organizations." *Journal of East Asian Affairs* 7, no. 2 (Summer/Fall 1993): pp. 498–544.

Arase, David, *Buying Power: The Political Economy of Japanese Foreign Aid.* Boulder, Colorado: Lynne Rienner Publishers, 1995.

———. "Japan's Evolving Security Policy After the Cold War." *Journal of East Asian Affairs* 8, no. 2 (Summer/Fall 1994): pp. 396–420.

Armstrong, David. "Chinese Perspectives on the New World Order." *Journal of East Asian Affairs* 8, no. 2 (Summer/Fall 1994): pp. 454–481.

Bodbrow, Davis B. "Playing for Safety—Japan's Security Practices." *Japan Quarterly* 31, no. 1: pp. 33–43.

Brown, Eugene. "Japanese Security Policy in the Post–Cold War World: Threat Perceptions and Strategic Options." *Journal of East Asian Affairs* 8, no. 2 (Summer/Fall 1994): pp. 327–362.

Calder, Kent E. "Japanese Foreign Economic Policy Formation: Explaining the Reactive State." *World Politics* 40, no. 4 (July 1988): pp. 517–541.

Ellings, Richard J., and Edward A. Olsen. "A New Pacific Profile." *Foreign Policy,* no. 89 (Winter 1992–93): pp. 116–136.

Funabashi, Toichi. "The Asianization of Asia." *Foreign Affairs* 72, no. 5 (November/ December 1993): pp. 75–86.

Hanami, Andrew K. "Japan and the Military Balance of Power in Northeast Asia." *Journal of East Asian Affairs* 8, no. 2 (Summer/Fall 1994): pp. 363–395.

Hornik, Richard. "Bursting China's Bubble." *Foreign Affairs* 73, no. 3 (May/June 1994): pp. 28–42.

Ikle, Fred Charles, and Terumasa Nakanishi. "Japan's Grand Strategy." *Foreign Affairs* 69, no. 3 (Summer l990): pp. 81–95.

Khampoo, Chaiwat. "Japan's Role in Southeast Asian Security." *Pacific Affairs* 64, no. l (Spring 1991): pp. 7–22.

Kristof, Nicholas D. "The Rise of China." *Foreign Affairs* 72, no. 5 (November/ December 1993): pp. 59–74.

Lavin, Franklin L. "Negotiating with the Chinese." *Foreign Affairs* 73, no. 4 (July/August 1994): pp. 16–22.

Mahbubani, Kishore. "Japan Adrift." *Foreign Policy,* no. 88 (Fall 1993): pp. 126–144.

Nye, Joseph S., Jr. "Coping with Japan." *Foreign Policy,* no. 89 (Winter 1992–1993): pp. 96–115.

Okita, Saburo. "Japan's Role in Asia-Pacific Cooperation," *Annals of the American Academy of Political and Social Science* (January 1991): pp. 25–37.

Segal, Gerald. "China's Changing Shape." *Foreign Affairs* 73, no. 3 (May/June 1994): pp. 43–58.

Shinohara, Miyohei. "Japan As a World Economic Power." *Annals of the American Academy of Political and Social Science* (January 1991): pp. 12–24.

Silk, Leonard, and Tom Kono. "Sayonara, Japan, Inc." *Foreign Policy,* no. 93 (Winter 1993–94): pp. 115–131.

Sing, Lai Sing. "From Mikhail Gorbachev's Policy to China's Regional Role." *Journal of East Asian Affairs* 7, no. 2 (Summer/ Fall 1993): pp. 498–544.

Taira, Koji. "Japan, an Imminent Hegemon?" *Annals of the American Academy of Political Science* (January 1991): pp. 151–163.

Wong, Amy. "Japan's National Security and Cultivation of ASEAN Elites." *Contemporary Southeast Asia Study* 22, no. 4 (March 1991): pp. 306–330.

Zakaria, Fareed. "A Conversation with Lee Kuan Yew." *Foreign Affairs* 73, no. 2 (March/April 1994): pp. 109–126.

## NOTES

1. See Gerald Segal, "China's Changing Shape," *Foreign Affairs* 73, no. 3 (May/June 1994). Segal notes that the World Bank has a reputation for conservative estimates. The size of China's current economy is also hidden by official currency exchange rates. As a result of undervaluation, the World Bank and the International Monetary Fund believe that real purchasing power is three times as high as its official GNP per capita would indicate.

2. See Merrill Goozner, "Don't Be Blinded by Bright Talk of a Japan on the Wane," *Chicago Tribune,* July 3, 1994, Section 7, pp. 17, 20.

3. Merrill Goozner, "In Asia, Lack of Coherent Strategy May Prove Costly," *Chicago Tribune,* July 3, 1994, section 1, pp. 1, 20.

4. Jennifer Cody, "Big Japanese Retailers Rush to Set Up Operations in Asia's Developing Markets," *Wall Street Journal,* July 8, 1994, p. A4.

5. Jennifer Cody, "Bid Japanese Retailers Rush to Set Up Operations."

6. See Fareed Zakaria, "A Conversation with Lee Kuan Yew," *Foreign Affairs* 73, no. 2 (March/April 1994): pp. 109–126.

7. For an analysis of Japan's emerging role as an activist state on security issues, including Sino-Japanese security relations, see Stephen J. Anderson, "Japan As an Activist State in the Pacific Basin: Japan and Regional Organizations," *Journal of East Asian Affairs* 7, no. 2 (Summer/Fall 1993): pp. 498–544.

For a discussion of Japan's shift from the Yoshida to the Miyazawa Doctrine, with implications for Sino-Japanese relations, see Eugene Brown, "Japanese Security Policy in the Post-Cold War World: Threat Perceptions and Strategic Options," *Journal of East Asian Affairs* 8, no. 2 (Summer/Fall 1994): pp. 327–362. For an explanation of why informal Asian security arrangements are more feasible than formal ones, see John R. Faust, "The Emerging Security System in Asia," *Journal of East Asian Affairs* 8, no. 1 (Winter/Spring 1994): pp. 56–89.

8. Charles F. Doran, "Security and Political Economy in US-Asian Relations," *Journal of East Asian Affairs* 8, no. 2 (Summer/Fall 1994): p. 240.

9. Andrew K. Hamani, "Japan and the Military Balance of Power in Northeast Asia," *Journal of East Asian Affairs* 8, no. 2 (Summer/Fall 1994): p. 375.

10. See David Arase, "Japan's Evolving Security Policy After the Cold War," *Journal of East Asian Affairs* 8, no. 2 (Summer/Fall 1994): pp. 413–415. Selig S. Harrison, "A Yen for the Bomb?" *Washington Post,* October 31, 1993, p. C1. "Official Says Japan Will Need Nuclear Arms if North Korea Threatens," *Los Angeles Times,* July 29, 1993, p. A4.

11. Quoted in Andrew K. Hamani, "Japan and the Military Balance of Power in Northeast Asia," p. 374.

12. Andrew K. Hamani, "Japan and the Military Balance of Power in Northeast Asia," p. 374.

13. Each of the five permanent United Nations Security Council members provided 100 personnel, which were later reduced to 50 each. [J. Faust interview with U.S. officers serving as UN observers in Kuwait, March 1992.]

# Emerging Global Regimes

The present-day world is at a vital turning point. The old structure has come to an end while a new one has yet to take shape. The world is moving in a direction of multipolarization. World peace, national stability, economic development are the aspirations shared by the people everywhere.

—*Li Peng, speaking before the summit meeting*
*at the UN Security Council, January 11, 1992*

In August 1991 the world order, as it had existed since 1945, collapsed. The bipolar world, in which two superpowers maintained a balance of power and kept their client states in check, dissolved, leaving uncertainty and, in some parts of the world, chaos. Today, no new world order has emerged. The international system is still unsettled, which is inherently dangerous. Each of the world's largest powers, including the members of the United Nations Security Council, is trying to redefine its role in the emerging world regime.

## PEACEFUL COEXISTENCE

China's philosophy of the proper relationship among states in the international system is summarized in its Five Principles of Peaceful Coexistence:

1. Each country should have the right to choose its own political, economic, and social system in line with its own circumstances.
2. All nations of the world, and especially the big powers, should strictly abide by the principle of not interfering in other nations' affairs.
3. All nations should respect and treat others equally, cherish mutually beneficial cooperation, exist in harmony, and seek common ground while resolving differences.
4. International conflicts should be fairly resolved through peaceful means, not through the use or threat of force.

5. Each country, no matter how big or small, strong or weak, should have the equal right to participate in consultations to settle world affairs.[1]

## The Westphalian System

The norms of the Westphalian system include the following: each state is sovereign in its own territory; each state is equal in its relations with other states; there is no higher authority above each state; sovereignty within states resides in the ruling elites; the people are subjects of their government, which derives legitimacy through good government; international security is based on a system involving a balance of power in which states pursue their self-interest but do not interfere in the internal affairs of other states; international transactions are conducted by governments, not individuals or groups within states; and a citizen of one state traveling in another state is subject to the latter's jurisdiction.

China's principles of interstate conduct are in accord with the basic norms that have guided Europe and therefore the international system for the past 350 years. The Treaty of Westphalia, signed in 1648, established the accepted principles of state sovereignty and equality of nations. Throughout the Cold War period, China and other Third World countries struggled to maintain the norms of the Westphalian System in order to allow freedom of action in a world dominated by the two superpowers. Ironically, the end of the Cold War both strengthens and weakens elements of the Westphalian system.

The collapse of the Soviet Union should theoretically have freed the less powerful nations of the world from their previous role as pawns in the Cold War battle. Each nation's freedom of action within its borders and in the international system should have been enhanced. Yet many Third World nations, China included, fear that they will be the losers in the post–Cold War era as well. In the United Nations Security Council, Russia has joined the Western voting bloc on several crucial occasions, such as the vote to authorize a war against Iraq, leaving China as the only self-professed advocate of the Third World. One nation alone cannot uphold the interests of the Third World, and because the poor nations of the world are of less importance to the security interests of the United States and Russia, economic aid is likely to disappear as well. The new order may well leave the Third World with less power and influence than ever.

## Interdependence

Even before the collapse of the Soviet Union, the Westphalian system was being eroded by increasing global interdependence. China itself, since the implementation of its open economic policy, has become tied to the international trade and financial system. Overseas Chinese interact freely with all levels of Chinese society, and their enormous financial investment in China gives them tremendous influence. Thus, China's once proudly self-reliant economy is now influenced by world trade trends and the financial interests of Chinese living outside the jurisdiction of the Beijing government.

In an era of mass communication and mass movement of people across boundaries, Chinese interest groups and individual citizens increasingly interact with their counterparts in other countries independently from the Chinese government. Tourism, educational exchanges of students and faculty members, and electronic communications also limit the powers of the Beijing government. For example, during the Tiananmen Square incident, Chinese students used fax machines to inform the outside world about what was happening, even after the transmissions sent by foreign reporters were cut off by the national news agency. In addition, videocassette recorders are used to show movies critical of the regime. Though party authorities are concerned about the "spiritual pollution" brought in from outside China's borders, they can no longer completely control the flow of information. No government is truly autonomous, even within its own borders, in this era of increasing global interdependence.

## The Global Commons

Increasing global interdependence underscores the commonality of global resources. Traditionally, each nation has controlled the resources present within its borders and used these resources for its own benefit, even though the future consequences of such use might affect the well-being of a far wider population. Immediate benefit to one nation or one group outweighs future costs, which are charged to the global community. For example, seventeenth-century English farmers all grazed their cattle on the village commons. Even though they realized that overgrazing would be the ruin of them all, the farmers still sought the immediate benefit of increasing their own herds. Such behavior has come to be known as the "tragedy of the commons."

Protection of the environment and a fair division of the global commons are both such complex issues that the current international system has only recently begun to grapple with them. Each and every attempt to develop an equitable division of the global commons and to assign responsibility for cleanup of past environmental misdeeds has been fraught with controversy, often between the major Western powers and the nations of the Third World. The many controversies associated with the Law of the Sea (which regulates economic rights to sea regions), the 1992 global environmental conference in Rio de Janeiro, etc., illustrate the problems only too well.

A just resolution of global commons issues may require establishment of global institutions with supranational authority. This, in turn, would require that each nation abandon some of its sovereignty to the international system in contradistinction to the Westphalian system of rule. Voluntary global regimes based on mutual self-interest rather than national self-interest will have to be accepted by all nations of the world.

In an era of transition, all nations will have to adapt their national policies to meet the demands of the emerging global regimes. China, too, will have to adapt to the new world environment. No one approach, whether it be state sovereignty, interdependence, or voluntary global regimes, will be sufficient. Rather, China's leaders will have to balance the demands of the hardliners, who favor greater Chinese independence from the international system, with those leaders who believe that in the future no nation can afford to remain aloof from global institutions or economic and political transactions.

## CHINA, THE UNITED NATIONS, AND COLLECTIVE SECURITY IN THE NEW ERA

After being denied entry into the United Nations for twenty-two years, the General Assembly voted to designate the People's Republic of China as the official holder of its China seat in 1971. The Republic of China (Taiwan) then withdrew from the United Nations Security Council. At the same time that the vote was taking place in the General Assembly, President Nixon's national security adviser, Henry Kissinger, was visiting Beijing. No better symbolism of the distance China had traveled could be imagined. Once condemned by the United Nations General Assembly in absentia for "aggression" in Korea, the People's Republic had become one of the five most important actors responsible for world order.

The Western world feared the presence of a Communist China on the Security Council. Yet China behaved conservatively once in the Security Council, often abstaining rather than vetoing controversial votes. Ironically, China became a strong advocate for the Third World by virtue of its membership in the United Nations, but it also became a major player in the international system that many in the Third World abhorred because of the system's inequality.

When the Soviet permanent seat in the Security Council was given to Russia, Beijing's leaders found themselves facing new opportunities and new dangers in the United Nations. Russia began to join the United States, Britain, and France in promoting United Nations security initiatives. China was now the sole permanent member that professed to view Security Council actions from a Third World perspective.

In the emerging global system, traditional sovereignty issues are giving way to new challenges to international security and the global commons. The end of the Cold War has lessened fears of a major world war. Instead, new and dangerous problems are developing: regional wars; instability within nations; growing violations of human rights caused by a return to extreme forms of nationalism; a surge in racial and ethnic hatreds; and threats of economic warfare as states struggle over whether to pursue mercantilistic economic policies or open up their economies to global competition based on comparative advantage. For Chinese decisionmakers, policy choices are especially difficult. In the confusion of the post–Cold War world, Security Council initiatives have often been sponsored by the United States and its allies, and these initiatives seem to have enhanced the global role of the West. China and the Third World have lost their ability to influence the two superpowers by awarding allegiance during their Cold War battle for allies. However, at a time when many Third World nations are faced with increasing economic and political problems at home, the United Nations is in many ways less responsive to their needs than in the past.

> ### Changing the UN Security Council
>
> Several proposals for a restructured Security Council have been offered, including the following: creating a revolving European seat to be shared sequentially by France, Germany, and the United Kingdom; having permanent seats for both Germany and Japan; and giving permanent Security Council seats to Brazil, Nigeria, Egypt, Japan and Germany, although only the original five would have veto power.

## Changing the UN Structure

China, along with the other 163 members of the United Nations that pay less than 20 percent of the organization's budget, would no doubt vigorously oppose any measures to change the "one member, one vote" provision in the UN Charter to reflect more accurately contributions to the operating budget. China's uncertain role on the Security Council is reflected in its contribution to the United Nations budget. Whereas the other four permanent members contribute nearly half of the United Nations' regular budget, China contributes less than 1 percent. Most states of both the First World and the Third World would oppose any amendments to make representation proportional to population because China and India would gain the most seats in the

General Assembly. And virtually all members of the United Nations are strongly opposed to any Charter changes that would maintain or enhance Western dominance of the organization.

China's position on reforming the Charter is complicated by its membership on the Security Council. Though China seeks leadership of the Third World, it does not relish the prospect of sharing permanent membership in the Security Council with other Third World nations, especially with India, one of its two greatest potential rivals for dominance in Asia in the twenty-first century. A permanent Security Council seat for Japan also makes Chinese leaders uneasy. Yet the demands for restructuring the Security Council to reflect the post–Cold War era will undoubtedly increase. Paradoxically, China, which has long been an advocate of greater power for the Third World in the United Nations, will lose more than any other permanent member if Third World membership is increased in the Security Council. Although China could veto any proposed change to the structure of the Security Council that it does not approve of, in reality China's options are limited.

## United Nations Peacemaking and Peacekeeping

There are numerous details concerning the range of actions the United Nations can take to promote peacemaking and peacekeeping:

- Article 41 of the UN Charter provides authority to impose political and economic sanctions such as breaking off diplomatic relations or limiting exports or imports (binding actions by the United Nations Security Council).
- Article 42 provides authority to take military action to prevent or resist aggression (binding actions taken by the United Nations Security Council).
- Under the Uniting for Peace Resolution, which was passed by the United Nations General Assembly in 1950, the General Assembly can recommend sanctions of a political, military, or economic nature. These recommendations are nonbinding on UN members. Under this precedent, the General Assembly could recommend any other actions listed below on a voluntary basis including both peacemaking and peacekeeping operations.
- The Security Council can create military forces to take limited military actions to restore or maintain order.
- The Security Council can create multilateral forces to observe or conduct elections.
- The Security Council can create multilateral forces or deputize national forces to disarm combatants in order to restore order.
- The Security Council can provide government services such as

administration, finance, communications, and health care in order to restore effective government where services have broken down. Such operations have included the Belgian Congo from 1960 to 1964 and Cambodia beginning in 1992.

- The United Nations can create multilateral forces to observe armistice agreements and report any violations of such agreements. This has usually been done by the Security Council, but it also has been done by the General Assembly, which created the United Emergency Force in the Middle East in 1956.
- A number of practices have developed in deploying peacekeeping operations, including the following: at least one of the countries that is a party to the peace agreement must be willing to allow the UN forces to be deployed on its soil; the lightly armed UN observers are instructed to use force only in self-defense; and the membership of the peacekeeping force must be acceptable to all the parties to the peacekeeping agreement.
- Peacemaking and peacekeeping operations are financed through a combination of sources including the following: assessments through the General Assembly budget, voluntary contributions by individual states, and partial or total financial support for forces being deployed by the troop suppliers.

Beijing's role in United Nations Security Council activities is complicated by the changing nature of the post–Cold War era and the growing demand for global solutions to regional and local instabilities. In spite of what President Bush said during Operation Desert Storm, there is no new world order. Instead, as instabilities emerge in the post–Cold War era, the United Nations reacts on an ad hoc basis.

During the Cold War years, United Nations security activities were largely limited to peacekeeping operations that were acceptable to the two opposing superpowers. Both the United States and the Soviet Union readily used their veto powers to stop any actions detrimental to their interests. Thus, by the time peacekeeping forces were deployed, the danger of the situation was generally defused to the point where UN observers were acceptable to both the combatants and the superpowers.

In contrast to the many peacekeeping operations since 1956, the United Nations has undertaken collective security actions only two times since its establishment. The first time was in Korea in 1950, when the Security Council voted to send a UN force to defend South Korea. Authorization was forthcoming only because the Soviet Union was boycotting the Security Council to protest the continued presence of Taiwan, rather than Beijing, in the China seat. Not until the end of the Cold War was another collective security operation possible. Much to the surprise of Iraq, S.C. Resolution 678 authorized the use of force to restore the sovereignty of

Kuwait. In order to gain economic assistance from the West, the Russians abandoned their Iraqi allies and voted for the resolution.

China's leaders wish to play an active global role along with other major world actors, but China has largely avoided intervening in affairs other than those along its recognized boundaries. The United Nations condemnation of Chinese actions during the Korean War further reinforced Beijing's suspicions of global actions initiated by the West in the Security Council. Once on the Security Council, the People's Republic has generally avoided involvement in peacekeeping operations. In 1990 and 1991, Chinese leaders therefore viewed Western-sponsored anti-Iraqi resolutions with grave misgivings. Though condemning the invasion of Kuwait, Beijing favored limited sanctions against Iraq rather than the use of force. When it became clear that S.C. Resolution 678 would pass unless the Chinese vetoed it, Beijing's leaders chose to abstain. In return for this favor, the United States worked to end the moratorium on further World Bank loans to China that had been in place since the Tiananmen incident.

China has also faced other difficult voting decisions in the post–Cold War Security Council. For example, China abstained rather than support a resolution authorizing sanctions against Libya that sought to bring alleged Libyan terrorists to trial in the United States or France. China has traditionally affirmed its support of the Arab world, but it was not willing to veto the resolution and alienate the West. Beijing has also supported limited Security Council resolutions related to humanitarian relief operations in former Yugoslavia, while abstaining on economic sanctions against Belgrade. Because many Islamic countries were in favor of the strongest possible anti-Serbian sanctions, China's position on the Yugoslavian issue lost China some of the Arab goodwill that it had been accorded for its position on Libya. Concerning Somalia, Beijing's leaders finally supported the U.S.-sponsored Security Council resolution authorizing a U.S.-led coalition force to restore order and ensure that food supplies reached the hungry. Beijing always prefers actions under the UN flag, but it was not willing to veto the U.S.-led Somalian force.

The reasons for China's inconsistent voting pattern on the post–Cold War Security Council are clear. Beijing, unable to take the initiative, has had to decide whether to support Western initiatives going beyond traditional peacekeeping operations or abstain. If China vetoes resolutions supported by the other four permanent members of the Security Council and their allies, it runs the risk of isolating itself from all major groupings within the United Nations. A Chinese veto might also lead the Security Council to invoke the Uniting for Peace Resolution, which allows a deadlocked Security Council to call the General Assembly into session to vote on the issue at hand. Although General Assembly resolutions are only recommendations and are nonbinding, it is hardly conceivable that Beijing would be willing to isolate itself from most of the world by forcing the United Nations to act through the General Assembly after a Chinese veto in the Security Council.

## The United Nations and Cambodia

Perhaps Beijing's most difficult decisions in the Security Council have come on the question of Cambodia. Whereas the authorities in Beijing long ago abandoned support for communist insurgents in most parts of the world, Beijing has always supported Pol Pot and the Khmer Rouge, even when they committed genocide against their own people. The issue for China is not ideological but political. China is and always has been opposed to any expansion of Vietnamese domination in Southeast Asia. It therefore opposed the Hun Sen Cambodian government that was established with Vietnamese backing. Beijing was also worried by Soviet support for Vietnam and Vietnamese proxy regimes.

The situation changed in 1989, however, as the Soviets withdrew from Vietnam and the Vietnamese withdrew from Cambodia. By 1991, with a Soviet veto no longer a problem, the Paris Accords were signed. The Security Council then authorized direct deployment of over 20,000 UN troops with authority to restore order and disarm the military factions. Order was to be reestablished in Cambodia, and elections were held to establish a democratic coalition government. Success is contingent, however, on neutralizing the Khmer Rouge, which is difficult because of the group's independent power base and its independent revenues from smuggling and other illegal activities.

Beijing wanted the UN effort to succeed and contributed a limited number of personnel to the Cambodian operation, but fears of Vietnamese influence in Cambodia continued. Because of this fear, China has refused to give up its support of the Khmer Rouge, even though this policy goes against the wishes of the West, most members of ASEAN, Japan, and India, all of whom provided UN contingents in Cambodia.

## The Future United Nations

In January 1992, leaders of the major world states held a summit at the United Nations to make recommendations on ways to promote international stability and peace. Li Peng, China's premier, was a major participant. He and the representatives of other permanent members of the Security Council sponsored a proposal asking the UN Secretary-General to develop a plan for more effective utilization of the United Nations system for the maintenance of peace and the prevention of war. The Secretary-General's final report, however, called for the creation of a permanent UN peacekeeping force of 50,000 for immediate use in crises. Because this proposal would require a joint UN high command, the United States and probably other powers as well are unlikely to accept it. Although global UN military operations multiplied to over 60,000 personnel in 1993, voluntary participation is likely to continue on an ad hoc basis. Beijing is likely to remain a free rider, choosing which peacekeeping operations it will participate in with great care.

In the future, events outside China are likely to be the primary determinants of China's UN policy. Although interdependence may grow, China and the other large and small nations in the international system continue to react to global problems on an ad hoc basis. What distinguishes Beijing's leaders from those in the West is the continuing hesitancy to join regional or global regimes that will reduce sovereignty or control over each state's destiny. As in the past, Beijing continues to be more reactive than proactive with respect to global and regional events, whether political, economic, environmental, or humanitarian. National self-interest, the dominant value of the international system since the Treaty of Westphalia in 1648, remains the key to understanding China's actions in the UN and other international fora. However, in the 1990s, deciding what constitutes the national self-interest for China and other world actors may be more uncertain than during the Cold War years, when the East-West rivalry provided a compass for determining regional and global power balances.

## ARMS CONTROL OR ARMS RACES: CHINESE ALTERNATIVES

The end of the Cold War has greatly reduced the danger of world war and has resulted in extensive military restructuring in both the United States and the former Soviet Union. Both to lessen tensions and as a result of lessened tensions, Mikhail Gorbachev and George Bush agreed to reduce troop deployments in Europe, to destroy intermediate-range nuclear weapons, and to drastically cut back on the number of strategic nuclear weapons. Although the collapse of the Soviet Union has complicated implementation of these accords, the new republics have stated their commitment to the terms of the agreements in words, if not always in action.

China's military and security position has been fundamentally altered by the events of 1991 as well. After years of vigilant anti-Soviet defenses on its borders, China is now no longer threatened by a major military power on its northern or western borders, although the new republics may develop small arms races of their own. This, combined with the phased withdrawal of U.S. troops from Asia, poses both opportunities and risks for Beijing. For the first time since the Western imperialists first visited China, China's leaders find themselves in a position to influence events beyond their borders rather than be pressured by superior external military forces.

At a time when Western nations and Russia are slashing their military budgets because of a reduced security threat, China is expanding its own military capabilities and increasing its military budget. Its reasons are internal as well as external. Ever since the Communist Party began its Long March to power, the military has played an important role. Mao's people's army was a peasant army—overstaffed, underequipped, and poorly trained. Yet it performed well in Korea, and reliable troops were used to clamp down on the worst excesses of the Cultural Revolution. More recently, the military again played a crucial political role when it crushed the protestors at Tiananmen Square.

> **China's Nuclear Policies**
>
> China now has something of a public relations problem. Before the Soviet Union and the United States agreed to cut their nuclear stockpiles drastically, Beijing claimed it would reduce its nuclear arsenal if Moscow and Washington agreed to destroy half of their nuclear arsenals. After the Start II agreements, China changed its position, arguing that Russian and U.S. nuclear capabilities are still so large that further reductions are necessary before Beijing could consider entering into serious negotiations to reduce its own stockpile.

Military budgets, however, have not always been commensurate with the military's political role. Deng Xiaoping drastically reduced the number of troops from four million to three million, both to reduce personnel costs and to reform the military into an educated professional force. Only after the military displayed its loyalty at Tiananmen Square did military budget allocations start to rise dramatically. Despite the reduced external threat, the regular Chinese military budget has increased in real terms by over 10 percent every year since 1989. Moreover, large purchases of Russian military equipment have allegedly been paid for from a secret fund controlled by the Central Military Commission.[2]

The years of low military budgets have had unintended side effects, both within China and in the international system. During the early years of Deng's reforms, those remaining in the military did not receive pay increases. Morale plummeted because of a loss of purchasing power. To supplement limited government funding, many military units sought outside funding sources. In cities such as Guangzhou, military units operated nightclubs, tourist hotels, and other enterprises—even shooting galleries. More dangerous, many Chinese military units began to sell weapons on the international market, especially in the Middle East and Asia. Competitively priced conventional weapons, as well as dual-use nuclear technology and short- and medium-range missiles, were marketed to eager nations stymied by Western arms embargoes (See Table 8.1). Using *guanxi* (personal gifts and rewards)—often the military export corporations are staffed by the children

**Table 8.1    Top Ten Weapons Exporters and Importers in 1990**

| Exporters | Importers |
|-----------|-----------|
| 1. United States | 1. Saudi Arabia |
| 2. Soviet Union | 2. Japan |
| 3. France | 3. India |
| 4. United Kingdom | 4. Afghanistan |
| 5. West Germany | 5. Spain |
| 6. China | 6. Turkey |
| 7. Czechoslovakia | 7. Greece |
| 8. Netherlands | 8. North Korea |
| 9. Sweden | 9. Angola |
| 10. Italy | 10. Czechoslovakia |

*Source:* Center for Defense Information, "We Arm the World: U.S. Is Number One Weapons Dealer," *The Defense Monitor* 20, no. 4 (1991).

of senior Chinese leaders—the military often completed these transactions without the knowledge of the Ministry of Foreign Affairs.[3]

Though domestic stability is a major reason for increasing military resources in the 1990s, there are other reasons as well. Beijing has always reserved the ultimate right to use force if a peaceful solution to reunification with Taiwan is not achieved. Despite greatly improved relations between China and Taiwan, particularly trade relations, recent U.S. and French arms sales to Taiwan have very much upset Beijing. In September 1992, President Bush announced a $6 billion deal to sell 150 F-16 fighter planes to Taiwan, which Beijing denounced as a clear violation of the 1982 Sino-U.S. agreement in which the United States agreed not to upgrade its military sales to Taiwan. This was followed by a multibillion dollar deal in which France agreed to sell sixty Mirage fighter jets and 1,000 short- and medium-range missiles to Taiwan. China responded by purchasing Russian military hardware. Its message is clear: Beijing's leaders intend to maintain a military position strong enough to convince Taiwanese leaders that a declaration of independence from China is not feasible.

Just as important is China's sense of honor and pride. Beijing believes that as an emerging world power it is entitled to play a larger regional and global role. China believes all states are entitled to up-to-date military forces. Beijing argues that its military buildup is not only justified but poses no danger to the world balance of power.

## Regional Arms Sales: A Chinese Perspective

Although China may develop a more formidable military force by the year 2000, Western observers are most concerned by China's emerging role as a major arms merchant in the Middle East, West Asia, and South Asia. Prior to the collapse of the Soviet Union, China played a relatively minor role in the Middle East, but Beijing's arms merchants have recently become an important factor in regional balance-of-power structures. China's diplomatic activities have also greatly increased. In 1991, Beijing established diplomatic relations with a number of key Arab states such as Saudi Arabia. Playing both sides, China also established diplomatic relations with Israel in 1992.

China justifies its arms sales to the Middle East by pointing out the enormous amount of military equipment sold by the United States, the former Soviet Union, and the nations of Western and Eastern Europe. In light of the large sales by these states since Operation Desert Storm, Beijing believes it also has the right to sell arms to the Middle East. China's arms industries, like those in Russia and the West, need hard cash, and China therefore believes that the United States and its allies are unjustified in trying to prevent China from selling arms and military technology to Iran, Syria, Sudan, and other states in the Middle East. From Beijing's perspective, Western and especially U.S. leaders speak with two voices—what is acceptable for Israel, including a probable nuclear stockpile, is not acceptable for the Arab states.

## Nuclear Weapons and Delivery Systems

In actuality, China behaves no differently from other actors in the international system with respect to arms sales and transfer of dual-use technology. It is now widely acknowledged that U.S. businesses sold Iraq a wide variety of components that Saddam Hussein used in his atomic bomb and missile-building projects. Similarly, critics claim that "Beijing is turning these dictatorships in the Middle East and Asia into missile producing and missile-transferring states themselves—North Korea for instance."[4]

At the same time, after considerable negotiations with the United States, China finally ratified the Nuclear Non-Proliferation Treaty of 1968 in March 1992. It is now formally obligated not to help other countries acquire nuclear capability. Although China reached agreements with Iran and Algeria in the early 1990s to assist with the development of nuclear power plants under the supervision of the UN International Atomic Energy Agency, it has provided Pakistan with dual-use technology for more than twenty years.

Similarly, Beijing supported the 1987 Missile Technology Control Regime after the Bush administration offered the incentives of sales of U.S. supercomputer technology to China and U.S. use of Chinese satellites for space launches. The MTCR, an effort by the United States and its allies to prevent further escalation of the arms race in the Middle East and South Asia, seeks to prevent the exports of advanced missiles into these regions. By 1992, however, U.S. intelligence reports indicated that Beijing was violating the spirit, if not the letter, of the law by selling missiles to Iran and Pakistan.

Further reports of missile sales to Pakistan in December 1992 created a high-level debate in the Bush administration just as it was about to leave office. The commerce and state departments wanted to go ahead with the sale of high-speed computers, but they were opposed by the Pentagon and the Arms Control and Disarmament Agency, which were concerned both by Chinese failure to keep its promises and by the potential use of the high-speed computers to upgrade Chinese military capabilities.[5]

### INTERNATIONAL FINANCE: THE INTERNATIONAL MONETARY FUND AND THE WORLD BANK

China's role in global economic regimes stands in marked contrast to its somewhat secretive and isolated role on security and arms issues. Prior to 1978, most of Beijing's economic and security relationships were bilateral, but with Deng Xiaoping's opening to the outside world, China changed its view on global economic institutions in what amounted to a revolutionary transformation. After Mao came to power in 1949, China supported the revolutionary overthrow of capitalist systems and viewed international economic regimes such as the World Bank and the International Monetary Fund as stooges of the Western capitalists. When the Soviets became the primary threat to Chinese security and Beijing started working with Washington in the early 1970s to contain Moscow, the Chinese position shifted to reformation rather than transformation of the global economic system.

After reclaiming the Chinese United Nations seat in 1971, the People's Republic also gained observer status in the Third World Committee of 77 and strongly supported its demands for a New International Economic Order (NIEO). Since 1978, Beijing has again changed its approach and indicated a desire to join existing global capitalist institutions such as the International Bank for Reconstruction and Development (IBRD a division of the World Bank) and its affiliated agencies: the International Development Association (IDA), which makes soft loans to less developed countries; the International Finance Corporation (IFC), which helps underwrite investments in the private sector; and the International Monetary Fund (IMF), which facilitates the international exchange of currencies and makes short-term loans based on conditionality (i.e., compliance to the IMF's recommended economic practices).

What was the reasoning behind this radical change in Beijing's thinking? Apparently Deng Xiaoping and his supporters had come to the conclusion that these capitalist multilateral regimes were not only an important source of capital but also of technical assistance, technical training, and information on how to develop and modernize China. Beijing decided that if these international economic regimes helped China finance infrastructure projects such as energy, education, power, communications, and transport, this would give foreign governments and private investors greater confidence in investing inside China.[6] China was further integrated into the global economic system when its request was approved by the United Nations Development Programme (UNDP) in 1978 to change its status from an aid donor to an aid recipient, enabling it to receive funding for a wide range of technical assistance for which it previously had not been eligible.

Since reclaiming its UN seat in 1971, Beijing has developed close working relationships with the various special UN agencies for projects such as those carried out by the World Health Organization, the United Nations Food and Agricultural Organization (FAO), and the United Nations Educational, Scientific, and Cultural Organization (UNESCO). Because of limited UNDP funding, which comes mostly from vóluntary donations from Western UN members, this aid has been much less important to China than funding received from the World Bank Group and the International Monetary Fund, which China joined in 1980.

Beijing has also extended its multilateral ties to the regional level. For example, its application for admission to the Asian Development Bank (ADB) was accepted in May 1986. However, membership in this organization posed a serious problem because Taiwan was a charter member of the ADB and also a major source of ADB funding for development projects throughout Asia.[7] Other ADB members, while supporting Beijing's admission, wished to keep Taiwan in the organization. In the past, when the issue of dual membership with Taiwan arose, Beijing had refused to participate in any organization where Taiwan was also a member, but in the case of ADB, it accepted an arrangement in which Taiwan would continue its membership under the name "Taipei, China." This provision conformed to the principle of "one China, two systems." Separate membership by Beijing and Taipei in the ADB, where the two regimes have gradually learned to get along with each other, may be a precedent that will help bring further reconciliation between the two governments. Taiwan has also expressed interest in rejoining the World Bank Group. Because Taiwan is one of the world's major economic success stories in achieving economic modernization and development, as well as an important factor in world trade and investment, the membership of both Beijing and Taipei in these organizations would further strengthen them and help to spur international economic integration and development, not only in Asia but also in other regions of the world.

## China and the International Monetary Fund

Beijing's admission to membership in the IMF in 1980 brought immediate benefits that have been very important to the success of China's Open Door policy and internal development (see Table 8.2). After paying in its financial obligations to the IMF, Beijing was able to draw sizable allotments of hard currency interest-free to help shore up its balance-of-payments deficits.

**Table 8.2    China's IMF Drawings, 1980–1987**

| Date of Inception/ Expiration | Source/Amount | Terms |
|---|---|---|
| December 1980 | Reserve tranche,  $278 million | Interest-free; no service fee; indefinite repayment schedule (already repaid) |
| January 1981 | Reserve tranche, $200 million | Same as above (already repaid) |
| March 1981/ December 1981 | First credit tranche (standby), $550 million | 6.4% interest: 0.5% service fee; 3–5 year repayment (repaid 1984) |
| March 1981/ March 1991 | IMF Trust Fund, $365 million | 0.5% interest, 10-year repayment |
| November 1986/ November 1987 | First credit tranche (standby), $717 million | 5.97% interest; 0.25% service fee; 3–5 year repayment |
| Total IMF drawings, 1980–1987 | $2,110,000,000 | |

*Sources:* Friedrich W. Wu, "External Borrowing and Foreign Aid in Post-Mao China's International Economic Policy: Data and Observations" *Columbia Journal of World Business* 19 (Fall 1984): 57; and William R. Feeney, "Chinese Policy Toward Multilateral Economic Institutions," in Samuel S. Kim, ed., *China and the World: New Directions in Chinese Foreign Relations* (Boulder, Colorado: Westview Press, 1989), p. 243.

Because China's record of repayment to the International Monetary Fund has been excellent, it has been able to obtain short-term drawings from the IMF at reasonable rates while at the same time avoiding stringent IMF conditionalities for borrowing additional money. China's relations with the IMF stand in stark contrast to many Third World countries, which because of their difficulties in repaying IMF loans have had to accept IMF-proposed economic reforms as a condition of getting further financing.

## China and the World Bank

China's admission to the World Bank came at the same time as its admission to the IMF, and China has benefitted not only from large IBRD loans at reasonable rates but also from extensive World Bank studies of the Chinese economy done in cooperation with Chinese planning agencies. The World Bank has instituted macro and sectoral studies of China's economy on a continual basis since 1980. Beijing's leaders have been especially pleased with a monumental three-volume report entitled *China: Socialist Economic Development,* which analyzed five important sectors: education, health, and populations; agriculture; petroleum, coal, and electricity; transportation; and industry.[8] In 1992, the World Bank, in collaboration with the Development Research Center (DRC) in Beijing, published a detailed report on China's economic industrial policies, which were designed to guide the country during the transition to modernization and a fully developed economy.[9] In the same year, the World Bank published another study analyzing in detail a number of economic sectors with recommendations for improvement and greater efficiency: rural collectives and private industry; urbanization; technical and vocational education; management and financial problems in higher education; improving the quality of education; challenges in health care; the role of the waterways and coastal shipping in China's transport system; coal pricing problems; and reforms of power prices.[10] A year earlier, the World Bank published a detailed analysis with recommendations on China's world trade, including statistical data on China's comparative trade advantage on a wide range of raw materials and industrial goods.[11]

Events such as Tiananmen Square have not changed Beijing's Open Door policy and utilization of the World Bank and International Monetary Fund to get loans and valuable assistance in transforming China's economy. China has become one of the largest recipients of IMF and World Bank funding. China also succeeded in having 50 percent of its World Bank lending come through the IBRD's soft loan window—the International Development Association, which does not charge interest for needed projects in countries with very low living standards. Other Third World countries complained, however, that China was much better off than them, and in the late 1980s IDA loans to China were reduced to 40 percent of World Bank funding (see Table 8.3).

**Table 8.3   World Bank Lending to China (in millions of dollars)**

| Year | Number of Loans | World Bank | Number of Loans | IDA | Comparative Numerical Ranking |
|------|-----------------|------------|-----------------|-----|-------------------------------|
| 1981 | 1 | 100.0 | 1 | 100.0 | 70/125 |
| 1982 | 0 | 0 | 1 | 60.0 | 63/125 |
| 1983 | 5 | 463.1 | 1 | 150.4 | 28/128 |
| 1984 | 5 | 616.0 | 5 | 423.5 | 18/132 |
| 1985 | 7 | 659.6 | 5 | 442.3 | 14/136 |
| 1986 | 7 | 687.0 | 4 | 450.0 | 11/136 |
| 1987 | 8 | 867.4 | 3 | 556.2 | 8/137 |
| Total | 33 | 3,393.1 | 19 | 2,182.4 | |

*Source:* William R. Feeney, "Chinese Policy Toward Multilateral Economic Institutions," p. 246. Reprinted with permission.

After the Tiananmen Square incident, Washington did convince the World Bank to suspend further aid to Beijing. By 1990, however, the Japanese prime minister took the initiative in persuading the G-7 countries (United States, United Kingdom, France, Germany, Italy, Canada, and Japan) to support new World Bank lending to China. Later in 1990, Beijing was able to bring further pressure on the United States to support IBRD loans for China by making such support a condition of China's abstaining rather than vetoing the Security Council resolution authorizing the use of force to remove Iraq from Kuwait. From the Chinese point of view, tying bank loans to events inside China is an illegal interference in China's internal affairs. Therefore, they believed that they were entitled to use leverage against the United States on other issues as a means of stopping these illegal actions. China was successful in changing U.S. policy and restoring its World Bank funding.

U.S.-led efforts to use the World Bank to penalize Beijing after the Tiananmen Square events in 1989 were only a temporary setback for China. Both before and after Tiananmen, Beijing was moving further toward privatization of the economy with the assistance of the International Finance Corporation. The IFC lends seed money to private ventures in Third World countries for the purpose of promoting private investment. In China, these are usually joint ventures between Chinese businesses and multinational corporations with headquarters in Hong Kong, Taiwan, South Korea, Singapore, Japan, the United States, and Western Europe. For example, in the mid-1980s, IFC money provided part of the capital for a joint venture between Peugeot, a French auto maker, and a Chinese partner in Guangzhou (in Guangdong province). This venture then served as a precedent for further IFC financing of private investment in China—multinational corporations are more inclined to risk venture capital when part of the funding comes from one of the World Bank lending windows.

IBRD and IMF aid to China since 1978 has been instrumental in helping the People's Republic achieve annual growth rates averaging 8–9 percent in GNP. And World Bank lending continues to grow. In 1992, Beijing announced that the World Bank Group authorized an additional $2.5 billion in proposed projects for fiscal year 1992/93, with total Chinese borrowing having reached $13.2 billion for 109 projects.[12] Ironically, while China, a communist country, continues to receive IBRD and IMF aid, former communist countries in Eastern Europe and the former parts of the Soviet Union, such as Russia and the Ukraine, have difficulty in getting World Bank lending because economic conditions inside their countries fail to meet World Bank standards.

## INTERNATIONAL TRADE: OPEN OR CLOSED SYSTEMS?

One of the most remarkable developments in recent international trade has been the more than 250 percent increase of Chinese exports between 1980 and 1987 (see Table 8.4). Chinese trade has continued to increase very rapidly in the 1990s, with exports of over $20 billion to the United States alone in 1992. Global reactions to events at Tiananmen Square in 1989 have had little effect on China's external trade relations, as exports continue to increase even more rapidly than China's annual 8–9 percent increase in GNP.

**Table 8.4**    **Composition and Destination of the PRC's Exports, 1987 (value of exports from China in millions of dollars)**

| Commodity Group | European Economic Community | European Free Trade Association | Japan | United States |
|---|---|---|---|---|
| All products | 5,562 | 762 | 7,386 | 6,910 |
| All foods | 837 | 66 | 1,461 | 310 |
| Fuels | 82 | 11 | 2,107 | 530 |
| Manufacturers | 3,869 | 647 | 2,642 | 5,721 |
| Agricultural raw materials | 546 | 18 | 699 | 94 |

*Source:* Alexander J. Yeats, "China's Foreign Trade and Comparative Advantage," *World Bank Discussion Paper No. 141* (Washington, D.C.: World Bank, 1991), p. 7.

**Table 8.5**    **Destination of the PRC's Total Exports (value of imports from China in millions of dollars)**

| Importer | 1965 | 1975 | 1980 | 1983 | 1985 | 1987 |
|---|---|---|---|---|---|---|
| Hong Kong | 406 | 1,374 | 4,401 | 5,806 | 7,537 | 15,048 |
| Japan | 224 | 1,533 | 4,323 | 5,087 | 6,483 | 7,386 |
| United States | | 159 | 1,161 | 2,477 | 4,222 | 6,910 |
| West Germany | 73 | 224 | 803 | 768 | 872 | 1,925 |
| Singapore | 73 | 288 | 623 | 827 | 2,260 | 1,416 |
| France | 44 | 173 | 468 | 432 | 499 | 1,101 |
| Italy | 38 | 129 | 437 | 415 | 589 | 1,025 |
| United Kingdom | 83 | 131 | 356 | 351 | 397 | 643 |
| Canada | 13 | 55 | 132 | 199 | 295 | 582 |
| Thailand | | 17 | 417 | 265 | 224 | 504 |
| Australia | 26 | 86 | 239 | 226 | 286 | 501 |
| Indonesia | 99 | 203 | 197 | 204 | 249 | 408 |
| Brazil | | 1 | 263 | 596 | 502 | 402 |
| Malaysia | 75 | 148 | 253 | 270 | 257 | 376 |
| Holland | 25 | 81 | 274 | 179 | 189 | 351 |
| Poland | | | 129 | 154 | 192 | 347 |
| Pakistan | 18 | 53 | 168 | 147 | 144 | 232 |
| Denmark | 11 | 22 | 60 | 96 | 111 | 232 |

*Source:* Alexander J. Yeats, "China's Foreign Trade and Comparative Advantage," p. 43.

Hong Kong is China's largest trade partner, serving as a transshipment point for Chinese exports to other destinations. Japan is second, closely followed by the United States (see Table 8.5).

By 1987, China had become the third largest developing-country exporter of manufactured products, exceeded only by Taiwan and Korea (see Table 8.6). By 1991, one-third of all toys and one-sixth of all clothing entering the United States originated in the People's Republic of China. Significantly, Hong Kong and Taiwan (both of which are Chinese and have special relations to the mainland), together with China, account for three of

**Table 8.6    Major Developing Asian Exporters of Manufactured Goods (exports to all countries, in millions of dollars)**

| Country | 1965 | 1975 | 1980 | 1983 | 1985 | 1987 |
|---------|------|------|------|------|------|------|
| Taiwan | 130 | 3,990 | 16,169 | 20,996 | 28,327 | 49,632 |
| South Korea | 72 | 3,448 | 12,669 | 16,604 | 19,509 | 39,020 |
| China | 554 | 1,896 | 7,712 | 9,899 | 13,022 | 28,420 |
| Hong Kong | 861 | 4,560 | 13,163 | 14,558 | 16,592 | 24,037 |
| Singapore | 57 | 1,442 | 5,143 | 7,141 | 8,683 | 13,990 |
| Malaysia | 24 | 476 | 3,010 | 3,847 | 4,786 | 7,466 |
| India | 607 | 1,331 | 3,877 | 3,591 | 4,160 | 6,666 |
| Thailand | 36 | 349 | 1,606 | 1,874 | 2,496 | 5,455 |
| Philippines | 72 | 358 | 2,149 | 2,569 | 2,960 | 3,800 |
| Indonesia | 10 | 66 | 466 | 948 | 1,357 | 3,277 |
| Pakistan | 108 | 436 | 990 | 1,121 | 1,218 | 2,246 |

*Source:* Alexander J. Yeats, "China's Foreign Trade and Comparative Advantage," p. 10.

the four largest exporters of Third World manufactured products. Since its normalization of relations and exchange of ambassadors with China in 1992, the fourth, South Korea, has also rapidly become one of China's major trading partners in the 1990s.

China's rapid foreign trade expansion has been one of its major sources of revenue and capital. In the 1980s, China's special export zones, where overseas investors can invest with few restrictions and also bring in raw materials and send out exports with few regulations or duties, have become China's greatest economic success story. Chinese exports have also come from agricultural commodities. In the 1980s the PRC became the world's second largest corn producer and exporter, with 14 percent of the global market. In 1993, the corn harvest was estimated at 93 million metric tons, with exports of 7.5 million metric tons. China is also the world's largest rice producer, with an estimated 185 million metric tons in 1993, as well as the world's largest wheat producer, with 101 million metric tons. Although China is a net exporter of rice, which brings a high price, it imports an estimated 10 million tons of wheat to help feed its growing population. Remarkably, China's overall grain production has doubled since Deng's reforms. China's importance as an importer of wheat in the 1990s and as a major customer of the United States and other wheat exporters is revealed by the probability that it will soon exceed Russia as the world's largest wheat importer.[13]

## Bilateral and Regional Trade Agreements

With the exception of China's adherence to the Multifiber Agreement (MFA) in January 1984, most of China's trade agreements have been bilateral.

Probably the granting of most-favored-nation status by the United States in 1980 was the single most important Chinese trade agreement since the beginning of Deng Xiaoping's Open Door policy. At a single stroke, average duties on Chinese exports to the United States fell from about 50 to 8 percent on a number of products, including toys and textiles. Since then, through bilateral negotiations, the United States and China have also signed a number of agreements protecting each others' trading rights, including copyrights, banning of prison-made exports, and the elimination of a number of nontariff trade barriers. In the past, China has had a wide range of restrictions on imports, and Beijing has preferred to make large purchases such as civilian jet airliners and wheat on a quid pro quo basis. For example, in 1993, Boeing Aircraft Corporation had an order of forty-three airliners from the Chinese government, which was 7 percent of Boeing's total production at a time when Western airlines were cutting back on orders because of competition and recession. Because of the size of the Chinese market, unlike most Third World countries, Beijing is able to exercise considerable leverage in its bilateral trade negotiations.

But future Chinese trade leverage may be limited because of the emergence of regional trading blocs in the 1990s. The European Community, having eliminated all its internal trade barriers by 1993, places numerous restrictions on a wide range of imports, especially agricultural products. At the same time, the European Community subsidizes certain exports such as wheat. The North American Free Trade Agreement (NAFTA), between the United States, Canada, and Mexico (signed in 1992 and ratified in 1993), makes North America the world's largest free-trade zone. Mexico, with its cheap labor, will compete for investments and trade that might otherwise go to China and other Asian Pacific Rim countries. Significantly, because of NAFTA, China is considering building manufacturing plants in Mexico.

Although the Pacific Rim is the world's fastest-growing economic region and is already a larger market for U.S. products than the European Community, there are almost no regional economic trade agreements in Asia, with the exception of limited arrangements among ASEAN. Asian states are dependent on either bilateral agreements or GATT for international trade. In the 1990s China has become a key actor in these bilateral arrangements, which now involve extensive bilateral agreements between China, Japan, Hong Kong, South Korea, Thailand, Taiwan, Indonesia, and even Vietnam, despite its border war with China in 1979. China has a common interest with other Asian countries in avoiding an Asian trade bloc dominated by Japan. In addition, because of its comparative cost advantage in the production of a growing number of manufactured products, China opposes the emergence of trading blocs, whether in Asia, North America, or Europe.

At the Asia-Pacific Economic Cooperation (APEC) forum, sponsored by President Clinton and attended by fifteen Pacific Rim trading partners in Seattle in November 1993, Chinese president Jiang Zemin opposed

Clinton's proposal for a Pacific Rim free-trade zone. Jiang was supported by most of the Asian representatives when he stated that although APEC was a useful forum to present different negotiating views, it should not seek to create a multilateral structure for negotiating elimination of trade barriers in the Pacific Rim. Beijing's Westphalian approach, based on bilateral negotiations, enables it to take advantage of its potentially huge domestic market. In return for access to this market, other nations may be willing to make major concessions, especially in an era of global recession.

## China and GATT

In contrast to its refusal to support regional economic trade agreements, since the 1980s Beijing has sought to reactivate its membership in GATT, which is designed to provide a multilateral forum through which states can negotiate reduction of tariff or nontariff trade barriers. The members of GATT invited China to become an active member of the organization when Beijing assumed the United Nations China seat in 1971, but Beijing at first refused. When Deng Xiaoping came to power, however, he viewed GATT and other global economic regimes as a means of gaining access to world finance and markets. In 1982, two years after joining the IMF and IBRD, Beijing was given observer status in GATT, and in 1986 China sought to reactivate its full membership.

Interestingly, Hong Kong, a British colony scheduled to be reintegrated with the Chinese mainland in 1997, received full membership in GATT in 1986, two years after the Sino-British agreement on Hong Kong. Taiwan is now also seeking membership in GATT based on the fact that it ranks fifteenth in world trade, ahead of most Third World countries (including China in 1993).[14] China's rejoining GATT is a logical step in its efforts to participate fully in the global market economy, but reentry will not be achieved until certain Chinese trading practices that currently fail to meet GATT trade and membership rules are reformed.

In the meantime Beijing participated as a nonvoting observer in the Uruguay Round of multilateral trade negotiations, involving over 100 counties, which were started in 1986 and completed in December 1993. These GATT agreements will clearly benefit China, perhaps even more than Japan and the United States. They will reduce not only restrictions on Third World textile shipments under the Multifiber Agreement, but also bilateral trade limits on a wide range of other labor-intensive goods shipped from China to Japan, North America, and Europe.

## DEALING WITH THE ENVIRONMENT

Environment and development are two major concerns of the international community. Through its arduous efforts of many years, especially those made since the industrial revolution, mankind has made brilliant achievements in transforming nature and developing economy. Yet neglect of environment in the course of industrialization, particularly the irrational exploitation and utilization of natural resources, has caused global environmental pollution and ecological degradation, posing a real threat to the survival and development of mankind. It is therefore an urgent and formidable task for all countries around the world to protect the ecological environment and maintain a sustainable development.[15]

The tension between development and environment is of overwhelming concern to all nations of the world, but particularly to the Third World. The nations of the Third World believe that their primary task is development and the elimination of poverty. Within these parameters, the Third World must take steps to protect their environment; yet many in the Third World believe the primary responsibility for environmental remediation should be taken by the industrialized world, which in the course of development has caused most of the world's environmental damage.

Even the definition of environmental damage differs in the industrialized world from that in the Third World and China. Many in the West devote their attention to climatic change, ozone depletion, biodiversity, and worry about the global environmental effects of each Chinese family owning its own car and its own refrigerator. The Chinese, however, define environmental problems in terms of pollution and ecological degradation in developing countries, such as soil erosion, desertification, diminished vegetation, droughts, floods,[16] and the problems of overpopulation.

China's record of dealing with its own environmental problems has been mixed. The problems are many. Any visitor to China during the winter can testify to the pervasive air pollution caused by heating with soft coal. Air pollution control equipment is rarely installed at industrial facilities. Water treatment is minimal if it occurs at all, and wastewater from domestic and industrial sources often flows directly into the nearest river without any treatment. In some highly industrial areas, health officials suspect that local area residents are suffering from pollution-related illnesses. China, therefore, has the same air and water pollution problems as most Third World countries going through the process of industrialization.

China also has degraded its environment. Population growth during the last two centuries has resulted in deforestation that is readily apparent to even the uninformed eye. The results can be dramatic. Rainfall is not absorbed but instead rushes down parched gullies into defenseless villages and towns. Lands become less fertile, and agricultural yields decrease. The increased use of chemical fertilizers, paradoxically a by-product of increasing wealth, results in contaminated rainwater runoff. A vicious cycle of ever-decreasing yields and greater pollution results.

Officially, the Chinese government advocates strict pollution control measures. At home, the government advocates a combination of planning measures at all levels, interministry coordination, and legal measures to control pollution. It has created the National Environmental Protection Agency (NEPA), and government experts interact regularly with foreign researchers to study the causes and cures for local pollution problems. On the international level, China regularly participates in environmental programs and conferences.

The reality, however, may be quite different. Claims that the government is paying attention to environmental problems have not always been borne out by field research. Four of the world's ten most polluted cities are in China. Coal dust emissions in northern China are five times World Health Organization standards. Drinking water for 60 percent of the Chinese people does not meet WHO standards, and acid rain is a severe problem in southern China. Beijing's funding for environmental spending in 1991 was 0.7 percent of the GNP, which was short of its planned 0.85 percent and well under NEPA's ideal figure of 1.5 percent.[17] One critic, He Bochuan, states that "false reporting, ineptitude and bad management are the main causes for the huge discrepancy between the impressive claims and the meager results of China's reforestation program."[18] Proper environmental management requires cooperative planning and monitoring by the government, a relatively uncorrupted legal system, environmental experts, and concerned citizens. As power in China becomes more diffused, the central government has lost much of its ability to enforce environmental protection measures.

Moreover, Beijing's real commitment to an overarching environmental policy is questionable. As the leaders of Eastern Europe discovered, environmental degradation is an issue around which political dissent can be organized. Green groups can become political parties that profess to speak for the ordinary person. Tellingly, after the Tiananmen Square demonstrations, Beijing's leaders banned He Bochuan's critique of its reforestation program. Beijing's commitment to environmental remediation extends only to technical solutions to specific problems, not to an environmental policy that can be adopted at the grass-roots as a political weapon.

## Population and the Environment

Even with one of the most comprehensive family planning systems in the world, 15 million people are added to China's population each year, almost one-fifth of the world's population increase. The Chinese people form one-quarter of the world's population. Yet only 11 percent of China's land is arable, and up to 10 percent of cultivable land has been lost to erosion and urbanization. With 70–80 percent of the Chinese population still living in rural areas, population density has risen to over 1,100 people per square kilometer in the densely populated provinces. "The amount of arable land per person has fallen by half, from a little less than half an acre in 1949 to just under a quarter of an acre in 1988."[19]

Population pressures have led to more intensive farming, which has been extended into marginal land. This, in turn, has contributed to forest degradation and soil erosion. Water supply for both the rural and urban populations is also becoming increasingly scarce. One-third of the wells in Beijing have gone dry!

Although initially Mao and the Communist leadership encouraged population growth, by the mid-1950s family planning and contraception were being encouraged. During the early years of the Cultural Revolution, all attempts at family planning were abandoned to the rigors of ideological purity—the Red Guards made love as well as war.

But by 1971, development of the Four Modernizations policy led China's leaders to launch a massive program that encouraged birth control and delayed marriage. The controversial one-child-per-family program, which used both coercive and monetary incentives to convince Chinese families that having only one daughter would not anger the ancestors, was initiated in 1979. Currently, over $1 billion is spent annually on family planning in both rural and urban areas. Almost all of the funding comes from domestic sources,

## China's Population

What should be done about China's inexorably increasing population? Experts offer a number of suggestions, including the following:

- More help should come from the international community because China's population problem is also a world problem.
- Additional funding is needed from both domestic and international sources.
- Investments are needed to achieve greater educational and employment opportunities for women.
- State-assisted pensions are needed for all.
- New types of high-quality contraceptives are needed.
- Foreign technical assistance is needed to develop clinical service and counseling networks.

although technical assistance, valued at less than $10 million per year, has been provided from international agencies such as the United Nations Population Fund. UN assistance has been limited by the refusal of the Reagan and Bush administrations to provide funding because of concerns that the Chinese government promotes abortion as a means of birth control. Some disturbing aspects of the campaign to slow birthrates are the dramatic drops in live births per 1,000 people and in women's fertility (from 22.4 live births per 1,000 people and 2.5 per woman in 1988 to 18.2 per 1,000 people and 1.9 per woman in 1992). Furthermore, after the government began vigorously limiting birthrates after 1989, there were 113.8 reported boy births for every 100 reported girl births.[20] This seems to indicate that female infanticide is occurring because of the age-old Chinese desire to have sons rather than daughters.

China's population growth rate did decrease during the early 1980s, but it began to climb again in the late 1980s before decreasing again in the early 1990s (see Table 8.7). Paradoxically, as the Chinese standard of living has increased, the desire for more children has become stronger, despite the dangers of overpopulation. Many rural families can afford to pay whatever fines and bribes are necessary to have more children, with the result that the average rural family now has three children. These children are needed to provide security to the elder generation in their old age—another side effect of privatization has been the abandonment of the social safety net that communism promised. In urban areas, the one-child policy has been more successful because government control is more established and because more people still work for state enterprises that provide social benefits for old age and unemployment.

**Table 8.7  China's Population Statistics**

| | |
|---|---:|
| Population (July 1994) | 1,192,000,000 |
| Births per 1,000 people per year | 18 |
| Annual population growth rate | 1.4% |
| Total fertility rate (average number of children per woman) | 2.0 |
| Percentage of couples using contraception | 83 |
| Infant deaths per 1,000 live births | 31 |
| GNP per capita | $370 |
| Population doubling time | 53 years |

*Source:* Shanti R. Conly and Sharon L. Camp, *China's Family Planning Program: Challenging the Myths* (Washington, D.C.: Population Crisis Committee, 1992), p. vii, updated by Nada Chaya at Population Action International (formerly Population Crisis Committee), November 1994.

When asked how this sudden shift from increasing to drastically decreasing fertility rates could occur, the head of China's State Family Planning Commission said, "Above all because party and Government officials at all levels paid greater attention to family planning and adopted more effective measures." These more effective measures included increased use of contraception and sterilization, as well as some methods reportedly used by local officials, such as forced abortions, much to the embarrassment of the central government.[21] Overall, the one-child family has been marginally effective, but given China's huge population problem, not effective enough. The environmental and economic costs of significant continued population growth are likely to far outweigh investments required to achieve only replacement-level fertility. Recent draconian family planning efforts aptly illustrate the problem facing China's leaders.

## Energy, Resources, and the Environment

China's 8–9 percent annual growth rate in GNP and 1.5 percent in population place a tremendous strain on all its resources, especially energy, water, and soil. As the economy expands, so do resource depletion and pollution. For example, China's people use coal and charcoal for 90 percent of their heating and cooking and for 50 percent of their generation of electricity. Mainly because of this coal usage, China is the world's third largest producer of carbon dioxide after the former Soviet Union and the United States.

Government subsidies have also had a deleterious effect on the nation's water supply. In Beijing, water is subsidized, costing only 2.5 cents a cubic meter. Yet since the 1970s, there has been an acute water shortage in northern China, as well as a drop in the water table. Chinese authorities estimate that northern China will need 78.9 billion cubic meters of water per year by the year 2000 but that the supply will be only 74 billion cubic meters. To meet the ever-increasing water needs, the Chinese government is now developing complex plans to divert water from central China to northern China through a series of channels.[22] The prohibitive expense of subsidizing water usage and rerouting water supply halfway across the nation is apparently less onerous than risking the wrath of China's city dwellers faced with a higher water bill. In dealing with these problems, China's leaders are faced with difficult choices when weighing economic development against environmental and resource problems. The World Bank has suggested approaches to increase energy efficiency and reduce pollution, including eliminating governmental subsidies on coal. Eliminating the subsidies would simultaneously ease the national deficit, increase the efficiency of coal usage, and reduce carbon dioxide emissions by 10 percent.[23] Ending coal subsidies would save the government $15 billion a year, but coal mining is one of China's major industries, employing three million people. The government is trying to close some of the least productive mines,[24] but judging each coal mine on a profit-and-loss basis raises uncomfortable questions about unemployment.

To solve its energy and resource problems, China is increasingly turning to multinational development agencies and to foreign investment. For example, China will use World Bank funds to build one of the largest dams in the world at the Three Gorges on the Yangtze River. Long debated as to its feasibility, the completed dam is expected to provide one-sixth of China's electricity. The environmental costs will be great, however, including relocation of over one million people who live in areas to be flooded. Until recently, however, the World Bank has ignored the environmental costs of the projects it funds. A recent example is the $10 billion Narbada Valley Dam complex in India, which according to the bank's own studies would cause serious environmental problems. Nevertheless, both India and the World Bank continued to develop the project.[25] Similarly, the Three Gorges project is expected to proceed despite many doubts.

Foreign assistance with oil field development is also being sought, even in areas of territorial dispute such as the Spratly and Paracel islands. Regarding these islands, the Chinese government signed a contract with a Denver-based oil company in 1992. In October 1992, the Chinese government signed a contract with a Japanese corporation to develop and ship oil from one of China's biggest oil fields in Xinjiang province in the far west to the eastern, populated part of China. An oil pipeline will be built, and eventually Japan will receive a large share of the oil. Beijing must choose between earning hard currency, aided by foreign investment, or developing energy resources through its own limited financial resources. It has chosen the former method, even though greater foreign participation limits Chinese freedom of action. It has also chosen to go ahead with oil exploration indiscriminately, even in areas where territorial claims could lead to hostilities.

Iron ore and steel are other "resources" that China is short of and that it is buying with its scarce foreign reserves. In 1992, the Capital Steel Corporation of Beijing (a state industry) purchased a Peruvian iron mining company for $312 million, more than the estimated value of the mines. To ensure a steady supply of high-grade iron ore at a constant price, China was willing to overpay for the raw materials needed to make steel, despite the slump in demand for steel on the world market. Ironically, a major threat to the mining complex comes from the Maoist Shining Path movement, which seeks to overthrow Peru's capitalist system and create a communist society. Purchases of entire steel mills, timber operations, and aluminum smelters are other examples of China's strategy to enter overseas markets to ensure supply for its growing economy. The dangers of this approach are obvious: outright purchase is generally more expensive than the spot market in the long run, and China's scarce foreign reserves are being used to prop up unprofitable ventures.

## POLICY OPTIONS

With the struggle for leadership succession in the 1990s, it will be difficult for China to do much more than react in an effort to protect its interests on global issues. Important issues include the role of the United Nations in promoting international security; arms sales; emerging global financial and trade regimes; and the growing linkage between the problem of global environmental damage and the policies of individual countries. Yet China is becoming more important as a major actor on all of these issues, even if most of the initiatives come from the First World, which clearly plays the dominant role in emerging global regimes in the post–Cold War era.

### Option 1: Damage Limitation

On questions of UN structural change, Beijing is likely to follow a policy of damage limitation, supporting the least unfavorable options initiated by other states for changing the role and structure of the Security Council, the

General Assembly, and the Secretariat. These bodies seem unable to deal effectively and efficiently with post–Cold War responsibilities, but proposed changes, including amendments to the UN Charter, could adversely affect Chinese interests and influence, especially in the Security Council:

- In the Security Council, Beijing may tactfully resist any proposal to eliminate the veto power of the five permanent members. Although this 1945 Charter provision seems an anachronism in the changing post–Cold War military and economic balance-of-power structure, China cherishes its privileged position as the only Third World power in the Security Council. So long as the other permanent members resist the elimination of the veto or the addition of other permanent seats, Beijing may be content to go along with the United States, the United Kingdom, France, and Russia.
- If change seems inevitable, especially because of growing demands by Third World members for a greater voice in the Security Council, Beijing may support changes strengthening Third World representation, both through the addition of permanent seats for countries such as Brazil, Nigeria, Egypt, and India and through the expansion of the Security Council to include more members of the General Assembly. Most of these selections would be Third World countries, the predominant bloc in the General Assembly.
- In response to pressures by the West to give permanent Security Council seats to Germany and Japan, China may bargain for a number of concessions. For example, China's leaders may simultaneously demand the admission of Third World powers such as Brazil, Nigeria, Egypt, and India but without the veto power of the five current members. China's leaders may also try to strike a deal with the new applicants for permanent seats, especially Japan and Germany, to gain long-term economic concessions from these states as a condition of supporting their applications.
- On the question of representation on the basis of financial contributions, China will lead Third World members in resisting changes to the current system, which allows one vote for each member despite the amount of each member's contribution to the UN budget. China would prefer representation based on population, but any such change would be resisted not only by the West but also by most Third World countries. Budget reform has been and continues to be a critical issue facing the United Nations.
- On the question of administrative reform of the UN Secretariat and the specialized agencies, China is unlikely to support Western demands for budget and staff cuts, as well as for depoliticization of the agencies. Generally, Beijing has adopted the Third World position on issues of administrative reform.

## Option 2: Limited Support of UN Security Operations

Expanding ad hoc peacemaking and peacekeeping operations also pose difficult choices for Beijing's decisionmakers. On the one hand, China's leaders wish to participate and be consulted on any new UN security operations. On the other hand, China, unlike India, has participated infrequently in these operations and it continues to be hesitant about committing funds or personnel to operations it believes will be controlled by the Western powers:

- China is highly unlikely to take the initiative in proposing new UN peacemaking and peacekeeping missions, but it is unlikely to veto missions supported by the other four permanent members of the Security Council.
- Should current efforts to democratize Russia's political institutions and to introduce market reforms fail, a highly nationalistic and anti-Western government could take power. Under these circumstances, the sudden increase in UN security operations in the 1990s might prove to be a temporary phenomenon. The permanent Security Council members might then become badly divided, with Russia no longer supporting Western initiatives. China's bargaining position then might increase, enabling it to work with both the West and Russia for policies more favorable to Chinese national interests.

## Option 3: China's Arms Sales

In a world in which China has no military allies, Beijing views the problem of weapons of mass destruction from a perspective that is not well understood in the West. Chinese leaders believe that arms races in places like the Middle East and South Asia are the result of local conflicts of interests that have traditionally been solved by military force. From the Chinese perspective, the United States, Russia, and their allies are primarily responsible for regional arms races. By taking sides, these countries have not exerted sufficient pressure to bring about an end to conflicts in these regions. In comparison, China's diplomatic role is minimal, and the total value of its arms sales is far below that of the United States, Russia, or a number of other countries. Similarly, China maintains that it has abided by the provisions of the Nuclear Non-Proliferation Treaty and the inspection requirements of the International Atomic Energy Agency:

- Because China has always been a secondary nuclear power, and because other states sell greater amounts of military technology in conflict-prone regions, greater efforts must by made by the United States, European powers, and former communist states to limit

their arms sales and respect the legitimate interests of all states in
these regions. The major initiatives in seeking peace based on
mutual self-interest must come from these states.

- Beijing is making a contribution to peace in these regions by taking into account the legitimate security interests of states in the
  Middle East and South Asia that are being ignored by Western powers. Arms assistance, which does not violate the nuclear proliferation treaty or specific agreements that Beijing has accepted, provides needed balance in these regions. The security interests of
  China are also promoted by giving Beijing the means to play an
  active role in political negotiations to bring about peace in these
  regions.

- Until greater efforts are made by the countries within these regions
  to end their conflicts, accompanied by greater efforts of the major
  arms sellers to support the legitimate interests of all parties to these
  disputes by reducing their own huge arms sales, a military version
  of the tragedy of the commons will continue. China will, in these
  circumstances, reserve the right to sell arms to those who want
  them as a means of promoting China's legitimate self-interests.

- Beijing's leaders will continue to insist that countries such as the
  United States have no right to link questions of arms sales and military security to terms of trade relations and trade agreements, such
  as MFN status. By 1993, the United States, with its Democratic congress and president, stood largely alone in making any such linkage. Interestingly, one of the questions facing Beijing is whether to
  impose trade penalties on France or the United States for their sales
  of military jet aircraft to Taiwan. At the time these sales were
  announced, Beijing threatened to cut back on U.S. grain purchases
  and French investment opportunities, indicating that China does
  link military and economic issues. From the Chinese point of view,
  however, because Taiwan has been recognized by Western countries as part of China, any sales of advanced military technology to
  Taiwan are an interference in Chinese internal affairs and a violation of international agreements prohibiting such sales.

- On the question of regional nuclear arms races, China has become
  indirectly involved in the negotiations going on between North and
  South Korea and between Pakistan and India. Beijing wishes to see
  relations improve between North and South Korea, but its long-
  standing commitments to North Korea prohibit any direct pressure
  on the Communist regime. There is no doubt, however, that Beijing
  would like to see increased stability in Northeast Asia and avoid
  any pretext for Japan to develop nuclear weapons because of a
  nuclear arms race on the Korean peninsula. As for South Asia, so
  long as India and Pakistan fail to resolve the danger of a regional

nuclear arms race, Beijing is likely to give low-key support to the Pakistani position. Interestingly, China previously did not support Pakistan's call for a nuclear-free zone in South Asia, which Pakistan supports and India opposes. The question is linked to India's refusal to give up the right to go nuclear so long as China refuses to eliminate its nuclear weapons.

- Beijing is likely to continue its demand for total elimination of all nuclear weapons. Such elimination is highly unlikely, however, given the danger of nuclear weapons proliferation throughout the world. Even with the reduction of U.S. and Russian nuclear weapons to 3,500 warheads each by the year 2002, these two countries would still have ten times China's current nuclear arsenal. Moreover, all nations speak about destroying nuclear weapons, but few seriously contemplate a complete elimination.

## Option 4: Participating in Global Financial and Trade Regimes

Although there are risks, especially from the perspective of the conservative wing of Chinese leadership, Beijing clearly has opted for further integration into the global economic system, in which the global regimes, whether international finance, investment, or trade, are clearly controlled by the Western World. The reformist wing, which seems to have gained the ascendancy during the Fourteenth Party Congress in the fall of 1992, seems convinced that the advantages of further integration into the global system clearly outweigh the disadvantages:

- The International Monetary Fund and the World Bank Group in the future, as in the past, are viewed as a valuable source of technical assistance and advice, as well as a major source of international funding. If China continues to develop in the future as it has during the past fifteen years, Beijing feels that China will be in a position to use its excellent record in paying off loans to gain new financing on very favorable terms.
- Although China will have to open its market further and eliminate many domestic restrictions on imports, its leaders are convinced that China will gain much more than it loses by joining GATT. China's domestic enterprises, whether public or private, will have to become more efficient to compete with overseas enterprises that will have greater access to Chinese markets. But Beijing seems convinced that as its own economy develops, comparative advantage will be in China's favor in both domestic and overseas markets.
- As a member of these global regimes, China is in a position either

to exclude Taiwan from participation or to orchestrate future arrangements for the participation of Hong Kong and Taiwan as associate members or observers (rather than as independent members) of the World Bank, the IMF, or GATT. Beijing seems convinced that as Taiwan increases its investment and trade with the mainland, Beijing's leverage with Taiwan, both bilaterally and at the multilateral level, will increase.

## Option 5: Limiting Population

Although there is no clear response to the conundrum of environment versus development, virtually all development experts and environmentalists throughout the world agree that population control is crucial to sustainable development. Population control not only reduces pressures on the environment, but also stimulates development, raises living standards, and helps to promote political stability. China's leaders would agree with all of these points. Their problem is not whether to promote family planning, but how vigorously and in what ways. In making policy choices, there may be a number of costs in vigorously pushing for smaller families:

- With the substantial increase in living standards since the economic reforms of 1978, people feel they can afford to have more children, especially in rural areas. They blame party leaders and officials for unpopular restrictions on having children. How can the party enforce strict birth control policies without alienating its rural constituency?
- The Chinese government already spends over $1 billion per year on family planning clinics and contraceptives. Given the seeming inability of the government to reduce rural family size below three children, might government resources be better spent for other purposes such as transportation, electric power, communication, and port facilities?

With China's high GNP growth rate and rising living standards, China's leaders may feel that it is not necessary to increase family planning efforts. Demographic research shows that as living standards rise, people will naturally have smaller families. This is already happening in Asian societies with relatively high living standards such as Taiwan, South Korea, Hong Kong, and Singapore. In Japan, birth rates are currently below replacement levels. Before abandoning the one-child campaign, however, China's leaders will have to consider the following:

- Even with current family planning efforts, the 15 million additional mouths to feed each year threaten to undermine stability, the environment, full employment, the provision of adequate social services, and the overall quality of life. China simply cannot wait for the demographic transition to lower birthrates resulting from higher living standards and less desire for children.

- Whereas negative threats and penalties are unpopular, a number of positive sanctions may improve the image of the party, the government bureaucracy, and the legitimacy of the leadership. For example, local government and production units, especially in rural areas, should be encouraged to provide more social services such as education (especially for women), retirement benefits, information about how family planning benefits society, and inexpensive and more modern means of contraception combined with less reliance on sterilization and abortion.

- Substantially increased funding from international sources is unlikely, but China's leaders may be able to benefit from greater use of foreign expertise and technology. With the change of administrations in Washington, the United States is more likely to provide technical and financial aid to China's family planning effort. Such an effort would have the added benefit of improving Sino-U.S. ties at a time of increasing political strain.

## Option 6: Promoting Sustainable Development

On issues such as energy, water quality and supply, deforestation and the timber industry, agriculture, and the mineral industry, Beijing may have a number of choices available for serious consideration:

- Simply by ending subsidies on fossil fuels, it may simultaneously be possible to create greater energy efficiency, reduce atmospheric pollution, and make renewable energy sources more competitive with coal and oil.

- While continuing reforestation efforts, China may also utilize currency gained from exports to either purchase timber or invest in overseas timber operations.

- While taking advantage of biotechnology and other techniques to increase agricultural production, China may purchase more agricultural products, such as wheat and feed grains, from overseas.

- China may carefully consider the cost and benefits of marketplace devices to reduce ground, water, and atmospheric pollution. With the assistance of both domestic and international environmentalists and economists, the current and future costs of pollution can be weighed against tax benefits or penalties that will motivate both public and private producers to become more efficient and utilize pollution controls. Perhaps China has an advantage over democratic societies in introducing marketplace incentives because these measures may be adopted with less public controversy and organized opposition than in Western societies. Extensive information programs can be helpful in gaining support for these environmental incentives.

## DISCUSSION QUESTIONS

1.  Should China change its policy of minimal participation in UN peace-making and peacekeeping operations? Should it follow the example of India and provide troops and personnel for these operations in different regions of the world?
2.  What stand should China take on the question of expanding the number of permanent members of the Security Council or doing away with the veto power of the permanent members?
3.  Beyond supporting international treaties on nuclear proliferation and biological and chemical weapons, should China support or oppose additional actions to eliminate weapons of mass destruction?
4.  What policy should China follow on the question of arms sales to regions such as the Middle East and South Asia?
5.  Although China is already a member of the International Monetary Fund, should it also agree to make its currency fully convertible?
6.  Taking into account that the Western powers control the International Monetary Fund and the World Bank, should China seek more or less advice and financial assistance from these organizations?
7.  Should China seek to comply fully with all GATT rules on the elimination of trade barriers in order to gain full membership, with all its advantages and disadvantages? Or is it more advantageous for China to negotiate trade agreements on a bilateral basis?
8.  Should China take a leadership role or largely be a supporter of Third World countries on environmental and development issues?
9.  In view of China's annual increase in population, should additional steps be taken to control population growth? If so, what steps?
10. Keeping in mind China's energy, resource, and developmental needs, what additional steps should China take to control population and maintain or improve the quality of its air, water, soil, and forests? In what ways should it work with international organizations and other countries in dealing with these problems?

## SUGGESTED READINGS

Berkley, Gerald W. "China As a Member of GATT: Historical and Contemporary Issues." *Asian Profile* 20 (August 1992): pp. 269–280.

Bitzinger, Richard A. "Arms to Go: Chinese Arms Sales to the Third World." *International Security* 17 (Fall 1992): pp. 84–111.

Boutros-Ghali, Boutros. *An Agenda for Peace.* New York: United Nations, July 1992.

Cai Wenguo. "China's GATT Membership: Selected Legal and Political Issues." *Journal of World Trade* 26 (February 1992): pp. 33–61.

Chen Qiuping. "Foreign Banks Branch Out in China." *Beijing Review* 35 (November 23–29, 1992): pp. 13–18.

"China's Demographic Dilemmas." *Population Bulletin* 47 (June 1992): pp. 1–44.

Chiu, Thomas C.W. "China and GATT: Implications of International Norms for China." *Journal of World Trade* 26 (December 1992): pp. 5–18.

Conly, Shanti R., and Sharon L. Camp. *China's Family Planning Program: Challenging the Myths.* Washington, D.C.: Population Crisis Committee, 1992.

Cormac, Susan Mac. "Eyeing the GATT." *China Business Review* 20 (March–April 1993): pp. 34–38.

Delfs, Robert. "Poison in the Sky: China Tops List of Acid Rain Suspects." *Far Eastern Economic Review* 156 (February 4, 1993): p. 16.

Dong Shi. "Water Crisis in North China and Counter-Measures." *Beijing Review* (April 2–8, 1990): pp. 31–33.

Dreyer, June Teufel, and Ilpyong J. Kim, eds. *Chinese Defense and Foreign Policy.* New York: Paragon House, 1988.

Fenney, William R. "Chinese Policy Toward Multilateral Economic Institutions," in Samuel S. Kim, ed. *China and the World: New Directions in Chinese Foreign Relations.* Boulder, Colorado: Westview Press, 1989, pp. 237–263.

Frieden, Jeffrey A., and David A. Lake. *International Political Economy: Perspectives on Global Power and Wealth.* 2d edition. New York: St. Martin's Press, 1991.

Gill, R. Bates. *Chinese Arms Transfers: Purposes, Patterns and Prospects in the New World Order.* Westport, Connecticut: Praeger Publishers, 1992.

Hom, Sharon. "Female Infanticide in China: The Human Rights Specter and Thoughts Towards Another Vision." *Columbia Human Rights Law Review* 23 (Summer 1992): pp. 249–314.

Kambara, Tatsu. "The Energy Situation in China." *China Quarterly* 131 (September 1992): pp. 608–636.

Larsen, Bjorn, and Anwar Shah. "Combatting the Greenhouse Effect." *Finance and Development* (December 1992): pp. 20–23.

Lensen, Nicholas. "All the Coal in China." *World Watch* 6 (March–April 1993): pp. 22–29.

Lewis, John Wilson, and Hua Di. "China's Ballistic Missile Program." *International Quarterly* 17 (Fall 1992): pp. 5–40.

Luk, Shiu-hung, and Joseph Whitney, eds. *A Case Study of China's Three Gorges Project.* Armonk, New York: M.E. Sharpe, 1992.

Pomfret, John. "Chinese Army Now Major U.S. Arms Merchant." *Washington Post* (March 4, 1993): pp. A1, A18.

Qu Geping. "China's Dual-Thrust Energy Strategy: Economic Development and Environmental Protection." *Energy Policy* 20 (June 1992): pp. 500–506.

Quin Ya. "GATT Membership for Taiwan: An Analysis in International Law." *New York University Journal of International Law and Politics* 24 (Spring 1992): pp. 1059–1105.

Renner, Michael. "Preparing for Peace," in *State of the World 1993.* Lester, Brown and the Worldwatch Foundation, eds. New York: W.W. Norton, 1993, pp. 139–157.

Ross, Lester. "The Politics of Environmental Policy in the People's Republic of China." *Policy Studies Journal* 20 (Winter 1992): pp. 628-642.

Smil, Vaclav. *China's Environmental Crisis: An Inquiry into the Limits of National Development.* Armonk, New York: M.E. Sharpe, 1992.

Tessitore, John, and Susan Woolfson, eds. *A Global Agenda: Issues Before the 48th General Assembly of the United Nations.* New York: University Press of America, 1993.

Tung, Ricky. "Peking Should Abandon the Three Gorges Project." *Issues and Studies* 28 (April 1992): pp. 104–108.

## NOTES

1. Embassy of the People's Republic of China, Press Release No. 27, December 27, 1990.

2. Willy Wo-Lap Lam, *South China Morning Post,* November 19, 1992.

3. Peter Grier, "China Arms Policy Puzzles West," *Christian Science Monitor,* July 3, 1992.

4. A. M. Rosenthal, "Missile Mongering," *New York Times,* April 10, 1992, p. A19.

5. For an analysis of U.S. concerns about Chinese missile sales in 1992, see *New York Times,* January 31, 1992, p. A1; April 19, 1992, p. A19; September 11, 1992, p. A3; December 4, 1992, p. A5.

6. For an analysis of the role played by multilateral economic regimes in the modernization of China, see William R. Feeney, "Chinese Policy Toward Multilateral Economic Institutions," *China and the New World: New Directions in Chinese Foreign Relations,* 2d edition, Samuel S. Kim, ed. (Boulder, Colorado: Westview Press, 1989), pp. 237–263.

7. William Feeney, "Chinese Policy Toward Multilateral Economic Institutions," pp. 252–254.

8. William Feeney, "Chinese Policy Toward Multilateral Economic Institutions," pp. 241–242. Also see World Bank, *China: Socialist Economic Development,* 3 vols. (Washington, D.C.: World Bank, 1983).

9. Interjit Singh, *China: Industrial Policies for an Economy in Transition: World Bank Discussion Papers No. 143* (Washington, D.C.: World Bank, 1992).

10. Shahid Javed Burki and Shahid Yusuf, editors, *The Sectoral Foundations of China's Development* (Washington, D.C.: World Bank, 1992).

11. Alexander J. Yeats, *China's Foreign Trade and Comparative Advantage: Prospects, Problems, and Policy Implications: World Bank Discussion Papers No. 141* (Washington, D.C.: World Bank, 1991).

12. Washington Embassy of the People's Republic of China, *Newsletter,* No. 21, July 10, 1992, pp. 3–4.

13. The data on China's grain production, exports, and imports come from Scott Kilman, "U.S. Steadily Losing Share of World Trade in Grain and Soybeans," *Wall Street Journal,* December 31, 1992, pp. 1, 6. In 1991, the former Soviet Union, prior to its breakup, imported 259 million bushels of wheat, whereas China bought 209 million bushels. [Joe Grant, "U.S. 5th in Wheat Production Worldwide," *Charleston Illinois Times Courier,* December 3, 1992, p. A8.]

14. For a detailed account of Beijing's and Taipei's relationships with GATT up to 1989, see William Feeney, "Chinese Policy Toward Multilateral Economic Institutions."

15. Premier Li Peng, Rio Summit Meeting of the United Nations Conference on Environment and Development, June 2, 1992, Chinese Embassy, Washington, D.C., Press Release No. 7, June 15, 1992.

16. Premier Li Peng, Press Release No. 7.

17. David Weaver, "Chinese Spar over How Best to Tackle Environmental Problems," *China Information Bulletin* (March 1993): p. 5.

18. Barbara Crossetts, "What Some Preach in Rio Is Not What They Practice at Home," *New York Times,* June 15, 1992, p. A5.

19. Shanti R. Conly and Sharon L. Camp, *China's Family Planning Program: Challenging the Myths* (Washington: The Populations Crisis Committee, 1992), p. 3.

20. Nicholas D. Kristof, "China's Crackdown on Births: A Stunning, and Harsh, Success," *New York Times,* April 25, 1993, pp. A1, A12.

21. Nicholas D. Kristof, "China's Crackdown on Births."

22. Dong Shi, "Water Crisis in North China and Counter-Measures," *Beijing Review* (April 2–8, 1990): pp. 31–33.

23. Bjorn Larsen and Anwar Shah, "Combatting the Greenhouse Effects," *Finance and Development* (December 1992): pp. 20–21.

24. Nicholas D. Kristof, "China Plans Big Layoffs of Coal Mine Workers," *New York Times,* December 12, 1992, p. C1.

25. "World Bank War on Pollution Faces Even Sharper Criticism," *New York Times,* November 12, 1992, p. A6.

# Alternative Scenarios: 2000 and Beyond

The rise of China, if it continues, may be the most important trend in the world for the next century. . . . China is the fastest growing economy in the world, with what may be the fastest growing military budget. It has nuclear weapons, border disputes with most of its neighbors, and a rapidly improving army that may—within a decade or so—be able to resolve old quarrels in its own favor. The United States has possessed the world's largest economy for more than a century, but at present trajectories China may displace it in the first half of the next century and become the number one economy in the world.

—*Nicholas D. Kristof in* Foreign Affairs

## THE RISE OF CHINA

As China's leaders look forward to the twenty-first century, they see both great challenges and opportunities. Within China itself, the challenges and opportunities are perhaps greatest because the external environment appears more favorable to China than at any time in modern history. As Machiavelli, the Italian political realist, pointed out in the sixteenth century, the choices of decisionmakers involve both opportunities and dangers, but may be determined largely by "fortuna" (circumstances beyond the control of decisionmakers). Machiavelli believed the key to effective leadership was how decisionmakers chose their course of action based on the availability of options at the time. The previous chapters have examined the dangers and opportunities facing China's leaders up to the present. This concluding chapter examines China's future role in the emerging global system, a world that looks very different from that of the Cold War era.

## CHINA'S ROLE IN THE EMERGING
## INTERNATIONAL SECURITY SYSTEM

China is experiencing a period of vigorous development, with economic construction as the focus. Its foreign policy must help create a long-

> standing and steady international environment of peace for its econom-
> ic construction. . . . At present, all nations, developed or developing,
> share the view that a country's national strength, especially in the eco-
> nomic sense, will decide its status in the 21st century. Therefore, they
> are generally turning their attention to domestic affairs, attaching great
> importance to economic construction and cooperation. All nations are
> becoming more interdependent, harmonious, complementary and mutu-
> ally restricted.[1]

In the above statement, Chinese foreign minister Qian Qichen reveals the
essence of China's security approach in the emerging global system. The key
seems to be internal stability and economic development in an era in which
domestic success is related to good relations and growing economic interdependence with others based on mutual self-interest. In the 1990s, Beijing
seems more concerned with internal factors that may destabilize the Middle
Kingdom than with any military threat from beyond its boundaries. But
security, which depends on well-being, also depends on continuing Deng
Xiaoping's Open Door policy. Trade and foreign investment are essential to
China's development, rising living standards, and ability to develop a modern military capable of protecting China in the twenty-first century. By
maintaining an authoritarian order at home while encouraging economic
interdependence and a market economy, Beijing's leaders hope to avoid the
Russian syndrome through which the changes introduced by Mikhail
Gorbachev appear to have weakened the former Soviet Union's security and
well-being.

Although observers mostly agree that there is no emerging global
order that ensures security at home and among nations in the 1990s, they
also mostly agree that security in the 1990s needs to be defined more broad-
ly than as violence and protection against outside interference in one's internal affairs (all Westphalian values). These concerns will remain important in
the twenty-first century, but security increasingly will also mean a sustainable environment—the maintenance of spaceship earth. The relationship
between humankind and its earthly environment—which provides adequate
air, water, soil, and biodiversity to sustain human life and well-being—is the
ultimate security envelope.

China's current leaders apparently agree with this broader definition
of security, which will involve international cooperation to preserve the
earth's essential resources. At the same time, although China's leaders
include economic, social, and environmental factors in their definition of
security, they have not yet chosen to include democracy or freedom of political expression as part of their broader definition of security.

Two Arabic words, *sullah* and *salaam,* may provide a key to China's
international security role. In many regions of the world the practice of sullah signifies the use of force and coercion, actions designed to solve disputes
through domination. On the other hand, salaam signifies a willingness to

seek security through solutions based on mutual self-interest, trust, and multiple-sum bargaining games in which everyone benefits. In short, one cannot be secure unless one's neighbor is also secure. The fact that China continues to hesitate in supporting the global security role of the United Nations suggests that Beijing may believe that bilateral relations are the best means of promoting Chinese security, especially if China's economy grows more rapidly than that of others, including Japan and the United States, in the twenty-first century.

At the global level, China is mainly a consumer of security rather than a major contributor to efforts to help provide security for those less fortunate and unable to protect themselves, as in Bosnia, Somalia, and Kuwait. China seems leery of the effort of others, especially the West, to use global institutions to eliminate or at least control security threats, especially if this means international efforts to protect human rights inside the borders of states. In the 1990s others may become increasingly disenchanted with China's view that it is making a major contribution to global security simply by abstaining rather than vetoing UN peacekeeping and peacemaking efforts.

## CHINA AS A REGIONAL POWER

> Now China's relations with Northeast, Southeast, South and Central Asia and Russia are all growing and its security environment has improved fundamentally. It is pointed out in a report to the 14th National Congress of the Chinese Communist Party that China's surrounding environment is in the best period since the founding of the People's Republic in 1949.[2]

In the above quotation, Qian Qichen emphasizes China's regional situation, which he says is highly favorable in the 1990s. Based on China's overall regional role as it approaches the twenty-first century, however, China may face a number of difficult choices in Asia. Currently, Chinese policy follows a dual line. Some even call it a Janus-faced policy, one in which China simultaneously pursues military buildup and threats while promising bilateral cooperation with its neighbors. For example, increased Chinese naval capabilities, in view of China's past actions against Vietnam both along its northern border and in the South China Sea, as well as rumors that China may build a naval base in Myanmar, could be harbingers of limited conflicts in the region.[3]

Samuel Kim, who has been writing about Chinese foreign policy for many years, observes that "China's regional security policy seems no more than a blurred image of its changing definition of the world situation."[4] In the future, China will find it increasingly difficult to maintain both policies. To maintain good relations with its Asian neighbors, China's leaders must decide whether bilateral cooperation is more important that military buildup.

## A Regional Security System in Asia?

In contrast to Eastern Europe and the former Soviet Union, where the disintegration of communist regimes has resulted in economic dislocation, political chaos, and even open warfare, Asia outwardly appears to be relatively stable in the post–Cold War era. Yet Western Europe's goals of economic and security integration still elude Asia. In comparing the two regions, a European writer, Peter Sturm, observes that there is little chance that regional economic and security arrangements can be created in Asia similar to those emerging in Europe. He notes that there is no leader in the region that Asian states would be willing to follow. If Asian countries were forced to defend their interests, he believes, they would be more likely to align with actors outside the region rather than accept the leadership of either Japan or China.[5]

China, too, has been loathe to accept a regional security system. To date, Beijing's leaders have rejected all such proposals by regional neighbors, including those put forth by Russia and Japan. From the Japanese perspective, an Asian security system is needed in the 1990s to ensure regional stability. But Japan would seek a regional security system only if it included China because no other arrangement could provide military stability in Asia. Because China seems unwilling to subordinate its security and military interests to a regional organization, the alternative, from the Japanese perspective, will necessarily be continued security arrangements between Asian countries with outside powers such as the United States.[6]

## A Regional Economic System in Asia?

Although China has rejected any multilateral approach to security in Asia, it is more likely to agree to multilateral economic cooperation. There are several possibilities, all based on the remarkable economic development in the region, including China. First, China could join others in seeking a narrow and structured regional market system, which might eventually resemble NAFTA. Malaysia's prime minister, Mahmood Mahatir, has advocated a plan known as the East Asian Economic Grouping (EAEG) that would "be a narrow regional grouping of East Asia that excluded North America and Oceana." It would seek "to invigorate regional economic transactions by promoting market liberalization and setting up common standards [for the region] . . . in the face of United States–led market liberalization attempts."[7]

A second approach to regional economic cooperation might be a looser arrangement to eliminate trade barriers among all the participating states, which would include North America and Oceana (Australia, New Zealand, and Pacific island states). The Asia-Pacific Economic Cooperation conference could be the basis for such an approach because it includes Asian countries as well as Australia, New Zealand, Canada, and the United States. The advantage of this type of arrangement would be that Asia would look outward in its trade relations rather than become a closed Asian trading bloc. APEC is unique in that it is currently the only international structure that includes China, Hong Kong, and Taiwan. Should the European Community impose further trade restrictions against both North American and Asian products, then an APEC-type structure could bring these two regions together as a counterforce against European protectionism.

A third approach, which is the one China seems to be pursuing at the present time, is reliance on bilateral trade arrangements while at the same time seeking to participate fully in the promotion of a global liberalized market system through membership in GATT. Beijing is so eager to renew its membership in GATT that it might even be willing to accept some type of associate status for Taiwan short of membership as an independent state. This would have the advantage of helping China, as a member of GATT, work out agreements that would enable it to take advantage of the tremendous market potential of Greater China. Examples of this might be additional international financial assistance, more overseas investment, and a greater opening of markets for Chinese products.

Japan's policy views will be a major factor in determining which of the three alternatives eventually emerges. Japanese observers recognize that a more open global trading system would be preferable for most Asian countries, including both Japan and China, than a closed Asian trading bloc. The latter alternative would presume Japanese leadership because Japan is the largest trader and investor throughout Asia as a whole. This is something China and the rest of Asia might object to. Japan, like the rest of Asia, would therefore benefit more from global liberalization of the market rather than a limited system in Asia or one including Asia and North America.[8]

## CHINA AND THE THIRD WORLD

A genuine peace that the people of the world have longed for has not come with the end of the Cold War. . . . New problems [are] added to the old ones and armed conflicts [arise] one after another as a result of disrupted equilibrium. Hegemonism and power politics continue to exist; the attempt of some big powers to control developing countries politically and economically has become more and more obvious; the long-hidden ethnic conflicts have surfaced with a vengeance; and the North-South contradictions have further aggravated. The road to peace and development . . . is covered with thorns.[9]

In 1955, China's prime minister, Zhou Enlai, participated in a conference in Jakarta, Indonesia, that was the forerunner of the nonaligned movement. The purpose of the conference, and later of the nonaligned movement, was to separate participating nations from both superpower blocs as a third force independent of the imperialist West and the "hegemonical" East. The latter term has been used by Beijing to categorize Soviet attempts to dominate Third World regions.

With the end of the Cold War, the nonaligned movement seems to have lost part of its reason for existing. Nonetheless, Third World leaders, including China, talk about the emergence of neoimperialism—Western economic domination after their soldiers have gone home. China has always seen itself as part of the Third World. In varying ways, it has sought to play a leadership role within the Third World, largely based on a common desire to change the global economic system so that poorer developing states would receive more help and fairer treatment from the rich Western countries who currently dominate the system.

When the non-Western developing states became a majority in the United Nations General Assembly in the early 1960s, they sought to promote their economic interests by calling for the United Nations Conference on Trade and Development, a forum dominated by the Third World. China was not an original member of the group, and as the movement continues its efforts, other members of the movement seem uncertain about their relationship with China; they are not sure whether China is a rival or a partner. Third World concerns have been further complicated by the collapse of the Second World (the Soviet Union and its satellites). In the 1990s, the former communist countries, as well as China, vie with Third World countries for bilateral and multilateral aid and investment. Like China, the Eastern European countries and the former parts of the Soviet Union need help in making the transition to marketplace economies. Aid and investment going to these regions lessens the amount available to Africa, Latin America, the Middle East, South Asia, and Southeast Asia.[10] Chinese statements about solidarity with the Third World are therefore unconvincing to many members of UNCTAD.

## China and the Third World: Similarities and Differences

Although China is less developed than some of its neighbors such as South Korea, Taiwan, Hong Kong, and Singapore, it is much more developed than a majority of Third World states, including most of Africa, parts of South Asia, and some areas of Latin America. China, which previously sought to serve as a model to the Third World for self-reliant socialist development, now seeks to show the Third World how to combine authoritarian political control with spectacular economic growth.

*Nationalism and subnationalism.*    A recent study of self-determination and nationalistic ideologies in different regions in the wake of the Cold War identifies nationalist ideologies as the great force both uniting and dividing peoples throughout the Third World and the former Second World.[11] In the 1990s, there are severe conflicts between subgroups and self-determination problems in nearly every region of the world.

In comparison with India and many other Third World countries, despite serious problems in outlying areas such as Tibet and Xinjiang,[12] China has a high degree of ethnic unity. The danger of disunity based on subnationalist and ethnic sentiments seems much greater in India, as well as in many other parts of the Third World, than in China. The large Chinese Han majority controls the heartland, and the odds are heavily against successful revolts by China's small minorities, which have been oppressed whenever they have resisted Beijing. Conflict inside China is more likely to result from growing unemployment, inequities in economic development, Communist Party corruption, and loss of support for party rule.

*Democracy versus authoritarianism.* One of the most controversial debates raging in China and the Third World involves the advantages and disadvantages of democracy during the transition from traditionalist to modern societies.[13] Many scholars and politicians concur that democracy, based on Western ideas of representative government and individual freedom, is essential to the full development of marketplace competition and economic success. From this perspective, the competitive marketplace of ideas, personal freedom, and competitive popular selection of leaders provide the environment in which the production and distribution of goods is most likely to succeed. However, others believe that democracy must be tempered by respect for authority and willingness to subjugate individual rights to the common interest.

Following the end of World War I, the English political writer Lord Bryce announced the triumph of democracy over other forms of government. In the remaining years of the twentieth century, however, democracy has suffered a series of setbacks. In the 1990s, the full extent of democratization remains in doubt in the former communist countries and many parts of the Third World. The correlation of modernization and development with democracy, touted by theorists in the 1960s, has not become apparent. Indeed, not only has democratization from within been slow to come, but external pressures for change have been muted. For example, during the debate over renewal of China's most-favored-nation status, U.S. business interests strongly lobbied against a link between human rights issues and trade issues. Capitalists who invest in China and many other Third World regions are often indifferent to how democratic the political system is. They may actually prefer authoritarian regimes, which promise stability and an absence of democratic labor or other populist movements.[14]

China's leaders believe that the key to human progress is not in the

form of political structures, but in economic growth. Beijing notes that
although India calls itself a democracy, as does the Philippines, rural peasants are still exploited by traditional ruling classes, with little effort by government to protect the people's interest and their well-being. A comparison
of living standards in rural China, especially with those in countries such as
the Philippines and India, shows that conditions in China seem to be more
favorable. In many parts of Africa, Latin America, and South Asia, despite
efforts to establish democracies, there also seems to be little hope for immediate improvement of life in rural areas.

Should Third World countries seriously consider the Chinese model as
an alternative means of achieving development and higher living standards,
as well as stability and order? How should Third World countries view
Chinese claims that the most important human rights are those such as order,
literacy, education, food, clothing, housing, the right to a job, and health
care? Chinese foreign minister Qian Qichen, speaking before the Forty-
Seventh Session of the United Nations General Assembly in 1992, said:

> It is obviously irresponsibly one-sided and harmful to make irresponsi-
> ble comments about the human rights situation in developing countries
> in disregard of the difference in historical background and cultural tra-
> dition as well as the actual conditions in these countries. For the people
> of developing countries, the right to subsistence and the right to devel-
> opment are undoubtedly the fundamental and the most important
> human right of all. In those areas hit by severe natural disasters for
> years, people are starving; in those war-ridden areas, millions are turned
> into refugees. How can the people living in such conditions enjoy
> "human rights?"[15]

States like India and the Philippines, with large rural populations, high
birthrates, and high levels of unemployment in rural areas, may wish to emulate China's rural development model. For example, they may see the advantages of adopting Deng Xiaoping's policies of encouraging peasants to create their own rural industries, either as collectives, joint ventures, or private
businesses. They might also take note that as a result of these reforms since
1978, over half of all income in rural China now comes from nonagricultur-
al work. Furthermore, they may wish to consider both the advantages and
disadvantages of China's dual economic system, in which the public sector
is either gradually being privatized or subjected to the discipline of the market through the elimination of special government loans, subsidies, guaranteed employment, and guaranteed prices. In view of what is happening in
former communist states, Third World countries may also wish to weigh
carefully the contrasting Chinese and Russian approaches. Would China be
better off if it had attempted to establish Western-type democracy, as the Russians tried to do, before trying to carry out marketplace
reforms?

## China as a Third World Leader: Partner or Rival?

At the global level, China has aligned with the Third World on development issues. In the 1970s, Beijing's delegates to the United Nations strongly supported Third World calls for a New International Economic Order. Virtually all developing countries felt that the global economic system was unfairly tilted toward the industrialized nations, and they resented the latter's control of the international regimes in trade, finance, and investment. China supported these views and agreed that the industrialized world should provide more aid and better terms of trade and finance. Then, later on in the 1980s, as the mood in UNCTAD shifted from a policy of confrontation, Beijing did likewise, joining other Third World states in seeking to become part of the global economic system as partners rather than challengers.

This is the core of Deng Xiaoping's Open Door policy. Instead of rejecting or seeking to reform the World Bank, the IMF, and GATT, Deng sought to join these international regimes in order to get more international aid and investment. In Latin America, Mexico is following a similar policy, as is India in South Asia. China is therefore, in many ways, their rival.

As noted earlier, despite professions of peaceful intent, Beijing sometimes seems to follow a "tragedy of the commons" approach. Especially in arms sales, China is in fact helping to stimulate arms races between Third World countries. Iraq and Iran illustrate the problem. Beijing sold arms to both sides in order to get hard currency. China has also been a major arms seller to a number of Third World countries that have a reputation of using force to suppress dissent within their borders.

In nonmilitary trade, China has also had a major impact on a number of Third World countries because of its comparative economic advantage, especially in light industrial products, which other Third World countries also wish to sell to Japan, North America, and Western Europe.[16] In the 1990s, as the world paradoxically becomes both more multipolar and more interdependent, the Third World (including China) seems to be united only at the rhetorical level. Third World nations seem to be increasingly divided amongst themselves on political-security as well as economic issues. Capitalism in the 1990s has won out over Marxism nearly everywhere. But this may lead to an economic version of the tragedy of the commons as the Third World countries compete against each other for exports, foreign investment, and aid from the First World. Each will be forced to offer more concessions to lure trade, aid, and investment away from its neighbors. In this competition, China frequently seems better situated to offer the West what it wants—larger markets, greater stability, and disciplined but cheap labor. Other Third World countries might believe they have to lower their standards to compete with China. Working conditions, including child labor, safety regulations, reasonable working hours, and good wages, are likely to be sacrificed in the process. A new international economic order is largely a mirage in the 1990s because Third World nations are unable or unwilling to bargain collectively for better economic terms. In a world of underemployment, unemployment, high Third World birthrates, and the overproduction of most commodities, China's comparative advantage in the marketplace may come not only from its disciplined and cheap labor but also from stability and order provided by its highly authoritarian regime.

## CHINA AND THE NEW WORLD ORDER REDUX: PROBLEMS AND SOLUTIONS

As China's leaders face the future, uncertainties abound over domestic and international challenges that, at best, must seem overwhelming to the aging leaders in Beijing. In the 1990s, the external world looks very different from that of the 1980s, but the real challenges appear to be within China's own borders. The leaders in Beijing must feel like they are riding the back of the tiger. They cannot get off for fear that they will be consumed by the forces they have already unleashed. Few ideological guideposts remain from the Maoist era to provide a compass in a sea of storms. Marxism is largely discredited in fact, if not in theory, and Leninism, based on party dictatorship, is also being questioned inside China; this is especially the case with China's youth and intellectuals, even if public protest is forbidden.

Fortunately, as challenges seem to grow from within, the outside world seems less threatening. Except for rigid adherence to Leninist party rule, Beijing's leaders seem willing to proceed pragmatically, adjusting their policies to avoid sudden dangers. Above all else, as China moves into the twenty-first century, its leaders—whether conservatives, moderates, or reformers—keep looking over their shoulders at events in Eastern Europe and the former parts of the Soviet Union. Gorbachev's approach is not a role model for any of China's potential leaders in the post-Deng era. All China's leaders wish to avoid, at almost any cost, the economic and political difficulties facing those living in these former communist lands.

## Future Challenges from Within

In looking to the future, Beijing's leaders can take considerable pride in what has been accomplished inside China since 1978. Although living standards vary by region, many parts of rural China and most of urban China are clearly better off than prior to the Communist revolution. Conditions in rural China compare favorably with rural conditions in much of the Third World, and this is also true in urban areas. China's people seem to have new energy, especially at the village and township levels, where life is clearly more prosperous than under Mao.

Another important development is the rise of consumerism. Technological innovation, increased production of better quality goods, and greater availability of a wide range of agricultural and industrial products have helped to create a cultural fad in which the Chinese masses are becoming addicted to material things as well as the pop culture of the West. The consumerism phenomenon is closely related to the rise of global capitalism, in which not only the middle classes but the masses seek satisfaction in mass consumption of goods and services. But with this increased desire for material things comes the danger of future disorders if China's strained infrastructure, accompanied by resource shortages, is unable to satisfy these growing demands for a better life.

Collapse of the economy would no doubt bring new demonstrations and disturbances, something that is always on the minds of China's leaders since the days of Tiananmen Square. Beijing's leaders will have to make difficult decisions. At one end of the spectrum are past ideologies and practices based on Marxism and Leninism. At the other end of the policy continuum are choices closer to Western values and practices. As China's society modernizes and becomes more complex, China's leaders must feel much like politicians in Western countries in the 1990s. There seem to be no good choices, but only a combination of options in which some are less damaging than others, or choices in which it is hoped the good will outweigh the bad.

How China deals with its internal dilemmas will have a major impact on its global and regional role in the twenty-first century. If these problems can be managed, China will be able to make a major contribution to the international community in promoting stability and economic prosperity. But if there is a breakdown of order, with the possible emergence of regional warlords, it would be difficult to predict China's future. Should power devolve from the center to the different regions, however, China's international role might be changed in a number of ways:

1. Political and economic rivalry inside China might substantially reduce China's influence as an international actor, especially at the regional level.
2. Instability could reverse China's remarkable success in attracting international investment.
3. Instability could also cause discontent and threaten party rule.
4. Some regions, particularly the coastal regions, might seek closer ties with the West in order to protect and promote trade and investment.
5. Domestic instability and decline in party rule is unlikely to bring about Western-type democracy and political freedoms in the foreseeable future. During the past 400 years, China's periods of both stability and instability have been characterized by authoritarian rule. With open political conflict within and between different regions, the personal well-being and rights of the people are likely

to suffer severely, just as the post–Cold War era has brought suffering in many regions with the collapse of international communism and the domestic disorder in Africa, the Middle East, Eastern Europe, and Russia.

In spite of China's rapid rise in living standards since 1978, there are unfortunately many signs of discontent that could very well lead to domestic instability in the 1990s. For example, there are over 100 million people, mostly peasants, who have not benefitted from the increased agricultural production and industrialization of the last decade. Many of them, without work permits, have migrated to China's rapidly developing coastal regions, where they have been unable to find work. As corruption seems to become more rampant in both the political and economic systems, those who are less well off show signs of greater impatience. Ominously for the CCP, which historically claims to draw its authority from the peasantry, peasants have recently demonstrated against local corruption and nonpayment for crops. There are also signs of discontent among China's intellectuals, many of whom have not shared the benefits of Deng's economic reforms and who regret the failure to achieve greater political freedom and individual rights after Tiananmen Square. Further evidence of current discontent in the 1990s is the willingness of thousands of Chinese in both rural and urban areas to give up their life savings to smugglers who help them migrate illegally to the West in search of a better life. Should there be a major breakdown of order inside China, one result might be a mass international migration of Chinese, dwarfing current levels and creating yet another international refugee crisis.

## Future External Challenges

In the post–Cold War era, geopolitics (the conduct of foreign policy based on how resources, geographical location, and changing technology affect the relative capability of states) plays a continuing role in Chinese foreign policy. According to Harold and Margaret Sprout, in their classic study of how environment affects international politics, not only real capabilities are important, but also how decisionmakers perceive each other's capabilities and intentions. Decisionmakers may sometimes decide what to do on the basis of false perceptions.[17] Beijing's current leaders are concerned about the changing perceptions of leaders in countries such as the United States, Russia, and Japan—perceptions that could seriously affect Chinese relations with these countries. To protect itself from policy changes in any particular country, Beijing seems to be trying to balance its relations with key countries such as Japan, the United States, and those in Western Europe in order to avoid relying heavily on any one of them.

Balancing its relations becomes even more important as China becomes increasingly sensitive to the policies of others beyond its shores.

Two U.S. international relations theorists, Robert Keohane and Joseph Nye, point out that states are becoming increasingly interdependent as their relations become more complex. Because of this, countries such as China, Japan, and the United States are not only sensitive but sometimes vulnerable as a result of each other's policies. According to Keohane and Nye, a state is sensitive to another's actions if those actions threaten to harm the state's vital interests. A state becomes vulnerable when it is not possible to take corrective actions to avoid these sensitivities, which can result from things such as increased communications, movement of people across international borders, foreign investments, and changes in export and import policies. Sometimes these transnational interactions take place without foreign offices and national authorities even being aware of what is occurring.[18]

Beginning with Deng Xiaoping's Open Door policy in 1978, this is what has been happening between China and the outside world. Even with its Leninist authoritarian government, Beijing is losing an increasing amount of control over social and economic transactions taking place across China's borders, especially at the local and regional levels. China's further integration coming from global trade, finance, investment, communications, and tourism will only speed up the process. Already, millions of overseas Chinese move in and out of China every year, along with hundreds of thousands of other tourists, investors, and professional people.

## Conflicting Policies?

China's regional and global policies may in fact be contradictory. On the one hand, China pursues a Westphalian policy to avoid outside cultural pollution and dependence on others for security. On the other hand, with China's Open Door policy of complex economic interdependence, including joining global economic regimes, China becomes increasingly sensitive and possibly vulnerable to the actions of others.

Even though China makes minimal contributions to global security (through the United Nations), it nevertheless wishes to be consulted, with the right to disapprove global security policies initiated by others. But if China continues at its current rate of economic development and increased economic interdependence with the outside world, China's future leaders may also find it necessary to increase their participation in multilateral political-security fora, both at the regional and global levels, in order to protect China's economic interests. From the Chinese perspective, complex interdependence may be good or bad, depending on China's ability to play outside forces against each other, including investors, traders, and governments. Beijing's leaders, by accepting interdependence in the economic sphere, seem to be betting that China will grow increasingly powerful in the economic sphere and therefore be better able to use its market leverage to promote its interests, preferably through bilateral transactions but also through global regimes if there is a clear economic advantage. Beijing's leaders are also betting that economic success will ensure the continuation of the Communist Party's political rule over the long term, which was the basic reason from the start for Deng Xiaoping's economic reforms.

## POLICY OPTIONS

Throughout this book a number of conclusions have been drawn about internal and external challenges facing China's decisionmakers. Now we will look at some of the more general policy options as China moves toward the twenty-first century:

### Option 1: Playing a Minimal
### Role in Global Security Operations

In the foreseeable future China faces no major external threat, and others have played a more active role in organizing United Nations security activities. With its currently limited capability to project power beyond its borders, Beijing may therefore wish to minimize its role, except where its own vital interests are at stake:

- At some future date when China has much greater capability, it may wish to assume greater responsibilities. Currently, a low profile seems to best suit China's interests. China is essentially a free rider on global security issues—it lets others do the work.
- China, as a permanent UN Security Council member, nonetheless wishes to be consulted and reserves the right to approve or disapprove initiatives taken by others.

### Option 2: Participating
### More in Global Economic Regimes

Beijing's leaders seem committed to playing an even larger role in global economic structures such as the World Bank Group, the IMF, and GATT:

- Even if these regimes are market oriented and controlled by the West, China's leaders believe that they have more to gain than lose by supporting them. In fact, Beijing believes that China will benefit from these regimes because as China develops economically, it will be able to exercise greater leverage in international investment, finance, and trade.
- Membership in organizations such as GATT may also help China reduce bilateral threats to use trade restrictions or avoid regional

trade structures (an Asian trade bloc possibly dominated by the Japanese) that might regulate trade in ways detrimental to Chinese interests.

## Option 3: Avoiding Entangling Alliances at the Regional Level

With an Asian post–Cold War balance-of-power system in which China faces no major threats, bilateral relations seem preferable to multilateral regional approaches in both political-security and economic relations:

- If China is able to continue its current rate of economic growth, it will be able to exercise more leverage on both security and economic policies through bilateral transactions with its neighbors.
- For the foreseeable future, regional political-security regimes seem, from the Chinese perspective, more likely to serve the interests of other Asian states than China (for example, Japan or the ASEAN states in Southeast Asia).

## Option 4: Seeking Good Bilateral Relations with All Countries in the Post–Cold War Era

Historically China has had no permanent friends or enemies and has been suspicious of entangling alliances. Beijing believes that its interests, with few exceptions, are best served by bilateral relations based on pragmatic agreements promoting mutual self-interest. Westphalian values are the cornerstone of such bilateral relations. Beijing seems convinced that political-security as well as economic mutual self-interest can be promoted by non-interference in each other's affairs.

## Option 5: Concentrating on Domestic Security, Maintenance of the Chinese Communist Party's Mandate of Heaven, and China's Continued Economic Development

Beijing's foreign policy is clearly dictated by domestic concerns.

- Without continued economic development inside China, party leaders believe they will have no chance to retain power, which traditionally is based on the popular perception that the rulers are meeting the needs of the people.
- A foreign policy designed to achieve minimal Chinese international obligations but considerable economic interdependence best serves China's internal development and its domestic needs.

- China's continued economic development depends on further elimination of domestic contradictions resulting from the dual economy, uneven regional development, and political corruption.
- Beijing's leaders are convinced that Western-style democracy is ill suited to Chinese needs, which can best be met through an authoritarian political system and the absence of organized political opposition or open challenges to continued party rule.

## DISCUSSION QUESTIONS

1. From the Chinese perspective, what are the favorable characteristics of the emerging global system? What are the unfavorable characteristics?
2. What role does China seek to play in the emerging global security and economic system?
3. How does Beijing view efforts to create regional political-security and economic structures in Asia? Explain the reasons for this point of view.
4. In the case of China, as well as other Third World countries, is Western-style democracy essential to the development and practice of marketplace economics?
5. How relevant is the Chinese model of development to the needs of other Third World countries in the post–Cold War era?
6. To what extent do other Third World countries recognize China as a leader of the Third World?
7. How are the following concepts applied in the making of Chinese foreign policy in the emerging global system: (a) the Westphalian system of values; (b) geopolitics; (c) complex interdependence?
8. Why are domestic challenges likely to pose greater risks than international challenges to China's leaders in the 1990s?
9. In the promotion of world peace and international security, in what ways is China part of the problem or part of the solution?

## SUGGESTED READINGS

Boutros-Ghali, Boutros. *Agenda for Peace.* New York: United Nations, 1992.

Decker, D., J. Frieden, S. Schatz, and R. Sklar. *Post Imperialism: International Capitalism and Development in the Late Twentieth Century.* Boulder, Colorado: Lynne Rienner Publishers, 1987.

Faust, John. "The Emerging Security System in East Asia." *The Journal of East Asian Affairs* 8, no. 1 (Winter/Spring 1994): pp. 56–89.

Halperin, Morton H., David J.Scheffer, and Patricia L. Small. *Self Determination in the New World Order* Washington, D.C.: Carnegie Endowment for International Peace, 1992.

Kaplan, Morton. *System and Process in International Politics.* New York: Wiley, 1957.

Kim, Samuel S., ed. *China and the World: New Directions in Chinese Foreign Relations.* Boulder, Colorado: Westview Press, 1989.

Klare, Michael T. "The Next Great Arms Race." *Foreign Affairs* 72, no. 3 (Summer 1993): pp. 136–152.

Kristof, Nicholas D. "The Rise of China." *Foreign Affairs* 72, no. 5 (November/ December 1993): pp. 59–74.

Pi, Ying-hsein. "Peking's Foreign Relations in the New International Situation." *Issues and Studies* 28 (May 1992): pp. 13–28.

Robinson, Thomas W., and David Shambaugh, eds. *Chinese Foreign Policy: Theory and Practice.* New York: Oxford University Press, 1994.

Shih, Chih-yu. *China's Just World: The Morality of Chinese Foreign Policy.* Boulder, Colorado: Lynne Rienner Publishers, 1992.

Sklair, Leslie. *Sociology of the Global System.* Baltimore, Maryland: The John Hopkins University Press, 1991.

Snow, Donald M. *Distant Thunder: Third World Conflict and the New International Order.* New York: St. Martin's Press, 1993.

Sorensen, George. *Democracy and Democratization: Dilemmas in World Politics.* Boulder, Colorado: Westview Press, 1993.

Stokes, Bruce. "Challenging China." *National Journal* 24 (September 19, 1992): pp. 2106–2109.

Whiting, Allen S. "China's Foreign Relations." *Annals of the American Academy of Political and Social Science* 519 (January 1992).

## NOTES

1. Chinese foreign minister Qian Qichen, responding to questions by a Xinhua correspondent in an interview on Chinese foreign policy on December 29, 1992. [People's Republic of China Washington Embassy, Press Release No. 11, December 30, 1992, p. 1.]

2. Qian Qichen, Press Release No. 11, pp. 1-2.

3. See Nicholas D. Kristof, "China Builds Its Military Muscle, Making Some Neighbors Nervous: Filling a Perceived Power Gap in Southeast Asia," *New York Times,* January 11, 1993, pp. A1, A4. Kristof notes that "the growing strength of the People's Liberation Army would not be so much of a concern if China did not have border disputes with at least seven neighbors." Referring to the possibility of Chinese naval facilities in Myanmar, he notes a growing concern from "mounting intelligence that China may be selling weapons to Myanmar in exchange for the right to set up naval facilities and listening posts in islands off the Burmese coast." Also see David Stenberg, "China Cultivates Its Burmese Connection," *New York Times,* January 19, 1992, p. 14.

4. Samuel S. Kim, "China As a Regional Power," *Current History* (September 1992): p. 248. Also see Michael T. Klare, "The Next Great Arms Race," *Foreign Affairs* 72, no. 3 (Summer 1993): pp. 135–152. Klare believes that China's military buildup and seizure of islands in the South China Sea is stimulating a regional arms race in which the ASEAN countries in Southeast Asia are now building up their own military forces in response to China's military actions. He also notes a renewed interest amongst Asian countries in seeking security assurances from countries outside the region. By refusing to support the development of a regional security system based on multilateral consultation, Beijing seems to raise suspicions that it is not really interested in joining its neighbors in preventing regional arms races or creating Asian-wide fora to solve regional disputes.

5. Peter Sturm, "Risks of Conflict Increasing As Asia Becomes Less Stable," *Frankfurter Allegemeine Zeitung für Deutschland,* December 4, 1992.

6. See Takashi Inoguchi (professor of political science, Tokyo University), "Japan's Foreign Policy in East Asia," *Current History* (December 1992): p. 412. Also see his book *Japan's International Relations* (Boulder, Colorado: Westview Press, 1991).

7. Takashi Inoguchi, "Japan's Foreign Policy in East Asia," p. 411.

8. Takashi Inoguchi, "Japan's Foreign Policy in East Asia," pp. 407–412.

9. Chinese foreign minister Qian Qichen, speaking before the Forty-Seventh

Session of the UN General Assembly, Press Release of the People's Republic of China Mission to the United Nations, September 23, 1992.

10. A major problem facing the Third World is that most foreign direct investment (86 percent) is between First World countries. However, of the remaining 14 percent, China's importance as a competitor for this investment is revealed by the fact that in 1989 it was the largest recipient of foreign direct investment going to Third World countries (16 percent), followed by Mexico (12 percent), Brazil (10 percent), and Egypt (7 percent). [Rosmarie Philips and Stuart K. Tucker, *U.S. Foreign Policy and Developing Countries: Discourse and Data 1991* (Washington, D.C.: Overseas Development Council, 1991), p. 33.]

11. Morton H. Halperin, David J. Schaffeer, and Patricia L. Small, *Self-Determination in the New World Order* (Washington, D.C.: Carnegie Endowment for International Peace, 1992).

12. Because of Beijing's encouragement of Han migration to these outlying regions, the native populations are becoming minorities in their own lands. Han Chinese are already a majority in Tibet, and in Inner Mongolia the indigenous Mongol population is only 16 percent of the total. [Halperin, Schaffeer, and Small, *Self-Determination in the New World Order,* pp. 133–134.]

13. See Donald M. Snow, *Distant Thunder: Third World Conflict and the New International Order* (New York: St. Martin's Press, 1993).

14. See D. Decker, J. Frieden, S. Schatz, and R. Sklair, *Post-Imperialism: International Capitalism and Development in the Late Twentieth Century* (Boulder, Colorado: Lynne Rienner Publishers, 1987). Also see Leslie Sklair, *Sociology of the Global System* (Baltimore, Maryland: The John Hopkins Press, 1991) and George Sorensen, *Democracy and Democratization: Dilemmas in World Politics* (Boulder, Colorado: Westview Press, 1993).

15. Foreign Minister Qian Qichen, Press Release, September 23, 1992, p. 6.

16. See Alexander J. Yeats, *China's Foreign Trade and Comparative Advantage: Prospects, Problems and Policy Implications,* Report No. 141 (Washington, D.C.: The World Bank, 1991).

17. Harold Sprout and Margaret Sprout, *Toward a Politics of the Planet Earth* (New York: Van Nostrand Reinold Co., 1971), pp. 97–107.

18. Robert O. Keohane and Joseph S. Nye, *Power and Interdependence,* 2d ed. (Glenview, Illinois: Scott Foresman and Company, 1989), pp. 3–37.

# Chronology of
# Most-Favored-Nation Status

| | |
|---|---|
| 1934 | Most-favored-nation (MFN) status was applied to U.S. trading partners. |
| 1951 | Trade Agreements Extension Act (P.L. 82-50), Section 5, required the president to suspend MFN status of the Soviet Union and all countries of the then Sino-Soviet bloc. |
| September 1, 1951 | United States suspended MFN status for China. |
| July 14, 1952 | United States suspended MFN status for Tibet. |
| 1974 | Jackson-Vanik amendment curtailed president's ability to extend MFN status to communist countries; to do so, president has to negotiate a commercial trade agreement subject to congressional approval and either certify that the country is allowing free emigration or waive this requirement on the grounds that the country is improving its emigration policies. |
| October 23, 1979 | President Carter transmitted to Congress a trade agreement with China (signed on July 7, 1979) and the executive order extending to China the Jackson-Vanik waiver. |
| January 24, 1980 | Congress approved the trade agreement with China. |
| February 1, 1980 | Trade agreement entered into force and restored MFN status for China conditionally under the Jackson-Vanik freedom-of-emigration amendment of the Trade Act of 1974. |
| October 1990 | H.R. 4939 passed House (384-30), requiring Chinese government to take a number of steps to correct human rights abuses in order to be eligible for MFN |

renewal. Senate did not take up this bill or adopt a measure of its own.

February 1, 1992
Trade agreement with China renewed (through January 31, 1995).

March 2, 1992
President Bush vetoed H.R. 2212, which set conditions for China's MFN status. Veto was overridden in House (357-61) but sustained (60-38) in Senate.

September 28, 1992
President Bush vetoed H.R. 5318, which withdrew MFN status for products of Chinese state-owned enterprises only; products of private Chinese companies and foreign joint ventures could still be imported under MFN status whether conditions were met or not. Veto was sustained by Senate (59-40) on October 1, 1992.

April 28, 1993
H.R. 1890 was introduced, prohibiting president from extending MFN status in 1994 to state-owned industries unless human rights and international security conditions were met; bill was referred to committees on ways and means and rules.

May 5, 1993
H.R. 1991 was introduced, prohibiting president from extending MFN status in 1994 to state-owned industries unless human rights and international security conditions were met; bill also specified cessation of coercive abortion or involuntary sterilization. Bill was referred to committees on ways and means, foreign affairs, and rules.

May 26, 1993
S. 1034 was introduced, prohibiting president from renewing China's MFN status in mid-1994 unless he could determine that China was not manipulating its currency to gain an unfair competitive advantage; bill was referred to Committee on Finance.

May 28, 1993
President Clinton issued a determination extending for one year China's Jackson-Vanik waiver and thereby its MFN status; Clinton also issued Executive Order 12850 extending MFN conditionally.

July 21, 1993
H.J. Resolution 208 was introduced to disapprove the extension of the waiver, but it failed to pass the House (105-318).

May 18, 1994
In a news conference, House Speaker Thomas S.

Foley said withdrawal of trade benefits would cause "a trade disruption" and would make the United States "less influential, not more influential" with the Chinese on human rights. One hundred six other House members, including Representative Lee Hamilton (D-Indiana), chairman of the House Foreign Affairs Committee; Robert Michel (R-Illinois), the minority leader; and Newt Gingrich (R-Georgia), the minority whip, signed a letter the week of May 16 urging unconditional renewal of China's MFN trade status and the creation of a bilateral commission to deal with human rights issues.

May 23, 1994     Secretary of State Christopher reported to President Clinton that China had met the two mandatory requirements of the executive order: cooperation on ending the export of prison-made goods to the United States and allowing close family members of certain dissidents to leave the country.

May 26, 1994     President Clinton announced he would extend MFN status and end the policy of setting human rights conditions as part of trade policy.

# Acronyms

| | |
|---|---|
| ADB | Asian Development Bank |
| APEC | Asia-Pacific Economic Cooperation |
| ASEAN | Association of Southeast Asian Nations |
| CAC | Central Advisory Committee |
| CCP | Chinese Communist Party |
| CSCE | Conference on Security and Cooperation in Europe |
| DRC | Development Research Center |
| EAEG | East Asian Economic Grouping |
| FAO | Food and Agricultural Organization |
| GATT | General Agreement on Tariffs and Trade |
| GNP | gross national product |
| IBRD | International Bank for Reconstruction and Development |
| IDA | International Development Association |
| IFC | International Finance Corporation |
| IMF | International Monetary Fund |
| LDP | Liberal Democratic Party |
| MFA | Multifiber Agreement |
| MFN | most favored nation |
| MTCR | Missile Technology Control Regime |
| NAFTA | North American Free Trade Agreement |
| NATO | North Atlantic Treaty Organization |
| NEP | New Economic Policy |
| NEPA | National Environmental Protection Agency |
| NIEO | New International Economic Order |
| NPT | Nuclear Non-Proliferation Treaty |
| PLA | People's Liberation Army |
| PRC | People's Republic of China |
| SDF | Self-Defense Force |
| SEZ | special economic zone |
| UNCTAD | United Nations Conference on Trade and Development |
| UNDP | United Nations Development Programme |
| UNESCO | United Nations Educational, Scientific, and Cultural Organization |
| UNHCR | United Nations High Commissioner for Refugees |
| VAT | value-added tax |
| WHO | World Health Organization |
| WTO | World Trade Organization |

# Index

# About the Book and Authors

This text introduces students to the history of China's foreign policy decisionmaking, its current policy agenda, and the factors that may influence the country's future decisions.

After discussing the PRC in the international arena through the 1980s, the authors focus on China's present relationships with the other Asian nations, the former Soviet republics, the United States, and international organizations. they consider its policy choices, outlining the ideological, political, security, economic, social, and ecological issues the country faces as a regional and aspiring Third World leader; they look, too, at how the shifting balance of power in Asia will affect China in the 1990s.

Each chapter of the book familiarizes students with the chinese framework for analyzing the issues in question. Alternate policy choices are suggested, along with supporting data for each course of action; students can thus decide for themselves which policy or combination of policies best promotes China's interests in today's world. Discussion and essay questions, as well as suggested readings, are also included.

**John R. Faust** is professor of political science at Eastern Illinois University. **Judith F. Kornberg,** a specialist in the history of Sino-U.S. relations, is Director of Sponsored Research at SUNY-Purchase and adjunct assistant professor at the University of Connecticut–Stamford.